EDINBURGH:
GORGIE AND DALRY

BY THE SAME AUTHOR

Marchmont in Edinburgh

Villages of Edinburgh Volume 1 (North)

Villages of Edinburgh Volume 2 (South)

Edinburgh: Sciennes and the Grange

Yerbury: A Photographic Collection 1850-1993

EDINBURGH:
GORGIE AND DALRY

MALCOLM CANT

MALCOLM CANT PUBLICATIONS

First published in 1995 by
Malcolm Cant Publications 13 Greenbank Row
Edinburgh EH10 5SY

Design by Sarah Merrill Mowat
Printed and Bound by Redwood Books Ltd
Trowbridge Wiltshire

Contents

To
Archie Robson
my late father-in-law
Director with Colin Macandrew & Partners Ltd.,
whose involvement with the
family and my books
is greatly missed.

Acknowledgments

Writing books on Edinburgh has taught me one thing, at least, and that is that it cannot be done without the involvement of a great number of people from many walks of life. It is customary to name those who have had the greatest involvement, although there are many others, too numerous to name.

It is probably easiest to name, first, the local and national repositories of information, which include Edinburgh City Archivist's Department; Edinburgh University Library; the Edinburgh Room of the Central Library; Edinburgh District Council, Department of Environmental Services; the *Edinburgh Evening News*; Historic Scotland; the National Library of Scotland; the National Trust for Scotland; the Royal College of Physicians; the Royal Commission on the Ancient and Historical Monuments of Scotland; the Royal Scottish Academy; the Scottish Record Office; the Scottish National Portrait Gallery; The Scotsman Publications Ltd.; and the Signet Library.

As I progressed through the various chapters of the book, the net caught an even wider range of people and organisations. The ministers, rectors and leaders of the many churches took an active interest in my work, as did the head teachers and staffs of the various schools. When it came to the chapter on industrial and commercial development, I was inundated with fascinating anecdotes from people who had worked in one or other of the many firms. Past and present managers and owners of businesses all supplied information on their particular sphere of activity. I found the same co-operation when I came to contact the sports clubs and places of leisure, entertainment and further education. Moira Reid kindly allowed me to make use of information on the Edinburgh Athletic Club which appeared in her recent article in *Scotland's Runner*. In my final chapter I relied heavily on the current organisations which make up the districts of Gorgie and Dalry as we know them today.

I also derived a great deal of assistance from several individuals who held many small pieces for the big jigsaw. Their contributions varied enormously, but I list the names alphabetically: Maurice Berrill; John Blakey; Janet Boyd; Alan Brotchie; Donald Campbell; John Campbell

Q C; Brian Donald; H.K. Fairless; Jimmy Fender; Jessie Flannigan; Mr and Mrs Foulis; the Forrest family; Patrick R. Gammell; D.L.G. Hunter; Danny McKay; Jean Moffat; Ian Morrison; J.K.S. Poole; Bill Rigby; Tom Scott; Patricia Scoular; Don Shaw; Mrs Shields; Sir J.C. Stormonth-Darling; Mrs M. Sutherland; John K. White; and Mary Wilson. I also thank the people who lent photographs: their names are credited throughout the book. Where no credit appears, the photograph forms part of the author's own collection.

I am indebted to the Rev. Bill Brockie, who has written the Preface, and answered a great many obscure questions during my research. John and Val Tuckwell have checked my script thoroughly and have helped bring the project to fruition. Finally, I thank members of my family: as usual my wife Phyllis has spent many hours typing the script; my daughters, Ingrid and Karen, have undertaken a range of administrative tasks; and my son Graham has drawn the map of Gorgie and Dalry. It has been a most rewarding experience just sitting here in my study watching it all happen.

MALCOLM CANT

Preface

In the front room of a tenement flat owned by a spritely lady in her nineties, a group of a dozen or so is talking. The subject is 'the Tiv'. It emerges that this is the cinema in Gorgie Road, now a bingo hall: and what went on in the back seats. Then someone protests that this must have been in the new Tiv because the old Tiv had 'forms' not seats. So the conversation goes on, about the lady street seller on the corner near the front of the old St Martin's, about the fire station in Angle Park Terrace . . . Old photographs are handed round, old newspapers produced. Precious family souvenirs and memories are now given extra value, as through the work of the historian, they take their rightful place as records of society. Throughout the meeting, Malcolm makes his notes.

Some of the group meet again, this time in the sheltered housing on Dalry Road with some of the residents there. Again memories of shops and factories, of work and of school days, of washhouses, of play places and events, are shared. Again Malcolm sits, makes notes and asks questions.

Malcolm and I went through the St Martin's Church records, minute books and registers, and examined memorabilia. When the congregation was begun in 1883 a men's club was started which included a shoe club with shoes provided by wealthy West End Episcopalians. This is an interesting insight into life in the 1880s in Edinburgh.

The memories and memorabilia of people and the documentation of ordinary life is the stuff of history. As Professor Christopher Smout, the Historiographer Royal, a former local resident and occasional visitor to St Martin's puts it, 'history is never about kings and queens, dates and battles, it is about the experiences of ordinary people finding their way through the difficulties and joys of life. Only when you know enough about individuals can you generalise about a people; and even after that you have to return to the known experiences of individual people fully to understand the colour of history'.

Malcolm's work, and the resulting book, are valuable contributions to our maintained knowledge of the past as it really was. If we are to have a sustainable future we must know and understand the past. He is to be thanked and congratulated for the work and the book much to be commended. I am proud to have been asked to write this preface.

REV. W.J.T. BROCKIE
RECTOR OF ST MARTIN OF TOURS,
TYNECASTLE, EDINBURGH

Introduction

When I first decided to study the districts of Gorgie and Dalry for a possible new book, I had no idea of the wealth of material which lay relatively undiscovered. The standard works on Edinburgh at the end of the nineteenth century, such as Grant, Wilson and Ballingall, do not devote much attention to the area. Although several comprehensive studies have been made of particular aspects of Gorgie and Dalry, many of them remain as private manuscripts. I therefore felt that there was a need to collate the available material and present it in a form which, hopefully, would be of use to people interested in knowing more about the districts. The result is *Edinburgh: Gorgie and Dalry*, which sets out to show that both Gorgie and Dalry have very ancient roots, and form an integral part of the way in which the city expanded from the Old Town of Edinburgh.

Many writers of local history face the dilemma of how best to present the available material. I have decided to adopt, as far as possible, a chronological approach in the first few chapters, so that readers can learn what is known of the area in the seventeenth and eighteenth centuries, and how the district was carved up in the nineteenth century by road improvements, the cutting of the Union Canal, and the construction of the railways. I have arranged subsequent chapters by subject matter: for example, schools, sport, entertainment and leisure, maintaining, where appropriate, a chronological sequence. Because of the complicated history of the churches, some of which had their origins in the Old Town, it was considered better to list them geographically on a route from Haymarket, westwards to Stenhouse. Of particular importance are the two chapters devoted to the industrial and commercial development of the area. The number of firms in the district is such that only a representative sample could be included of the main trades and processes. In the final chapter I have returned to a chronological approach for the twentieth century, observing some of the many changes which have taken place, and which are not specifically mentioned in the chapters on particular subjects.

In 1911, 'An Onlooker' published *Edinburgh Street Studies* from a series of articles which had previously appeared in the *Edinburgh Evening News*. He observed that 'from Dalry to Saughton is a goodly journey, and . . . there is less to attract attention there than in almost any part of Edinburgh'. I cannot quite make up my mind if the author was 'an onlooker' or 'an overlooker', but in either case I can assure my readers that he was certainly not a 'close looker'. With that assurance I hope you will read on.

MALCOLM CANT

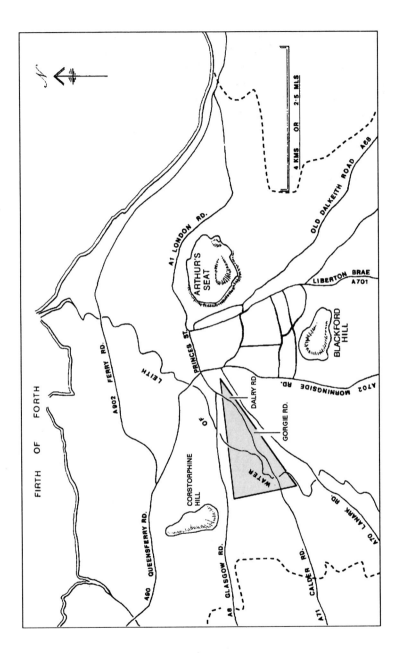

EDINBURGH SHOWING THE LOCATION OF GORGIE AND DALRY

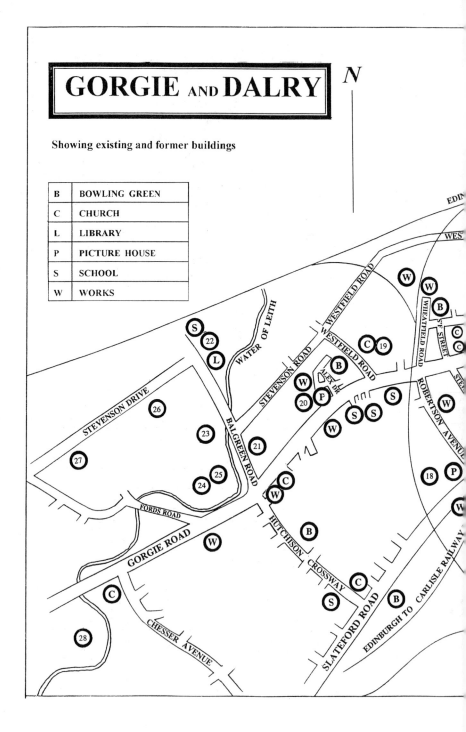

GORGIE AND DALRY

N

Showing existing and former buildings

B	BOWLING GREEN
C	CHURCH
L	LIBRARY
P	PICTURE HOUSE
S	SCHOOL
W	WORKS

HAYMARKET TERRACE MORRISON STREET
GROVE STREET
O GLASGOW RAILWAY LINE
RUSSELL ROAD
CATHCART PL.
SPRINGWELL PL.
DUFF ST.
DOWNFIELD PL.
DALRY ROAD
ORWELL TER.
ORWELL PL.
C. PLACE
C. ROAD
CRESCENT
CALEDONIAN
WEST APPROACH ROAD
FOUNTAINBRIDGE
CH ROAD
McLEOD STREET
MUR. CRES.
MUR. TER.
MUR. ROAD
HENDERSON TER.
ARDMILLAN TER.
ANGLE PARK TER.
BRYSON ROAD
WATSON CRESCENT
DUNDEE STREET
VIEWFORTH
UNION CANAL
GIE ROAD
WHITE PARK
SLATEFORD ROAD
HARRISON ROAD
SHANDON PLACE
AN RAILWAY LINE
L. ST.
TERRACE

1	FLORA HA'	15	GORGIE CITY FARM
2	GROVE HOUSE	16	MCLEOD ST. CENTRE
3	FOUNTAIN HOUSE	17	HEART OF MIDLOTHIAN
4	WAR MEMORIAL	18	GORGIE STATION
5	DALRY SWIM CENTRE	19	GORGIE MEM. HALL
6	EASTER DALRY HOUSE	20	GORGIE HOUSE
7	DALRY HOUSE	21	LYARSHALL
8	ST BRIDE'S CENTRE	22	TYNECASTLE CLUB
9	CANMORE	23	SAUGHTON GARDENS
10	A.L.P.	24	SAUGHTON HALL
11	DALRY CEMETERY	25	SCOTTISH NAT. EXHIB.
12	WEST. REFORMATORY	26	SAUGHTON PARK
13	MAGDALENE ASYLUM	27	S'TON SPORTS COMPLEX
14	N. MERCHISTON CEM.	28	STENHOUSE MANSION

1
The Early History of Dalry

To look at the modern district of Dalry, crammed as it is with houses, shops, industries and traffic, it is almost impossible to have any idea how it evolved from being a quiet rural backwater near the metropolis of Edinburgh. Yet much of that rural character was still evident up until the last quarter of the nineteenth century. Historically the Lands of Dalry stretched from Semple Street, near Tollcross, on the east side, to the boundary with the Lands of Gorgie on the west side. From the middle of the seventeenth century the dominant centre of influence was Dalry House, situated about midway between the east and west boundaries. As late as the 1860s Dalry House was a country estate with two access driveways from Dalry Lane (now Dalry Road). A third drive-way from Fountainbridge crossed the line of the Caledonian Railway and entered the estate grounds from the south. At the present day little evidence of the estate remains but Dalry House survives in Orwell Place, hemmed in on all sides by tenement buildings of the late nineteenth century. The way in which this transformation took place is the story of Dalry.

According to *Gaelic Place Names of the Lothians*, the name Dalry comes from *Dail Ruigh*, a field on the lower slope of a hill.

THE CHIESLIES

At the beginning of the fourteenth century the Lands of Dalry and Merchiston were owned by William Bisset and his family. During the reign of David II (1329-1370) possession was with William Mure of Abercorn, who in turn sold to William Touris and his wife Helenor Douglas.

In the seventeenth century, however, much more information is available concerning the Chieslie family who owned Dalry until 1696. The earliest record of the family in the district is 1656 when Walter Chieslie was living at Easter Dalry. It was probably Walter who built Dalry House in 1661. He was the third son of the Reverend John Chieslie, a minister in Lanarkshire, and in 1638 was apprenticed to an Edinburgh mer-

chant, James Nasmyth. His keen business acumen, bordering on sharp
practice, soon earned him an unenviable reputation over various commercial transactions. A veneer of respectability was acquired through
his marriage to Katherine Tod, daughter of Sir Archibald Tod, Lord
Provost of Edinburgh.

Walter's son John and his wife had ten children and various marital
problems, which eventually led to John being brought to court to answer a claim for alimony. The evidence was heard by Lord President
Lockhart who awarded the sum of £93. John Chieslie was so incensed
by the judgement that he lost all reason and openly avowed, in the
presence of Sir James Stewart, advocate, to kill the Lord President. Sir
James cautioned Chieslie that 'the very imagination of such a thing is a
sin before God', but the fiery retort was 'Leave God and me alone; we
have many things to reckon betwixt us and we will reckon this too'.
The Lord President was warned but did not take any special precautions. On Easter Sunday 31st March 1689 Chieslie loaded his pistols
and stalked the Lord President on his way from St Giles to his house in
Old Bank Close. As he was about to enter his house a shot rang out and
the Lord President fell. The ball or bullet had passed through his body,
and he died a few minutes later in the house. On being apprehended
Chieslie boasted, 'I am not wont to do things by halves and now I have
taught the president how to do justice'. He was sentenced to death but
had his right hand cut off first, and was hanged with the pistol tied
round his neck. His right hand was nailed on the West Port. Although
there is doubt about where the execution took place, it was strongly
suspected that Chieslie's supporters took possession of the body afterwards for a secret burial.

Two intriguing stories survive. Dr Daniel Wilson, in *Memorials of
Edinburgh in the Olden Time*, states that the body was brought back to
Dalry House which was thereafter haunted by a shadowy figure which
glided between the house and a recess in the garden wall. Some years
later when the garden wall was being repaired, an old stone seat was
removed and under it was found the skeleton of a man — complete in
every detail save the right hand! Dr Robert Chambers tells a slightly
different story in *Traditions of Edinburgh*. He says that when a hearth-
stone of an old cottage at Dalry Park was being removed, a skeleton
was found with the remains of a pistol 'near the situation of the neck'.
Whatever the true facts, Chieslie certainly lost his grip on the estate. A
descendant, Major Chieslie, sold the lands of Dalry in 1696 to Alexander Brand. In Greyfriars Kirkyard there is a Chieslie family tomb, but

Sir George Lockhart of Carnwath was Lord President of Session in 1689 when he was shot and killed by a disappointed litigant, John Chieslie of Dalry House. (Grant's Old and New Edinburgh.*)*

although several descendants are buried there, including Lord Provost
Sir Robert Chieslie, the inscription does not carry the family name.
Only the name of Walter Chieslie's wife appears, Katherine Tod, who
died ten years prior to the murder of the Lord President. At the present
day, the tomb, built against the west wall, is indecipherable owing to
erosion of the stonework and a thick growth of ivy.

DALRY BECOMES BRANDSFIELD

On the demise of the Chieslie family the Lands of Dalry were purchased in 1696 by Alexander Brand, son of Alexander Brand of Baberton
and Reidhall (Redhall). Alexander Brand, proprietor of Dalry, was a
very shrewd businessman whose exploits in the lace industry and in the
supply of armaments had made him a very rich man. On purchasing
Dalry he renamed the house Brandfield, and the estate Brandsfield, in a
vain attempt to secure continuity of the family name. In fact when his
ownership came to an end subsequent owners reverted to the original
name of Dalry. Some of his business dealings give an interesting insight
into the character of the man and the nature of business transactions at
the end of the seventeenth century, before he purchased Dalry.

Brand was Master of the Merchant Company in 1686. A few years
prior to that he obtained a monopoly for the manufacture of Spanish
leather which was stamped with gold and used as high-class room-
hangings. When the Merchant Company was setting up its new meeting place in the Cowgate in 1691, Brand used his influence as Master
to secure a lucrative contract under the guise of acting in the interests
of the Merchants. He offered £150-worth of room-hangings to adorn
the new building provided that the Merchant Company agreed to order and pay for whatever additional hangings were required. The overall transaction was very much to the benefit of Brand. He would, of
course, have been sufficiently astute to cross all the t's, learning from his
earlier brushes with the law in 1681 and again in 1683. On these occasions he was summoned before the Privy Council to answer charges
that he had imported prohibited cloth, but he was acquitted. His other
great exploit was the importation of firelocks or guns for the Lords of
the Treasury in Scotland. On this contract he had the assistance of two
partners, Sir Thomas Kennedy and Sir William Binning, both of whom
eventually rued the day that they ever got involved. The contract was
for the supply of 5,000 guns. When the guns were imported, Brand
claimed that they were of a quality superior to that stated in the con-

The tomb of the Chieslie family of Dalry, in Greyfriars Kirkyard, does not record the names of any of the family interred there after the killing of the Lord President by John Chieslie. (The Epitaphs and Monumental Inscriptions in Greyfriars Churchyard.)

tract and that in consequence he was entitled to a balance of £1500 above the original price. Brand was given the extra payment but disagreement arose with his partners over their shares. He eventually paid Kennedy but Binning had to sue before he got his rightful share.

The firelock affair and other dubious dealings eventually brought Brand to the brink of financial ruin. In a desperate attempt to avoid disaster he advertised in the *Edinburgh Evening Courant* of 2nd August 1706 to raffle his house and contents at £5 per ticket. It would appear that the raffle did not take place but his creditors were successful in having a factor appointed to the estate by the Court of Session. When another attempt to sell the house failed in 1711, Brand was forced to sell parts of his estate to persons who had previously taken a feu. He conveyed to John Watson, younger, on 22nd August 1711 'a tenement or great lodging' (probably Roseburn House) and the eastern half of the Lands of Dalry, called the Town of Dalry. In 1714 Dalry House, as distinct from the Lands of Dalry around it, was sold to Sir James Nicolson of that Ilk, Bart. From then on the house and lands devolved separately. Part of the 1714 deed gave an interesting description of Dalry House at that time:

> All and haill twelve full acres of arable land lying upon the south side of the Park — also two foot of ground around the said twelve acres for a dyke where on it is not already built — also All and haill the Mansion House and Manor Place of Dalry with the stable and coach house thereto belonging, the yard, park, current water or burn running through the same with the privilege and use of the spring well of Foull Bridge with power of conveying in pipes so much of the water to the foresaid mansion house as may serve for the possessors allenerly.

During Alexander Brand's ownership of the Lands of Dalry he did not develop the estate well. He should have taken advice and arranged for a formal feuing plan to be drawn up with specific conditions in the feu charters. Instead he developed the ground piecemeal, feuing individual plots from time to time without any restriction as to use. He appears to have made a conscious decision to feu for industrial and business use rather than for residential development. That could well have been a sound commercial decision had he controlled the matter properly. The area of the Old Town around Portsburgh and the West Port was very congested and the eastern side of the Lands of Dalry was well placed for an extension of industrial development.

DALRY HOUSE

Dalry House dates from 1661. The year, and various insignia, are incorporated in the ceiling plasterwork in one of the rooms on the first floor. The house was originally a simple z-plan of three storeys lying on a north-west/south-east axis. From the rectangular box of the main building, the z-shape was completed by an octagonal stair-tower on the north-west corner, and a small south-east jamb. The floor area was greatly extended in the early eighteenth century by the addition of a two-bay extension to the north, and an ogee roofed tower at the south-west corner. The original stair-tower on the north-west corner was probably given its ogee roof at the same time. Around 1800 a further extension was built to the south containing two storeys within the height of the original three. In 1877 John Watherston & Sons built school accommodation to the east of this and altered the roof of the south extension to create more space in the attic floor. Finally in 1965 Robert Hurd and Partners (now the Hurd Rolland Partnership) built an east wing behind the north part, replacing the 1900 wing which had been in need of renovation. This work included a completely replanned interior, and tying in the two towers which had been built simply butting onto the main walls. The opportunity was also taken to restore original features, and a new ribbed plaster ceiling with crests and motifs in the panels was designed for the first floor, based on a small area of seventeenth-century ceiling which still remained in the building.

After ownership by the Brand family, Dalry House devolved separately from the estate around it. The first person to own the house without owning the estate was Sir James Nicolson in 1714, followed by the 1st Earl of Rosebery in 1716. By 1724 Dalry House was owned by Mathew Lant, Chief Baron of the Exchequer in Scotland who became Lord Chief Baron in 1728. He was one of the first directors of the Royal Bank of Scotland when it was founded in 1727 and became the second Governor from 1737 to 1742, taking over from the Earl of Ilay.

Legal connections with Dalry House continued in 1741 when Lant sold to John Idle, Lord Chief Baron. It may well be that descriptive surnames are not always an accurate assessment of the holder's ability, but to be Baron Idle suggests that the implied shortcoming had been present since birth! The Earl of Mansfield was obviously not taking any chances when he wrote to Lord President Forbes on 18th November 1741:

> Idle is made Lord Chief Baron of Exchequer of Scotland by the Chancellor from the merit of old acquaintance and domestic concern. I have a mind you should take possession of him by all sorts of civility. He is a good natured man but not a man of business, or much parts, which will give you more opportunity of advising and protecting him. I wish you would introduce him to any people of distinction that happen to be in Edinburgh . . .

Having been appointed Lord Chief Baron, Idle remained so until his death in September 1755, when Dalry passed to his sister Francisca. The Signet Library in Parliament Square in Edinburgh retains legal papers which illustrate that towards the end of his life Baron Idle became embroiled in a lengthy dispute with David Laing, a wright at Crosscauseway. Laing had been employed by Idle to renew the roof of Dalry House during Idle's absence in England, on the strict understanding that the work would be completed without causing any damage to the interior of the house. When complications arose in Idle's absence, Baron Maul discussed the matter with Laing and directed that the old roof joists should not merely be strengthened: 'That would not do; the interjecting of a new Couple betwixt each two of the old ones behoved to be to the Chief Baron's Prejudice in regard the old Couples were so very insufficient that they would not support the Roof and consequently behoved in a short Time to fall down about the Chief Baron's ears'. In the process of the renewal work the interior of the house was damaged and Idle refused to pay for the new roof. It is not recorded how the dispute was eventually settled but it appears to have been unresolved at the time of Idle's death.

The next proprietor of Dalry House, in 1761, was William Kirkpatrick of Allisland, one of the Principal Clerks of Session who was called to the bar in 1728. He had a short parliamentary career and returned to the law in 1738, later becoming Sheriff of Dumfriesshire. It was Kirkpatrick who was involved in an abortive plan to feu out the ground around Dalry House in 1762. Only two feus were granted after the following advertisement appeared in the *Edinburgh Evening Courant* of 17th March 1762:

> Feus for Houses and Gardens — This is to give notice, that the proprietor of the Parks of Dalry intends to set off, for situations of houses and gardens, certain parts of the said inclosures upon the south side thereof, lying along from the turnpike road from Fountainbridge, and also upon the east side thereof, lying down from the said turnpike road northwards towards the Castlebarns road, in larger or lesser spaces as purchasers shall call up . . .

Some years later, in 1778, Dalry House was acquired by the Honourable Basil Cochrane, one of the Commissioners of Customs in Scotland, whose tall, slender figure made him an ideal subject for Kay, the caricaturist. Cochrane had a military background with the Hanoverian army and was taken prisoner by the Highlanders at the Battle of Prestonpans in 1745. Kay's etching shows Cochrane carrying his favourite gold-headed staff and wearing 'black silk-velvet straps, instead of garters, which added very much to his military appearance'. He lived at Dalry until his death on 2nd October 1788.

The Walkers resided at Dalry House longer than any other family and hung on to their mansion until it was completely surrounded by industrial development and tenement buildings. James Walker acquired a portion of the ground in 1790 and bought the mansion and other ground in 1812. He built up his holding gradually, including the lands of North

Dalry House in Orwell Place dates from 1661 and was the principal house of the Lands of Dalry. It is pictured here in 1964 when the Edinburgh and Leith Old People's Welfare Council began a £50,000 appeal for renovations. (Crown Copyright: RCAHMS)

Merchiston which adjoined the south boundary of Dalry. There were three members of the family called James Walker, all of whom resided at Dalry House at various times, and all of whom are buried in St Cuthbert's churchyard. The family tomb is on the south boundary wall a few yards east of the tower on the corner of Lothian Road and King's Stables Road. The first James Walker was a Writer to the Signet who died aged seventy-four on 9th May 1817. The second James Walker was his son by a second marriage, who became an advocate and died at Dalry House on 3rd May 1856 at age sixty-six; and the third James Walker was the eldest son of the second James Walker and died in 1900 at age seventy at Hanley Lodge in Midlothian. The second and third James Walker saw extensive changes in their ancestral home at Dalry, firstly by the construction of the Union Canal in 1822 and then by the Caledonian Railway. These undertakings attracted a lot of industrial development and long rows of houses for the working population.

In the early 1870s the old manor house of Walter Chieslie ceased to be a family home and was acquired by the Scottish Episcopal Church as a training college for teachers. It was used in this way for many years, incorporating what was known as the Normal Practising School. In 1964 the Scottish Episcopal Church gifted the building to the Edinburgh and Leith Old People's Welfare Council, details of which are discussed in Chapter 9.

EASTER DALRY HOUSE

Easter Dalry House is in Distillery Lane, off Dalry Road, near its junction with Haymarket. It is possibly older than Dalry House but its history is an enigma. It is likely that Walter Chieslie was living at Easter Dalry House around the time that he built Dalry House in 1661. Even if that is proved, there is, of course, no guarantee that the house in which he was living is the same one which has survived until today. The Edinburgh volume of *The Buildings of Scotland* places Easter Dalry House in the middle of the eighteenth century, although other opinion suggests the seventeenth century. It is difficult to say why the house has not attracted the attention of writers on Edinburgh over the years, other than its comparatively small size. It is not mentioned by Maitland (1753), Arnot (1779) or Kincaid (1787), nor a century later by Grant or Wilson.

There is, however, a short period in its history when the notoriety of its occupant was sufficient to gain it a place in history. In 1841 David Scott, R.S.A., the painter, took a lease of Easter Dalry House, which he used as a studio until his death, in 1849, at the age of forty-two. His style was to paint on vast canvases, so large that it was necessary to have an extra barn-like studio built beside the house. One of his works at Easter Dalry was *The Discoverer of the Passage to India passing the Cape of Good Hope*, measuring 17 ½ feet by 13 ½ feet, which was shown on its own at an exhibition in the Calton Convening Rooms. Unfortunately, the wide canvas did not have the same appeal, and Scott was angered by the critics' patronising comments. Although he was a powerful and talented artist, Scott never received the acclaim which he thought his work deserved. His short life was crammed with disappointment, isolation and self-doubt. Ironically, during the last year of his life, 1849, the Royal Scottish Academy exhibited his work *The Discoverer of the Passage to India passing the Cape of Good Hope*, which was subsequently bought, by public subscription, for Trinity House, Leith. The accolade had come too late, however: Scott was already in Dean Cemetery.

In the latter half of the nineteenth century, Easter Dalry House was occupied, firstly, by James Watherston, the builder, and later by John S

David Scott, R.S.A., the painter, lived and worked at Easter Dalry House until his premature death in 1849. (From a painting by Charles Lees, R.S.A. in the collection of the Royal Scottish Academy.)

Gibson, the architectural woodcarver, who remained there until around 1930. John S. Gibson retired in the early 1930s, after a lifetime of work as a woodcarver and cabinetmaker. Much of his work was on church interiors, including the Thistle Chapel in St Giles Cathedral and Old St Paul's in Jeffrey Street. He also did work on the figurehead and trailboards of an Egyptian yacht, built by Ramage and Ferguson of Leith around 1923. Also in Distillery Lane at that time was Carrick, the monumental sculptor: Alexander Carrick's work in Edinburgh includes the statue of William Wallace at Edinburgh Castle, parts of the Scottish National War Memorial and the figure of *Justice* at the Sheriff Court in the Lawnmarket. From the 1930s, Easter Dalry House, or its immediate policies, appears to have changed occupancy fairly frequently, usually to people with artistic interests. They included: Norman J. Forrest, woodcarver and modeller at Dean Studio; James McKenzie, sculptor and woodcarver; Mrs H. Wingate Thornton, designer; and the Britannia Yacht Works.

In the mid-1970s, the house was sold by the Murray family of Dalry, and converted to office use. It was acquired in 1991 by Patrick and Sally Gammell, property developers, who undertook renovation and restoration of all rooms and the elegant stairway and mahogany banisters. A single-storey extension, to the south, was added in 1992. The exterior of the building and its policies were also greatly improved by re-siting an electricity sub-station, removing the informal car park, and redefining the entrance with stone walls and railings.

Despite a recent renewal of interest in the historical importance of Easter Dalry House, there is still much to be discovered. Its exact age is uncertain, and there is confusion about the position of the front entrance. The *Ordnance Survey Maps* of 1851 and 1881 show the entrance driveway leading up to the south side of the house, where there is a small porch over the doorway. Internally, the main staircase also faces south. Exactly why, and when, the main entrance was changed to the north side is a matter of conjecture. It may have been at the time when the driveway from Dalry Road was closed off and repositioned from Distillery Lane. Legend has it that the reason is much more sinister. It is said that the owner of the house was killed on his doorstep, in 1745, by the followers of Bonnie Prince Charlie for having refused to provide the troops with victuals. From that day on, the main door, on the south side, was closed off, and the family used the 'rear' entrance on the north side.

FOUNTAINBRIDGE

Originally the name Fountainbridge was applied to the road which ran from Main Point at Lauriston, westwards, to what is now the top of Henderson Terrace. In relation to modern street names the roads are East Fountainbridge, Fountainbridge and Dundee Street. Although much of that area is no longer considered to be part of Dalry, there is no doubt that historically the Lands of Dalry extended eastwards as far as Semple Street. According to John Smith in Volume XX of the *Book of the Old Edinburgh Club*, Fountainbridge, during most of the eighteenth century 'was dotted over with pretentious and roomy mansions each having its own garden and orchard and stabling accommodation . . . and occupied by wealthy and influential citizens'. Particularly along the south side of Fountainbridge there was a small colony of English government officials, many of whom had come to Edinburgh after the Union of 1707. It may well be that Mathew Lant and John Idle at Dalry House had set a trend which other lesser officials were happy to emulate. Perhaps the most prominent official was Richard Dowdeswell who took up the position of Commissioner of Excise in 1730. He was one of the first directors of the Royal Bank of Scotland when it was formed in 1727 and became a burgess and guilded brother of Edinburgh. On his death at Fountainbridge in 1758 his mansion was offered for sale as 'that large house in Fountainbridge Street, lately possessed by Commissioner Dowdeswell, with a stable, coach-house, hay-loft, flower garden and small park thereto adjoining'. Sadly, there is no surviving record of where the house stood or when it was demolished.

The area was not, however, the exclusive domain of English government officials. Several of the Scottish gentry retired to the salubrious air of Fountainbridge from the rather cramped conditions of the Old Town. Some of their dwellings can be identified by name and position although none has survived.

GROVE HOUSE

The Grove, or Grove House, and its immediate policies stood near the west corner of Fountainbridge and Grove Street. The corner is now occupied by a very unusual tenement, built in 1864, and designed by Frederick T. Pilkington, architect of the Barclay Church, Grange Park House, and Claigend Park, in Edinburgh. The grounds of Grove House extended over several acres, northwards to Morrison Street, but were

Lord Gardenstone lived at Grove House before moving to Morningside in 1789. He is shown here riding to the court in Parliament Square followed by his young attendant who looked after the horse while his lordship was on the bench. (Kay's Original Portraits.)

dissected in the middle of the nineteenth century by the Caledonian Railway. Although no illustration of Grove House has been traced, some idea of its size and importance can be gauged from the status of its occupants and also from advertisements for the sale of the house.

Grove House was built on land feued by Sir Alexander Brand in 1718. Its first tenant was Baron Kennedy of the Court of Exchequer who lived there until his death on 19th May 1754 at the age of eighty-one. In his obituary he was described as 'an eminent lawyer, a just judge and a good man'. After the death of Kennedy the house was let to Patrick Boyle and in 1762 it was purchased by Allan Whitefoord of Ballochmyle. A subsequent owner was the Hon. Charles Colville, a distinguished soldier, who died at Fountainbridge on 29th August 1775. On his death the property passed to his nephew, John, Lord Colville, who gave it the name 'The Grove'. When Colville sold the house in 1784 the advertisement stated that the house had been let to Lord Gardenstone. Many stories are told of Lord Gardenstone, notably his alleged habit of keeping a pig in his bedroom which lay on his clothes

On the left is Andrew Bell, the engraver, unkindly portrayed by Kay as having a large nose and deformed legs. He was the co-founder of the Encyclopaedia Britannica *which was produced in a printing works near Grove House. The figure on the right is William Smellie, the printer. (*Kay's Original Portraits.*)*

overnight and kept them 'pleasantly' warm for the next day. Gardenstone is more commonly known to have resided at Morningside House from 1789 and to have spent a considerable sum of money on the construction of St Bernard's Well at Stockbridge in 1788.

On 15th November 1796 Grove House entered one of its last phases when the property was purchased by the Bonar family. The first owner was Thomson Bonar, a Leith merchant whose brothers Andrew and Alexander were partners in the banking business of Ramsays, Bonar & Co. Thomson Bonar married a daughter of Andrew Bell the engraver and joint founder of *Encyclopaedia Britannica*. Bell bought ground near his son-in-law's house on which he erected a printing works where the early editions were produced. In Kay's *Original Portraits* there are two interesting caricatures of Andrew Bell, both of which over-emphasize his large nose and bow legs. The biographical notes which accompany the sketches show that Bell, far from being embarrassed by his unusual physical features, turned his deformed legs to some advantage: 'Once in a large company, when some jokes had passed on the subject, he said, pushing out one of them [his leg], that he would wager there was in the room a leg still more crooked. The company denied his assertion and accepted the challenge, whereupon he very coolly thrust out his other leg, which was still worse than its neighbour, and thus gained his bet'. On a more serious note Bell was a reasonably competent engraver but he made his fortune and reputation in the speculative publication of *Encyclopaedia Britannica*. It was said that he made £20,000 from one edition alone.

Andrew Bell died on 10th May 1809 and was survived by his son-in-law Thomson Bonar by only five years. When Thomson Bonar died on 25th July 1814 the house passed to John Bonar. By then the character of the district was under severe threat from the proposed construction of the Union Canal and later the railway. Some idea of the lay-out of Grove House at the beginning of the nineteenth century can be obtained from an advertisement for the sale of the house which appeared in the *Edinburgh Evening Courant* on 18th January 1816:

> To be sold or let for such time as may be agreed on. The house, offices and grounds of 'Grove' situated at Fountainbridge in the neighbourhood of Edinburgh. The house contains eight fire rooms besides kitchen, cellars etc with an excellent washing house and dairy adjoining, and the offices consist of gardeners houses, six stalled stables, byre and poultry house. The grounds consist of upwards of ten English acres and extend northwards from Fountainbridge to the Glasgow Road. About four acres are laid out in garden and pleasure grounds well stocked with fruit trees, and in the highest order. The remainder of the ground is divided into four parks, well fenced and surrounded with old trees under the shadow of which there is most delightful walks round the premises.

In the few decades after 1816 the district became progressively more industrial, and by the 1860s tenement dwellings were being erected in Fountainbridge and Grove Street. Grove House was probably demolished during this era.

FLORA HA'

The rural character of Fountainbridge, suggested by names like The Grove, was also evident in the neighbouring property Flora Ha', which survived until c. 1931. It lay to the east of Grove Street (near the junction with Fountainbridge) on land which was occupied partly by the Grange Cricket Club and partly as a market garden. The site is shown on *Kirkwood's Map* of 1817 as belonging to Mr Gordon. From 1846 Flora Ha' was occupied by Andrew Boyd, the millwright, whose son Thomas Boyd, Snr, was shown as occupier from around 1892. Thomas Boyd, Snr, married Christina Wright, and their son, Thomas Boyd, Jnr, was born in 1884. The Boyds' occupation of Flora Ha', after almost seventy-three years, came to an end shortly after the death of Christina on 29th November 1918. Although the house was demolished around 1931, it is still recalled by senior members of the Boyd family. The house was entered from the east side of Grove Street, immediately south of the former Mission Hall, and about one hundred yards from the junction with Fountainbridge. It was reached by a lane, running eastwards, wide enough to allow access by a horse and cart. At the Grove Street end there was a narrow gate for pedestrians and a wider gate for carts, which was always closed at dusk. The far end of the lane opened out into a courtyard with Flora Ha' on the north side enjoying a south-facing aspect. The yard was equipped for the horse era: stables along one side, a central well for water, and in the far corner, the midden. The house was of two storeys with bedrooms, a parlour, and a kitchen complete with box bed at one end. A bathroom was added at a later date.

After the departure of the Boyd family Flora Ha' and its policies were gradually incorporated into various business premises entered from the north side of Fountainbridge. The east corner of Grove Street and Fountainbridge was also the site of the bronze foundry of Sir John Steell, R.S.A. (1804-1891), sculptor of many famous Edinburgh statues, including the Duke of Wellington at the east end of Princes Street, and Lord Jeffrey in Parliament House.

At the present day nothing remains of Flora Ha' but its position can best be judged from the building No. 117 Grove Street, occupied as Clan House. A fading plaque above the entrance doorway states:

West Fountainbridge Hall
erected by
Barclay Church Congregation
1872

The entrance to Flora Ha' (at one time marked by a small arched doorway with the date 1753) was immediately to the south of No. 117. The site is now vacant and the archway has long since disappeared.

GARDNERS HALL

Gardners Hall completed the horticultural trio. It stood south of the junction of Ladywell Place and Morrison Street, and was reached by a long driveway opening into a circle in front of the house. The ground had originally been in the control of The Society and Fraternity of Gardeners in the Shire of Midlothian, whose members ran numerous commercial nurseries on the Lands of Dalry. Gardners Hall was built by the Society, probably in the early eighteenth century, but by 1785 it was owned by Nathaniel Donaldson who had just returned from the West Indies. It is possible, but by no means proved, that Tobago Street and Jamaica Street (now part of Morrison Street) were named from that connection. Donaldson became involved in an expensive lawsuit in 1787 with his neighbour William Morrison over the sale of two small areas of ground. At the conclusion of the court case he put Gardners Hall up for sale. The advertisement dated 4th January 1788 ran as follows:

> Villa to be sold. The house offices and parks of Gardeners Hall and Dowhill half a mile west of Edinburgh. The house is elegant for its size and commands a fine prospect. There are two enclosures consisting of five Scots acres, part of the ground is laid out in parterre and shrubbery.

By coincidence Gardners Hall was later owned by William Gardner W.S. He had the house demolished and the entire policies feued for the construction of Gardner's Crescent, described in the Edinburgh volume of *The Buildings of Scotland* as 'A simple and subtle master-work by R. and R. Dickson for William Gardner, 1822'. Gardner's Crescent was not completed until c. 1826, the year in which Gardner's Hall Church was erected at the south end for the United Associate Secession Church. Their first minister, the Rev. David Marr, lived at No.8 Gardner's Crescent. The Secession congregation moved in 1831 to Lothian Road Chapel (now the Filmhouse) and Gardner's Hall Church was acquired by St Cuthbert's Parish Church and renamed St David's. After St David's Church was demolished to allow through-traffic from Gardner's Crescent to Fountainbridge, the congregation removed to Viewforth Church on the corner of Viewforth and Gilmore Place.

When Gardner's Crescent was being developed, two streets were planned to the east but these were abandoned in favour of Port Hamilton, one of the basins of the Union Canal. The dividing line between the Lands of Dalry and the Lands of Tollcross was at Thornybauk and

Mrs Christina Boyd, around 1914, at her home Flora Ha' on the east side of Grove Street, near its junction with Fountainbridge. The Boyd family were at Flora Ha' from 1846 until the death of Mrs Boyd in 1918. (Courtesy of Mrs Mary Bruce.)

Semple Street, much further east than is generally considered to be Dalry at the present day. Much of the area of land bounded by Semple Street, Morrison Street, Gardner's Crescent and Fountainbridge has recently been cleared of old buildings in preparation for redevelopment, to include housing, offices and the possible reintroduction of waterfront properties. On the north-east corner of this piece of land a brewery was constructed in the early part of the eighteenth century. It was later acquired by John Semple followed by Robert Semple who gave their name to the adjacent street in 1766.

FOUNTAIN HOUSE

Fountain House, the last of the grand houses in or around Fountainbridge, was demolished as recently as 1934. It stood on the north side of Dundee Street almost opposite the junction with Viewforth, on ground which now belongs to Scottish and Newcastle's Fountain Brew-

ery. Fountain House was a well-proportioned building, standing back
from the main road, of three main storeys and a basement. There were
six bays or windows to the upper storeys and on the ground floor the
entrance doorway was offset to the right. At a later date a single-storey
wing was built to the east. The exact year of construction of Fountain
House is uncertain, but it was probably shortly after 1763 when the
plot on which it was built was feued off by William Kirkpatrick of
Dalry House to Alexander Bain, his wife Agnes Dunlop and their son
Alexander. It was offered for sale in 1774 and was acquired by Alexander Gardner, Depute Remembrancer of Exchequer in 1783. He died
at Fountain House in 1818 but the house remained in the family until
1862 on the death of his last surviving daughter, Miss Gardner.

   Fountain House was later acquired by J. & B. Greig, the engineers, at
what was later Nos. 26 and 28 Dundee Street. A surviving photograph
of Fountain House, taken shortly before its demolition in 1934, shows
on the left (west side) the original south entrance to Dalry House. The
entrance is flanked by high square fluted columns topped by ornamental vases. In the photograph the original gates have been removed and
replaced by timber doors with an inset door typical of the style used in
industrial properties.

BAINFIELD

Bainfield was not far from Fountain House, a matter of a few hundred
yards west and lying on the south side of Dundee Street. In relation to
existing streets it lay on ground now occupied by Murdoch Terrace,
Gibson Terrace and Yeaman Lane. The site is clearly shown in *Kirkwood's
Map* of 1817 as a rectangular piece of land bounded on the north by
what is now Dundee Street and on the south by the 'line of Canal
Proposed by Mr Baird'. The entrance gates were in the centre of the
north frontage and gave access by a long driveway to the main house.
There was a separate entrance and driveway from the south and most of
the available land was clearly under cultivation. To the east of Bainfield
was ground belonging to the Trades Maiden Hospital, and to the west
was the property known as North Merchiston.

   Bainfield was named after James Bain, a commercial gardener who
acquired six acres, part of the Lands of Merchiston, in 1728. He gradually converted most of the ground into a nursery which he worked
until his retirement in 1762. He was one of the founder members of
The Society and Fraternity of Gardeners in the Shire of Midlothian

*Fountain House stood on the north side of Dundee Street on land now occupied by Scottish & Newcastle's Fountain Brewery. It is shown here shortly before its demolition in 1934. On the left are the gate pillars which stood at what was the south drive to Dalry House. (*The Book of the Old Edinburgh Club, Volume XX.*)*

which built Gardners Hall near Morrison Street. In addition to his great interest in horticulture Bain was an ardent follower of the Secession movement, and his house at Bainfield was used from time to time as a place of worship. He was an elder at Bristo Street Church until his death around 1765.

From 1780 the house at Bainfield was owned by Bain Whyt W.S., whose advertisement to let the house in the same year gives a good description of the available accommodation:

> Country house to Let. The house of Bainfield a little south west of Fountainbridge consisting of a parlour and small room adjoining a large room with concealed bed and light closet, two large bedrooms with light closets and three smaller bedrooms with a good kitchen — a flower plot, a small kitchen and a piece of grass ground surrounded with shrubbery and a well of good water.

Bain Whyt was a colourful character who resided at Bainfield until his death on 26th December 1818. He never married and was survived by his sister Agnes Whyt who died in 1836 at the age of eighty-seven. Despite being very active in his own profession and holding the rank of major in the Royal Edinburgh Volunteers, Whyt is probably best re-membered as founder of the Wagering Club.

The Wagering Club was founded in January 1775 with twelve mem-bers and a constitution which directed that the membership should not exceed thirty. In fact it greatly exceeded thirty by a system of allowing 'visitors'. Membership was from a wide range of occupations, the only requirement being that the proposed member had 'the spirit of good fellowship'. Originally the value of a wager was not allowed to exceed 'the value of one bottle wine or half a mutchkin of punch' but this was later altered to a fixed limit of one shilling. Each wager was included on a sheet which had two columns for signatures, one for those voting 'yes' and one for those voting 'no'. The wagers were sealed until the next annual meeting (held on the last Monday of January) and were then opened and read out. The winners did not benefit financially but the losers paid one shilling into a common fund. Once the small ad-ministrative expenses had been deducted, the balance of money was given to a deserving cause in the city. The Club records show that the first meeting in 1775 was at Matthew Thomson's Tavern in Old Post House Close, and that in subsequent years there was a tendency for the meetings to be held in the hotels of the New Town in preference to the taverns of the Old Town. Wagers were on a wide range of issues of both national and local interest. The year and the result were usually, but not always, recorded in the books:

> That Miss Halket, niece of the late Miss Fletcher, shall be married in the course of the year, 1780. She was not.

> That there shall be a cessation of hostilities between Great Britain and the Dutch before the 1st August, 1781. There was none.

> That France shall be invaded during this Year, 1792. It was.

> That the Prince and Princess of Wales shall be reconciled and living together before next meeting, 1808. They were not.

> That Poland shall be an independent state at next meeting, 1832. She was not.

> That a railway betwixt Edinburgh and Glasgow shall be commenced before next meeting, 1832. It was not.

The history of the Wagering Club was reviewed in some detail by James B. Sutherland in Volume II of the *Book of the Old Edinburgh Club*.

The amenity of Bainfield was adversely affected by the construction of the Union Canal along its southern aspect in 1822, and even more so by the building of the Vulcanite Factory to the east in 1861. Within a short time thereafter the Bainfield policies were cleared for the construction of Murdoch Terrace, Gibson Terrace and Yeaman Lane. In the decade before its demolition Bainfield was occupied by Thomas Gibson & Son's Iron and Wire Works whose principal, Thomas R. Gibson J.P., resided at Bainfield, No. 94 Polwarth Terrace, Edinburgh. On the demolition of the old house of Bainfield the firm continued in business for many years at No. 18 Gibson Terrace, the street being named after the Gibson family.

NORTH MERCHISTON HOUSE

The property known as North Merchiston was built on the Lands of Merchiston and not on the Lands of Dalry. Nevertheless, their juxtaposition, and the fact that Merchiston and Dalry were in joint ownership for many years, justifies its inclusion here.

Around 1756 a large part of the Merchiston estate to the west of Bainfield was acquired by John Adam the architect, elder brother of the more famous Robert Adam who designed the north side of Charlotte Square. As is often the case with houses of this age, the only surviving description comes from an advertisement for sale in 1764:

> The House, offices, gardens and parks of North Merchiston being a feu of part of the estate of Merchiston. The whole consists of 27 acres (Scots measure) beautifully laid out. The House contains a hall, a dining room, drawing room, four bed chambers and closets, two bedrooms without fires, two good garrets, a housekeeper's room which serves for a storeroom, pantry cellar and larder, also a stable and coachhouse, has been formerly let at £40 a year. The ground which never was rented is reckoned at £5 per acre including the value of the trees, gravel walks, TEMPLES and ORNAMENTAL BUILD-INGS, upon it, so that there is a free rent of £126: 17s: 6d. Sterling after deducting £53: 2s: 6d. sterling of feu duty payable to Watson Hospital. The property of John Adam, architect, residing in the Cowgate, Edinburgh.

It is not clear how much time John Adam spent at North Merchiston but the house was advertised to be let furnished shortly before Adam died in June 1792. He was buried in Greyfriars Kirkyard, the family mausoleum near the Covenanters' Prison being designed and erected by John himself. The inscriptions were added by John Adam's son William in 1827. After the death of John Adam the house was occupied by Lord Bannatyne in 1807 and then the whole property was sold to James Walker of Dalry House in 1818. In 1822 the estate of North Merchiston was completely divided by the construction of the Union Canal, and the *Edinburgh & Leith Post Office Directory Map* of 1845 shows the proposed line of the Caledonian Railway cutting off the north-west corner of the estate. In the years between these two main developments North Merchiston House was used by the Royal Engineers Office but it was again residential in 1835 when it was the home of George Joseph Bell, advocate and professor of law at Edinburgh University. In the last quarter of the nineteenth century the amenity of North Merchiston deteriorated and the ground was eventually used for the construction of tenement buildings.

In relation to modern street names North Merchiston policies stretched along Dundee Street from Yeaman Lane (in the east) to Harrison Road (in the west), the entrance driveway and lodge being on the west corner of Fowler Terrace and Dundee Terrace. The ground extended south as far as Polwarth Gardens and returned northwards by Yeaman Place bordering the property of Bainfield. Almost the entire estate is covered by three streets of tenement buildings running east to west, namely Bryson Road, Watson Crescent and Temple Park Crescent. Temple Park Crescent is named after one of John Adam's temples erected on the estate and marked on *Kirkwood's Map* of 1819.

2
The Early History of Gorgie

Well within living memory Gorgie and its adjacent lands had three substantial houses dating from the seventeenth century: Gorgie House on the north side of Gorgie Road near Alexander Drive; Stenhouse Mansion at Stenhouse Mill Lane; and Saughton Hall which stood in what is now Saughton Park. Only one now remains. Fortunately, the surviving house, Stenhouse Mansion, is owned by the National Trust for Scotland and is, therefore, likely to remain in existence for a very long time to come.

Parts of the district of Gorgie were developed into suburbs of Edinburgh very much later than neighbouring Dalry. The eastern portions of the Lands of Dalry stretched as far as Semple Street at Tollcross and therefore came under the threat of development much sooner than parts of Gorgie. The *Post Office Plan of Edinburgh and Leith* for 1900-1901 shows that Gorgie's main centres of population did not extend further than the line of the Edinburgh Suburban and South Side Junction Railway, which crossed above Gorgie Road at the foot of Robertson Avenue. West of that point there was a fair amount of ribbon development on both sides of Gorgie Road and on the banks of the Water of Leith. Otherwise the area was mainly farmland. Most of this development consisted of communities which had existed long before the city's urban sprawl had reached so far west.

Starting at a point immediately west of the railway bridge carrying the suburban line, the first two buildings were the school and the church. Gorgie Board School lay on the left and the 'Little Church in the Field' lay on the right. A few hundred yards west at the first dogleg bend, Gorgie House sat in its own grounds on the north side of Gorgie Road, and Gorgie Mills (home of Cox's Glue Works) straddled both sides of the road. A cluster of houses lay between Cox's and Saughton Hall on the north side. At the point where Chesser Avenue now meets Gorgie Road was Delhaig, and west of that was Stenhouse Mill and Mansion. The outlying properties on the north side were Balgreen and Damhead, and on the south side, Gorgie Farm.

According to *The Streets of Edinburgh*, the name Gorgie is said to have been originally *Gorgyne* from the Welsh *Jorcyn*, meaning a spacious wedge of land—between Craiglockhart Hill and the Water of Leith.

LANDS OF GORGIE

The history of the Lands and manor house of Gorgie are recorded in a lengthy article by John Smith in the *Proceedings of the Society of Antiquaries of Scotland*, volume II of the 6th Series, 1927-1928.

Mr Smith records that the Lands of Gorgie were acquired in 1236 by Sir William Livingstone and remained in the family's possession for the next three hundred years. A sasine of the Lands of Gorgie was granted to William Livingstone in 1467 and another to Margrate Livingstoun in 1513. For reasons which are not now known Margrate Livingstoun granted a charter on 16th February 1527-28 in favour of her husband's cousin, James Hamilton of Schawfield, 'of the half lands and half mill of Gorgie'. When James Hamilton died shortly thereafter, the lands appear to have been unofficially annexed by Thomas Otterburn of Reidhall. Hamilton's heirs were not, however, unmindful of their claim. Many years later the problem surfaced again during negotiations over ownership of tithes, originally payable to the Abbey of Holyrood House, but acquired through a number of transactions by Thomas Otterburn of Reidhall in 1575. Otterburn thought his interest was secure but in 1605 his title to half of the lands was challenged by Sir Robert Hamilton, as heir of the late James Hamilton of Schawfield. When Otterburn refused to concede the claim, Hamilton took him to court and was granted a sasine on 20th March 1606. After a lapse of nearly eighty years the Hamiltons had regained their interest in the Lands of Gorgie, only to resign all that they had won—back to the Otterburns in 1609. No reason is recorded for this dramatic change of mind but it may have been on account of threatened litigation. Whatever the reason, the victor 'Otterburn de Reidhall' sold the lands immediately to James Duncan of Ratho, who in turn passed the property to his son, also James Duncan, in 1620.

A new chapter in the history of Gorgie began with the arrival of the Broun family, who remained there for several generations. They came to prominence, firstly as tenants and then as owners, from 1656. John Broun, the first, was a member of the Broun family of Hartrie near Biggar, whose female members married into the families of Otterburn of Reidhall and Foulis of Colinton. It was probably this family influence which secured the tenancy of the lands for John Broun as early as 1578. He married one of the Watsons of Saughton and died at Gorgy Mylne in 1592.

John Broun, the second, a 'werrie honnest, famous and ansuerable man', was very young when he succeeded to his father's tanancy. His local knowledge and integrity made him an obvious choice by the Privy Council to arrange the finance for the construction of a new bridge at Saughtonhall. In 1605 he was given power to collect dues for a period of nine years from everyone who used the fords across the Water of Leith. With the money collected he was under an obligation to build within three years thereafter 'a sure bridge for man and horse on the Water of Leith a little below Dalyellis mill . . .' In 1617 the completed bridge was approved by the Privy Council after a site inspection by Sir Archibald Napier of Merchiston, in the presence of other justices. Although the full contract had taken twelve years to complete, it resulted in a bridge which stood the test of time. It remained in use until the 1890s when it was swept away by flood waters, to be replaced by a light iron bridge. The creator of the original bridge, John Broun, the second, died in 1653.

In 1656 Isobel Foulis (wife of James Duncan the owner of the Lands of Gorgie) sold the lands to John Broun, the third. Unfortunately he died in 1658 leaving everything to the fourth John Broun, who benefited greatly from the accumulated efforts of his forebears. It was the fourth John Broun who was able to buy the Barony of Braid when it came on the market after the death of Sir William Dick of Braid. In 1684 the fourth John Broun was succeeded by his son Andrew, who in turn was succeeded by his own son, also Andrew. The second Andrew was unmarried and the family line became extinct.

For a short time the Lands of Gorgie were owned by Sir Alexander Brand of Dalry but in 1709 he was forced to sell the property to George Lind, a merchant from Edinburgh. He was succeeded by two generations of his own family who were in possession up to at least 1764. In the latter part of the eighteenth century the property was owned by the Cox family who began as corn millers on the north side of Gorgie Road and expanded their business into leather tanning and glue manufacturing on the south side of the road. Cox's Glue Works remained at Gorgie until 1969, after which the site on the south side of Gorgie Road was developed as Telephone House.

GORGIE HOUSE

When John Smith contributed his article on Gorgie to the *Proceedings of the Society of Antiquaries of Scotland* in 1927, he reported that Gorgie House was still in existence on the north side of Gorgie Road. In 1929 Gorgie House was included in the *Tenth Report of the Royal Commission on the Ancient and Historical Monuments of Scotland*, which reviewed the three-phase development of the house.

Despite the authoritative nature of both reports, they differ in some important respects. The two reports are, however, in agreement that there was a three-phase development. Originally the house was built on an L-shaped plan, then the L-shape was enlarged to a rectangle, and finally a completely new front was put on the old building. The relevant part of the *Tenth Report* runs as follows, now with italics added:

> The modern part of Gorgie House screens the remains of a much altered house of the 17th century, originally L-shaped on plan, having a main block lying *north* and *south*, and a wing projecting *eastward*, in alignment with the *south* gable. The re-entrant angle, infilled in 1710, opened to the *north-east* and presumably contained the staircase with the entrance at the stair-foot, but these details have been demolished.

Mr Smith's description refers to the three-phase development but states that when the house was L-shaped 'the principal entrance was on the *west* side of the L, as that faced the mill'. He then says that a later owner (George Lind) 'added a new part to the *south-east*'. Finally, in relation to the third phase he states that 'the incorporation of this new *east* front is clearly seen on its *south* end'. The *Ordnance Survey Map* of 1932 shows the east front protruding further south than the remainder of the building. Mr Smith's reference to the principal door being on the west side is not confirmed in the *Tenth Report*. He does, however, include in his draft article a photograph showing the new frontage, 'built in the Adam style'. It consists of a symmetrical elevation of three storeys (with the upper storey reduced in height), a central doorway and an embellished wallhead.

The confusing descriptions should not, however, detract from the interest in the house and its interior. The dining room, to the south, on the ground floor of the main block had walls panelled in eighteenth-century style, and a plaster ceiling divided into compartments, bearing the date 1661 and the initials C.R.2 (Charles II). Two other main areas of interest are recorded: the basement chamber of the wing retained a

*Ceiling rondel, with the date 1661 and the initials C.R. 2 for Charles II, at Gorgie House, prior to its demolition for the construction of Poole's Roxy Cinema on the south side of Gorgie Road. (*Crown Copyright: RCAHMS.*)*

stretch of seventeenth-century panelling; and there was a contemporary fireplace and over-panel in the northern chamber of the main block at second-floor level.

The *Tenth Report* also refers to the pedimented overdoor with the date 1710 below the entwined initials of George Lind and his wife Jean Montgomery. This pediment was inserted above the new doorway when George Lind extended the original L-shaped house. It was later set into the inner face of the garden wall south-south-east of the house, along with another unmarked pediment, probably at the time of the third phase.

John Smith concluded his report in 1927 by saying that it was owing to the care of each of the owners of Gorgie House 'that this fine old manor house is in such wonderful preservation'. He also observed, however, that 'signs are not wanting that the time is fast approaching when its removal and demolition will take place'. He was not wrong. For many years prior to 1927 the house had been in the possession of Finlay Dun (secretary to the Swan Land and Cattle Co. Ltd.), followed by the Misses Finlay Dun. By 1933 the occupier was James McArthur, and C.L. Patrick ran the Gorgie House Riding Academy from the stables. In 1937 the house was demolished, apparently without effective protest, to make way for a forthcoming attraction which could never have been anticipated by the old families of Gorgie House—the Poole's Roxy Cinema built in 1937 by Chadwick Watson & Co. of Leeds. The ground plan deposited with the Dean of Guild Court and dated 16th April 1937 shows Gorgie House, beside which are the words 'existing buildings removed'. Although some old garages or stables were exactly on the site of the intended cinema, Gorgie House is shown completely clear of the proposed building line. Nevertheless it was demolished and the Poole's Roxy Cinema was built in the garden ground.

LANDS OF SAUGHTONHALL

A very detailed account of the history of the lands of Saughtonhall and its mansion is given by Miss A.S. Cowper in Part Four of *Historic Corstorphine and Roundabout*. Miss Cowper reviews at length details of the various owners, and includes a myriad of well-researched data on their lifestyles and influence on the local community.

The lands of Saughtonhall were held by the Abbey of Holyroodhouse until the sixteenth century. Thereafter Saughtonhall was divided between various proprietors up to the mid-seventeenth century, several well-known family names appearing in the records: Watson, Winraham,

This group of buildings (part of 'the Auld Square') near to present-day Alexander Drive, probably survived until c. 1933. The large building on the left is clearly the oldest, beside the 'modern' appendage of John Henderson's wine and spirit store. On the right, the single-storey house (Ivy Bank) was occupied by Ben Bremner, the blacksmith at Murieston. (Crown Copyright: RCAHMS.)

Lawtie, Morison, Somerville, Wilkie, West, Dalzell and Moodie. William Watson and his descendants appear to have been a particularly troublesome family, frequently involved in disputes and litigation. The list is lengthy. William Watson set a bad example by getting into trouble with the authorities for being absent from the army musters of 1544 and 1546. This incident seems to have set the scene for his son, James, who became involved in several other disputes. In 1569 he fell out with Christian and Agnes Thomson over his failure to repay a loan, and in the same year he lost an action against Johnne Stanehope, the miller at Stenhouse, for the supply of oatmeal. A few months later he won a court case against John Thomson (the brother of Christian and Agnes) who was found guilty of having carried off Watson's livestock 'under silence of nyght'. Several years later, in 1590, the third generation, John, showed that the same blood ran in his veins. Following a land transaction with John Coutts of Dalry, Watson's conduct was severely criticised by the Kirk Session of St Cuthbert's.

Between 1600 and 1650 the lands of Saughtonhall had various owners, the Morison family taking over from John Watson and John Dalzell. The Morisons then sold the lands to Thomas Moodie of Dalry in 1639. It was Thomas Moodie who bequeathed a substantial sum of money for the erection of Canongate Kirk. In 1660 his daughter Janet sold Saughton Hall to Robert Baird, merchant and baillie in Edinburgh. This last transaction heralded a period of comparative stability for Saughtonhall, which remained in the possession of the Baird family for several generations.

Shortly after the arrival of Robert Baird, the lands of Saughtonhall became a barony (lands granted by the crown and given jurisdiction), incorporating various parcels of land which had previously been owned by families Watson, Lawtie, Dalzell and Morison. Robert was a successful merchant trading extensively with Holland in the 1660s and 1670s. He became a baronet of Nova Scotia in 1695, a title instituted by Charles I and conferred on persons contributing to the settlement of Nova Scotia. On his death in 1696 he was succeeded by his son James, who in turn was succeeded by his son, Robert. When the second Sir Robert took up residence at Saughton Hall in 1715 he was unmarried, but subsequently he married twice. The first marriage was to Janet Baikie in 1729, who died in 1733, and the second was in 1737 to Dame Helen Hope who died in 1741. On the death of Sir Robert in 1742 an inventory of his effects was compiled which showed the nature of his interests—fishing, archery, and a considerable library of books on travel and history. Sir Robert also owned a 'rotula', invented by George Brown, a minister who had been banished from Edinburgh for conducting irregular marriages. The rotula, whilst primitive by modern standards, was probably ahead of its time in claiming to 'teach those of a very ordinary capacity who can but read the figures, to add, subtract, multiply and divide'.

Sir Robert Baird was survived by his three children David, William and Mary. David was the heir but survived his father by only three years. As a lieutenant in the 1st Royal he died at Fontenoy in 1745 aged seventeen, following amputation of an injured limb. The subsequent marriages of his sister, Mary, and his brother, William, had a significant influence on the future of the family name. Mary Baird married David Gardiner, son of Col. James Gardiner of Bankton, and William Baird married Frances, the daughter of Col. James. From then on the family at Saughton Hall took the name Gardiner Baird. On the death of young David from his war injury the estate passed to his brother William, a captain in the Royal Navy. He died at Saughton Hall in 1771 and was succeeded by his son James Gardiner Baird, a lieutenant-colonel in the 28th Light Dragoons. Sir James Gardiner Baird died in 1830 and was buried in St Cuthbert's Churchyard where there is a monument on Mid Wall with the inscription:

> The burial place of Sir James
> Gardiner Baird, Baronet, of
> Saughton Hall, who died 23rd
> June 1830, aged 74 years; the
> last of the family interred here.

By the end of the eighteenth century the Gardiner Baird family had ceased to occupy Saughton Hall, having first come there as the Baird family in 1660. The family line continues to the present day, and several streets in and around Balgreen commemorate the name Baird.

SAUGHTON HALL MANSION

The main house or mansion on the lands of Saughtonhall was known as Saughton Hall. It was constantly confused with Saughton House which lay a mile or so to the west. Saughton House, on the west side of Saughton Road, was demolished several years ago for the construction of Broomhouse Primary School.

Saughton Hall was probably built by Robert Baird, the Edinburgh merchant, after he bought the estate in 1660. The original entrance to it was by what is now Ford's Road. By far the longest period of ownership was by the Baird family, but it had other significant uses in more recent times. Several descriptions, plans and photographs of the house survive, and Miss A.S. Cowper, in Part Four of *Historic Corstorphine and Roundabout*, includes details of an inventory, made in 1785, of the main contents of the house. The list includes the following apartments and items, among others: hall—a large mahogany table, six green painted chairs, six brackets, eight pictures of Alexander's battles, and a painting of our Saviour; parlour—four chairs, a large settee chair, a table and a grate; dining room—marble table, a cracked chimney glass and a grate; drawing room—twelve mahogany chairs, window curtains, a marble table, a carpet, a chimney glass with double branches, and two corner cupboards. The Green Room and the Yellow Room were also listed, obviously laid out as bedrooms with four-poster beds. The kitchen contained four crans (for supporting pots on an open fire), a jack, a perpetual oven, three dressers, tongs, and a grate.

By the end of the eighteenth century the Gardiner Baird family had ceased to occupy Saughton Hall, having first come there as the Baird family in 1660. During the nineteenth century the house was used as a mental hospital.

At the close of the nineteenth century the house and its policies were the subject of a report dated 27th June 1899 by Mr Thomas Hunter, Town Clerk of Edinburgh. He was reporting to the Public Parks Committee of Edinburgh Corporation regarding ground at Saughtonhall which it was proposed should be purchased for a public park. The total extent of the ground was some ninety acres, pleasantly situated, and clearly defined—on the north by the North British Railway, on the south and east by the Water of Leith, and on the west by a road leading northwards from the farm of Saughton Hall Mains. The proposed purchase was to include Saughton Hall Mansion and its grounds, Balgreen House and its grounds, and some fields which were let to Sir John Batty Tuke, the physician. There were, however, a few words of caution as the Town Clerk observed that 'although not close to the populous district which it is intended to serve as a place of recreation, it is readily accessible by good roads and tramways'. Probably anticipating that Edinburgh's urban sprawl would soon reach Saughton, Mr Hunter consulted the land valuator, James Inglis Davidson of Saughton Mains, who knew the ground well. A provisional arrangement was made with the owner, Sir William Gardiner Baird, Bart., to buy the land for £51,500, which worked out at about £570 per acre. As the land was entailed (restricted to a designated line of heirs), approval by the Court of Session was required for the sale. Transitional arrangements were made with Sir John Batty Tuke for him to continue in part occupation of ground not immediately needed for the public park. Later documentation suggests that the final deal at Martinmas 1900 was £52,900 for ninety-eight acres of land, some of which was used by Edinburgh Corporation for housing. Part of the extensive grounds was used to house the Scottish National Exhibition of 1908.

In 1929 Saughton Hall was included in the *Tenth Report of the Royal Commission on the Ancient and Historical Monuments of Scotland*. It was described as 'a large and rambling structure mainly modern, except the central portion, which dates from the late 17th century'. At that time the house was disused but conserved by its owners, the City of Edinburgh, who had bought it after a long period of occupancy as a mental hospital. The original seventeenth-century house was built on an L-plan, the main block (measuring 68 feet by 26 externally) lying on a

Saughton Hall Mansion in 1908. The oldest part of the house was probably built by Robert Baird after he bought the estate in 1660. On account of its semi-derelict state, it was razed to the ground in 1952 on the instructions of the owners, Edinburgh Corporation.

north-east/south-west axis. A wing projected in a north-west direction in alignment with the south-west gable. The re-entrant angle formed by these two structures contained a semi-octagonal staircase with a wheel-stair leading to the three main floors and the attic. All the rooms occupied the full width of the house which meant that they had to be intercommunicating. The only access was the wheel-stair. At the time of the *Tenth Report* very few original internal features remained. In the basement kitchen there was an arched fireplace, subsequently infilled, and also an eighteenth-century fireplace on the opposite wall. Perhaps the most interesting features were three ornate plaster ceilings in good condition, two at first-floor level and a third at second-floor level. The description of two of these ceilings in the *Tenth Report* runs as follows:

> The southern ceiling is quartered by moulded ribs with foliaceously enriched soffits, which run from semicircular panels at the walls to a central circular panel. The panels and quarters contain plaster ornaments, including vine, rose, and thistle motifs, and lion masks. The other ceiling is the richer and is more elaborately ribbed; the motifs

employed in enrichment are the lion rampant, the Seton dragon, the star, the cherub's head, and the curious Renaissance ornament comprising a nude human trunk and head, the former terminating in a rude variety of acanthus leafage, the latter 'horned' with rudimentary volutes. The most interesting enrichment, however, is a hunting scene, where the bare-legged hunter is clad in 17th-century garb, with a riding shirt, and urges on his mount with a three-tailed whip; below a hound gambols.

Many of these plaster ceiling features were included in drawings, made by the City Architect, A.A. MacCulloch, in April 1942. His plan also includes the various 'modern' additions referred to in the *Tenth Report*. In 1947 a later City Architect, E.J. Macrae, also included Saughton Hall in a publication, *The Heritage of Greater Edinburgh*, sub-titled *Report on Old Buildings or Works worthy of Preservation in Edinburgh outwith the Royal Mile*. Under Saughton Hall his entry reads: 'Main building semi-derelict. Old portion might be restored for community purposes'. Sadly his idea was never taken up and in 1952 nearly three centuries of history were consumed when Saughton Hall was razed to the ground by the Royal Engineers and the Fire Brigade on the instruction of the owners.

SAUGHTON HALL ASYLUM

Several documents survive which provide an interesting insight into the use of Saughton Hall during the nineteenth century as 'a private lunatic asylum exclusively designed for the reception of Patients of the higher ranks'. Much of the early work was undertaken by Dr W.H. Lowe, followed by Dr John Batty Tuke. At various times the separate property, Balgreen House (now the site of Balgreen School), was also used in connection with the mental hospital.

The life of William Henry Lowe, 1815-1900, was researched by Joan P.S. Ferguson for her article in the *Proceedings of the Royal College of Physicians, Edinburgh 1991*: 21: 483-7. William Henry Lowe was born in 1815, either at Whitchurch, Shropshire, where his older brothers and sisters were born, or at Burton-on-Trent where his younger brothers and sisters were born. He was one of fourteen children, his father, Samuel Lowe, being an attorney. Nothing is known of Lowe's schooling, but he came to Edinburgh University where he graduated M.D. in 1840 and became a Fellow of the Royal College of Physicians, Edinburgh in 1846.

Dr William Henry Lowe (1815–1900) was appointed resident physician, in 1840, at Saughton Hall Institute for the Recovery of the Insane, usually referred to as Saughton Hall Asylum. (Courtesy of the Royal College of Pysicians, Edinburgh.)

In 1840 Dr Lowe was appointed resident physician of the Saughton Hall Institute for the Recovery of the Insane, later known as Saughton Hall Asylum. On taking up the post at Saughton Hall, he noted that although the asylum had been in existence for many years it did not have regulations or a fixed code of practice. With the co-operation of the existing staff he set out to compile such a document which ran to several pages. The report describes Saughton Hall as having 'been very considerably enlarged, and baths of the best construction, airing galleries, and other conveniences added'. An ornamental garden and a botanic garden were created, the patients being encouraged to tend the plants and the grounds in general. Male and female patients were admitted but they were kept strictly apart with a separate staircase for each. Occasionally, at meal times, males and females could sit together, 'care being taken by the selection of the Patients that no impropriety [could] occur'. Each floor of the house was used for distinct functions so that the management was able 'to separate those who from greater eccentricities of character might annoy their companions, or who, from being regardless of the usual restraints of society, might disgust by their unpleasant habits'. It was found that the females were very much more amenable than the males to learning some useful pastimes. Patients could also attend lectures on chemistry and botany three times a week or play a wide variety of games—bowls, billiards, battledore and shuttlecock, cards, chess and backgammon. The report concludes with a list of staff rules and regulations, one of which, at least, was designed to concentrate the mind: Instruction 6—If an attendant permit a Patient to escape, he or she shall be fined £1. Dr Lowe also compiled information, divided into eight separate tables, giving statistical data between January 1824 and November 1840, on such matters as the ages and status of patients, duration of stay, cause of mental alienation, species of insanity etc.

Dr Lowe's report was obviously intended to act partly as a brochure for those persons who were about to entrust their relatives to his care. His confident assertion that the asylum was the best of its kind was generally borne out in two 1862 Reports by the General Board of the Commissioners in Lunacy for Scotland. On the second visit the Board reported that they 'found the asylum in its usual satisfactory condition'.

Joan P.S. Ferguson also traces in her article Dr Lowe's great interest in botany, a passion which he was well able to indulge, using the extensive gardens and hothouses at Saughton Hall. He became a member of the Botanical Society of Edinburgh, founded in 1836, and he constructed his own botanic garden at Saughton Hall. Dr Lowe was President of the Royal College of Physicians, Edinburgh from 1873 to 1875 after which he retired to Wimbledon. In his retirement he took up the study of Coleoptera (beetles) and held the position of President of the Botanical Society of the British Isles in London. He died in 1900, the year in which his beloved Saughton Hall was purchased by Edinburgh Corporation.

Saughton Hall Asylum was also fortunate to attract another doctor of considerable talent and varied interests, Dr John Batty Tuke, born in Staines, near London, in 1835. Tuke came from an old Quaker family and spent much of his early years in the East Riding of Yorkshire. In 1842 he was in Edinburgh under the care of his uncle Dr Smith at No.20 Charlotte Square. He attended Edinburgh Academy, and graduated in medicine at Edinburgh in 1856. After marriage at age twenty-one he emigrated to New Zealand where he was medical officer in charge of the colonial troops during the Maori War. He returned to Edinburgh in 1863 to work firstly at the Royal Edinburgh Hospital and then at Fife and Kinross Asylum. In 1873 he joined Drs Smith and Lowe at Saughton Hall Asylum and at Balgreen House where he was resident. It was at Balgreen House that Dr Tuke and his associates formed the nucleus of the Edinburgh Pathological Club in 1886. He was also instrumental in founding the Research Laboratory of the Royal College of Physicians, Edinburgh and became its President in 1898 for three consecutive years, during which time he received a Knighthood. Around 1910, after Edinburgh Corporation purchased Saughton Hall, Sir John Batty Tuke moved the asylum to Mavisbank near Eskbank, adopting the name New Saughtonhall. He was succeeded at Mavisbank by his son, also Dr John Batty Tuke.

In recent years two papers, relating to the confinement of inmates in Victorian asylums in Scotland, have touched on life at Saughton Hall Asylum. In 1978 Irene Rosie researched Thomas Balfour, M.P. for Orkney and Shetland, who was brought to Saughton Hall Asylum in 1837 suffering from the stresses of politics, religion and his intended marriage to one Eleanor Edmeston. Despite an early improvement in his condition he deteriorated rapidly and died at Saughton Hall in 1838. The second paper, considerably more detailed and authoritative, by Dr M. Barfoot and Dr Allen W. Beveridge, appeared in *Psychological Medicine*, 1990, 20, 263-284 under the title *Madness at the crossroads: John Home's letters from the Royal Edinburgh Asylum, 1886-1887*. Barfoot and Beveridge provide a detailed and critical discussion of the Edinburgh lawyer, John Home, a certified inmate of the Royal Edinburgh Asylum during the years 1886 and 1887. Home left the Royal Edinburgh Asylum on 7th September 1887 and was transferred to the care of Dr J. Batty Tuke at Saughton Hall Asylum where he died on 10th April 1890 from 'congestion of the lungs'. Home's extraordinary behaviour and thought-provoking correspondence are reviewed with dispassionate candour by the two doctors in their quest to establish whether Home was mad or wrongfully confined.

THE SCOTTISH NATIONAL EXHIBITION OF 1908

Shortly after 7a.m. on 1st May 1908 His Royal Highness Prince Arthur of Connaught arrived at Waverley Station, Edinburgh where he was met by Sir Robert Cranston, Chairman of the Executive Committee of the Scottish National Exhibition. His Royal Highness had travelled overnight from London to be in Edinburgh to open the Exhibition at Saughton Hall on the outskirts of the city. A grand lunch for three hundred guests was held at the North British Station Hotel (now the Balmoral Hotel), after which the entourage made its way out to Saughton Hall for the official opening at 3 p.m. After the Prince had declared the Exhibition open, Lord Provost James P. Gibson announced that the five-month event had already got off to a very good start: instead of the anticipated overdraft of £16,000 the Exhibition organisers had £780 in the bank; almost the total costs had been met by the advance sale of 38,558 season tickets at 10/6d each (52 ½ p). On the opening day the attendance reached over 125,000, made up of 122,500 season-ticket entries and 2819 day admissions of 1/- (5p) each. Transporting that number of people to and from the Exhibition put considerable pressure on the transport systems. Extra tramcars were laid on from the centre of Edinburgh at 2d per journey one way, quickly undercut by the North British Railway Company which offered the return journey for just 2½d (approximately 1p). The train left Waverley Station at regular intervals and arrived six minutes later at a specially constructed station at Balgreen near to where the line branched to Corstorphine. Gorgie Station on the Edinburgh Suburban and South Side Junction Railway was also one of the recommended routes, although it entailed a further journey of about half a mile, usually on foot. The various railway companies put on special trains and connections from most parts of Scotland.

The Exhibition was laid out on the garden ground of Saughton Hall Mansion to the west of Balgreen Road, on land now used as Saughton Rose Gardens and Saughton Public Park. There were two entrances: the main Gorgie entrance, with an imposing triple-domed gateway, was reached by a purpose-built bridge over the Water of Leith at the west corner of Balgreen Road and Gorgie Road; and the second entrance (to accommodate the train passengers to Balgreen) was near what is now the junction of Balgreen Road and Stevenson Avenue. Inside the main Gorgie entrance a short driveway led to the Royal Promenade which ran almost the entire length of the site. To the left (west) were fine views of Saughton Hall Mansion, and to the right were the Baby Incubator, the Senegalese Native Village, the Model Garden City, the Tea Room and the Winter Garden. At the north end, the Promenade opened out into a rectangular arena bounded by the main buildings of the Exhibition, all designed by the architects Walker & Ramsey of Glasgow: the Industrial Hall, the Club, the Machinery Hall, the Concert Hall, the Fine Art Building and Canada House. In the centre of the arena were the octagonal bandstand and Van Houten's Cocoa Pavilion where cocoa was available at 1d per cup including a

The Industrial Hall at the Scottish National Exhibition of 1908 which was held on ground now occupied by Saughton Rose Gardens.

The Water Chute at the Scottish National Exhibition of 1908 was a great favourite with young and old alike. No doubt it helped to boost the total number of admissions between 1st May and 31st October to 3.5 million.

biscuit. To the west of the main buildings were the Sports Ground, the Water Chute and the figure-8 Railway.

The Exhibition attracted a wide variety of interests, applications for space being received from France, Italy, Denmark, Holland, Russia, Serbia, Persia, Japan, China, the United States of America and Canada. The main topics were listed as Women's Work, Scottish Industries, Nursing and Care of Orphan Children, Education, Agriculture, Horticulture, Arboriculture, Nature Study, Housing of the Working Classes, Bee Keeping, Poultry Farming, Small Holdings and Artisans' Work. By far the largest covered area was the Palace of Industries, 100,000 square feet in total, constructed of timber and white fibrous plaster. In a supporting role was the Machinery Hall, about one-third of the size, but displaying a wide range of machinery pertaining to shipping, mining, gas, steam, electricity, water, sewage, baking and printing. The baking section had a distinctly Scottish flavour with machinery for making biscuits, scones, oatcakes and shortbread. Saughton Hall Mansion was used to house the Artisans' Collection, the Japanese Educational Section and the Mary Queen of Scots Exhibition. The Concert Hall was near the Balgreen entrance, a large circular dome-roofed structure with four towers leading to a horse-shoe shaped gallery. It also had a three-manual organ built by Abbot and Smith of Leeds and a 'fairy fountain' which produced an interesting rainbow effect when it was lit. The Fine Art Gallery was built on the very latest principles of fireproof construction, lined internally with asbestos from the foundations to the roof, at a total cost of £5,075. There were nine separate galleries, the loan section including work by some of Scotland's leading artists: Allan Ramsay (son of the poet), Sir David Wilkie, Sir Henry Raeburn, Alexander Nasmyth and the Rev. John Thomson of Duddingston. The Canadian Pavilion, with a domed roof and elegant pillars, was illuminated outside by hundreds of coloured electric lamps. The official guide stated that the displays 'show the progress of the Dominion in her various branches of manufactures, minerals, agriculture, horticulture, timber etc.'.

Entertainment was also high on the list of priorities, to cater for every taste—concerts, tournaments, pageants, displays, sports, kite flying, balloon ascents, water chute, illuminations and fireworks. By far the most popular entertainment was the figure-8 Railway built by T.M. Hartin & Co of Pittsburg, U.S.A. It boasted high-speed excitement, completely free from danger, for exactly 1 minute and 15 seconds. There were ten cars (examined at frequent intervals as a safety check) which climbed to a height of fifty-five feet above the showground. At its busiest time the railway produced receipts of £16 per hour which was considered to be very profitable. The Exhibition continued through the whole of the summer and autumn, to 31st October. On the last day there were 53,563 attendances, some of whom decided to stage their own grand finale, immediately after the formal closing by Sir Robert Cranston. Owing to an earlier disturbance at the Terrace Bar a decision had been taken to close the bar at 9.30 p.m. instead of 10 p.m. Unfortunately this restriction incensed the crowd to the point where the police had to move in to restore order. Customers were ejected, many of them still holding bottles and tumblers which they used to throw at the police. At the bandstand policemen, perhaps missing their usual beat, were forced to raise their batons as youths pitched in with chairs and music stands.

Despite the unruly behaviour on the last night on the Promenade, the Scottish National Exhibition of 1908 was considered to be a great success, the admissions from 1st May to 31st October totalling 3.5 million.

STENHOUSE MANSION

Stenhouse Mansion is a difficult building to research in the sense that it has been given different names throughout its long history. MacGibbon & Ross, writing in 1892, devote five pages to it under the heading 'Saughton Mills', in Volume IV of *The Castellated and Domestic Architecture of Scotland*. In 1929 the *Tenth Report of the Royal Commission on the Ancient and Historical Monuments of Scotland* also provides a very comprehensive description under the titles 'Saughton Mills or Stenhopes Mills'. On the other hand, modern-day writers have used the description 'Stenhouse Mansion', for example, Miss Joyce Wallace in *Historic Houses of Edinburgh* and Miss A.S. Cowper in *Historic Corstorphine and Roundabout*. The confusion is compounded by the variations in the spelling of the family name Stenhouse to include Stanehope and Stenhop.

In relation to modern street layout Stenhouse Mansion lies a few yards to the south of Gorgie Road opposite its junction with Stenhouse Drive. It stands within a natural loop of the Water of Leith, hemmed in by modern commercial buildings. Despite a chequered career its condition is now excellent and its future assured by the present owners, the National Trust for Scotland.

Stenhouse Mansion dates from the sixteenth century when the adjacent Saughton Mills were leased to the Stanehope family. In plan, the mansion forms the letter F, but like many similar buildings of that age, it has evolved from a much simpler design. It was built, probably by the Stanehopes, as a three-storey rectangular block lying north and south. In 1623 its new owner, Patrick Eleis (or Ellis) undertook extensive improvements. He doubled the length of the main block southwards and built a new stair-tower and offices projecting westwards from the centre of the main block. From the west gable of the stair-tower a range of offices ran north, parallel to the main block, thus creating a small courtyard. Its open north end was probably closed by a wall and gates but only remnants of this enclosure now remain. There are two doorways side by side in the re-entrant angle, facing north. The left-hand doorway is the grander of the two, giving access to the wheel stair. Above the door are the words 'Blisit Be God For Al His Giftis', and an armorial panel with the initials P.E. (Patrick Eleis) and the date 1623. The right-hand doorway, without embellishment, leads to what was the western cellar of the stair-tower. In 1700 a second wing was built westwards, in line with the south gable of the main block and parallel to the stair-tower, thus completing the F-shape. The stair-tower was built to three storeys but the south wing has two storeys only. Along the east lateral wall there are signs of an extension running eastward but no further details survive. Something similar is visible on the south gable.

Internally many of the original features have been removed over the years. The two northern cellars are vaulted, the inner one at one time containing a draw well. The outer one houses a beebole (a niche for nesting) in the north wall, sixteen recesses cut into the stonework which are thought to be hen boxes, and two triangular access holes to the outside. The kitchen on the ground floor is adjacent to what were probably brewhouses and bakehouses. Of the fifteen apartments, the grandest is the King Charles Room on the second floor. It has an ornate plaster ceiling with the initials C.R.2 high on one wall, made from the same moulds as were used at Dalry House in 1661. To the north of the mansion the ground was laid out as a kitchen garden and orchard. This ground, and that occupied at one time by a doocot, is now used for factory units.

There is little doubt that the first family to occupy Stenhouse Mansion was Stanehope. They sold the property to Patrick Eleis around 1623, but by 1690 the Eleis family had fallen on hard times and were in debt to the Watsons of Saughton. In 1691 Eleis sold Stenhouse to the Watsons for 34,000 merks. Subsequent tenants were the Brouns followed by the Cleghorns during the second part of the eighteenth century. In 1734 the mansion was let to William Murray for a weaving

Stenhouse Mansion c.1890 when it was in very poor condition. Above the left-hand doorway are the words 'BLISIT BE GOD FOR AL HIS GIFTIS', and an armorial panel with the date 1623 and the initials P.E. for Patrick Eleis. (Crown Copyright: RCAHMS.)

*Stenhouse Mansion in 1939 during restoration work by the architect, Ian Lindsay.
The work was interrupted by the Second World War and was not completed until
1965. (Crown Copyright: RCAHMS.)*

factory. During the nineteenth century Stenhouse Mansion entered a
long period of gradual decline, which continued into the twentieth
century. In 1892 MacGibbon and Ross began their report with the
words: 'This [Stenhouse Mansion] has been at one time a pleasant residence on the bank of the Water of Leith, about three miles west from
Edinburgh, but it has now fallen on evil days and has been cut up into
small houses for labourers'. By 1929 the position had not improved
substantially, as the *Tenth Report* described Stenhouse Mansion as 'now
reduced slightly in area and greatly in degree as it provides labourers'
dwellings'. In 1937 the surrounding land was purchased by the Grey-
hound Racing Association who constructed a racecourse on the site.
Having no use for the dilapidated building, the Association gifted it to
the National Trust for Scotland. Restoration work was undertaken by
the architect Ian Lindsay during 1937-1939 but was interrupted by the
Second World War. It was completed in 1965 when Stenhouse Mansion
became the home of the National Trust for Scotland Restoration Centre.
    The centre now operates under the name Historic Scotland Conser-
vation Centre—Stenhouse and South Gyle—as part of the Scottish

Office Environment Department. At Stenhouse Mansion work is undertaken on the conservation and restoration of paintings, prints and drawings. At South Gyle similar work is done on stonework and painted ceilings. The staff, taken jointly from the National Trust for Scotland and the Scottish Office Environment Department, work on projects referred to them by the Historic Buildings Council, the National Trust for Scotland, Regional and District Authorities, and the private sector.

3
Nineteenth-Century Development

During the nineteenth century, the districts of Gorgie and Dalry (but particularly Dalry) changed from being a farming community to one of Edinburgh's most densely populated, industrial areas. In the first few years of the nineteenth century, the road authorities of the day, in anticipation of increased traffic, commissioned a complete resurvey of the 'main highway' between Saughton and the West End of Edinburgh. In 1822 the Union Canal was opened, linking Edinburgh with the Forth and Clyde Canal, and twenty years later the Edinburgh - Glasgow Railway was built along the northern boundary of the district. Even more obtrusive was the line of the Caledonian Railway, which proposed to cut through the properties of Bainfield and North Merchiston. The combined effect of the new road, the canal and the numerous railways brought the districts into the limelight, with the result that several institutions became interested in the available ground. Dalry Necropolis was laid out in 1846 and North Merchiston Cemetery in 1874. Between these dates, the Western Reformatory and the Edinburgh Magdalene Asylum moved to Ardmillan Terrace in 1862 and 1863 respectively. One of the first industries to arrive was the Caledonian Distillery, which acquired several acres at Haymarket in 1855. With that level of activity, housing became a major priority. First to be constructed were the Terraces on the south side of Dalry Road, near Haymarket, followed by the streets around Caledonian Crescent. Public transport was extended from Haymarket around 1881 using horse cars to begin with, and then cable cars from about 1898.

By the end of the nineteenth century most of the available ground between Haymarket and Robertson Avenue was built up. The western part of Gorgie (i.e. the original village and its surroundings) still maintained much of its rural character well into the twentieth century.

EARLY ROAD IMPROVEMENTS

The Scottish Record Office holds the original sketch plan of 'The Improvements to be made on the Roads . . . From Lyarshall to Princes

This building stood near the present Wheatsheaf Inn in Balgreen Road. It may be the property referred to as Lyarshall in a sketch plan of road improvements, dated 1803, held by the Scottish Record Office. (Courtesy of Wilfred Grubb.)

Street by Whitehouse Toll', dated 1803. The course of the old road is shown with several proposed new sections, avoiding bends and congested properties. The route begins at Lyarshall (near the present-day Wheatsheaf Inn in Balgreen Road) to the east of which is the first new section of road, skirting the south of Gorgie Mills. The intention appears to have been to straighten the road between Lyarshall and the position of present-day Stewart Terrace, but only the western section seems to have been completed, leaving the dog-leg bend near Telephone House. No improvements were intended between Stewart Terrace and Ardmillan. The old road shows a property, apparently with the intriguing name Slockendrouth, on the south side of Gorgie Road, near White Park. In *Chambers Scots Dictionary* the meaning of the word *slocken* is given as 'to drench or to quench thirst of fire', and the meaning of the word *drouth* is given as 'thirst, dryness or a drunkard'. Tempting as it may be, the evidence seems hardly sufficient to confirm the existence of one of Gorgie's earliest pubs! East of Slockendrouth is Tynecastle Toll which is known to have stood on the north side of the road, where the Tivoli Picture House was later built. Ardmillan Terrace is proposed, completing the triangle with Angle Park Terrace and Henderson Terrace. To the east of Ardmillan, two main bends in the road are taken out, the one farthest east to avoid the property known as West Dalry. At this point a road, near the line of West End Place, runs south to meet what is now Dundee Street. At that time, of course, the road would not have had to contend with the Caledonian Railway, which was not built until very much later. Dalry House is shown on the south side of the road, and on the north side are properties owned by Mr Rigg, Mr Walker and Mr Robertson. At Haymarket, a building is shown on the site of Ryrie's Bar, and Whitehouse Toll is shown in what is now Haymarket Terrace. After Haymarket the proposed road removes a number of bends through Heriot's Hospital Lands, and proceeds to the West End of Edinburgh. Although the road has been widened on several occasions over the years, the 1803 line remains substantially unaltered to the present day.

THE UNION CANAL

As early as the end of the eighteenth century, several speculative reports had been compiled on the possibility of linking Edinburgh and Glasgow by a ship canal, suitable for freight and passenger services. At a meeting of interested parties in Edinburgh in January 1793, John Ainslie and Robert Whitworth were appointed to make the necessary survey. Four separate routes were suggested to which John Rennie, the bridge engineer, added a fifth, to the north of the others. Some years later, amid growing speculation as to the commercial viability of the scheme, Hugh Baird was commissioned to draw up another report with the assistance of Francis Hall, the surveyor. The result was a lengthy *Report on the Proposed Edinburgh and Glasgow Union Canal* dated 20th September 1813, in which Baird explained the line of the canal, the technical difficulties, the anticipated objections and, most importantly, the estimated costs and expected revenue.

Baird proposed a contour canal, without locks, from Lothian Road in Edinburgh to join the Forth and Clyde Canal at Falkirk, a distance of twenty-eight miles, being only four miles more than the turnpike road. To accommodate boats up to thirty tons, the canal had to be five feet deep, twenty feet wide at the bottom, and thirty-five feet wide at the surface of the water. The problem of providing that amount of

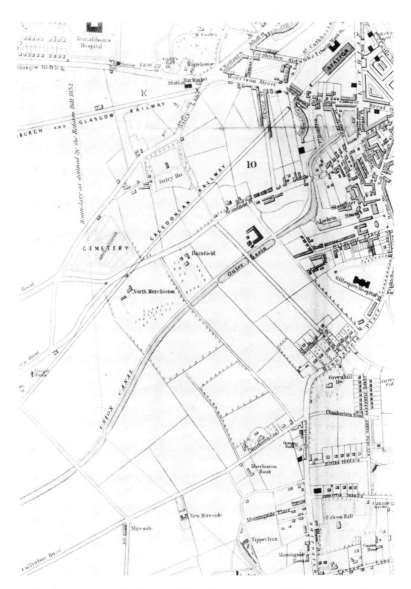

The Edinburgh and Leith Post Office Directory map of 1852 *gives a good idea of the districts of Gorgie and Dalry before the large-scale developments in the latter part of the nineteenth century.*

water constantly was more difficult than the layman might imagine.
Canals leak. They also lose millions of gallons of water by absorption,
evaporation and the effects of the wind. Baird also faced a daily loss of
water through the lock system linking the Union Canal with the existing Forth and Clyde Canal. He calculated that on the basis of ten boats
passing up, and ten boats passing down each day (i.e. twenty lockfulls
lost daily) the canal would require to be replenished to the extent of
seventy-two million cubic feet of water each year. That figure was required for only four months of the year as it was anticipated that for the
greater part of the year the canal could be topped up by the numerous
rivers and burns along its route. Substantial reservoirs were, however,
proposed, to deal with the summer months, and to negate complaints
from the mill owners on the Avon and the Amond rivers, who were also
dependent upon a good supply of water for their machinery. The total
cost of the canal, basins, aqueducts and reservoirs was estimated at £235,167.

Baird then outlined the economic reasons for building the canal.
One of his main arguments was that great savings had been made by
utilising the Forth and Clyde Canal instead of taking a direct route to
Glasgow. He also produced compelling figures on the uneconomic cost
of road transport between the two main cities in Scotland. A sum of
£30,000 a year was paid for coach passengers and parcels, with an
additional £40,000 paid for the carriage of heavier goods. Edinburgh
paid one third more for its coal than Glasgow, and three times as much
as was paid in localities along the route of the proposed canal. The
carriage of freestone from Hailes quarry alone required forty horses and
carts going twice a day to Edinburgh with an average load of sixty tons.
Special emphasis was also placed on the transport of valuable consignments of sugar, tea, coffee and rum, which by road were liable to pillage.

Baird's report was considered at a General Meeting of Subscribers at
the Town House of Linlithgow on 8th October 1813, but the following year the Magistrates of Edinburgh objected to the plans and appointed Robert Stevenson (grandfather of Robert Louis Stevenson) to
advise on a different route to connect with Leith Docks. Bitter controversy followed, with allegations that Baird's plan favoured his own
coalmining interests to the west of Edinburgh. By 1817, however, the
Union Canal Act was passed and Baird was instructed to begin work.
On Tuesday 3rd March 1818, the Committee of Management proceeded to the west end of Fountainbridge 'attended by a vast number
of people to witness the commencement of so grand an improvement
to the Metropolis'. A prayer was said by the Rev David Dickson, and

This aerial photograph shows the Union Canal terminating at the Lochrin Basin at the top right-hand corner of the picture. To the left of the Canal are Fountainbridge and Dundee Street, with the Morrison Street Goods Yard on the extreme left. (Courtesy of Patricia Scoular.)

Mr Downie of Appin, Chairman of the Committee, dug the first spadeful, proclaiming that the entire venture would bring much-needed employment to the city. The cost of the project increased from £235,167 in 1813 to £461,760 on completion in 1822.

Almost twenty years after the canal was opened, the Edinburgh and Glasgow Railway Company opened a line from Edinburgh to Glasgow with catastrophic results for the canal. Passengers travelling by boat ceased almost immediately and in 1849 the Railway Company bought the canal for £209,000—less than half the cost of its construction. Freight continued to be carried until the mid-1930s, but modern usage has been confined to pleasure craft only, and the supply of water for industries on the west side of Edinburgh. The Union Canal never really became an industrial waterway in Edinburgh, and its impact on the surrounding districts was not, therefore, as great as it might have been. In fact its influence on the districts of Gorgie and Dalry as we know them today was much less than the effect of the railways. The canal did, however, have a profound effect on that part of the Lands of Dalry which stretched along present-day Fountainbridge and Dundee Street. Particularly affected were the properties on the south side of Dundee Street, namely the Trades' Maiden Hospital, Bainfield and North Merchiston. Baird anticipated that the proposed line of the canal would attract criticism from these property owners, who saw the prospect of their extensive south-facing estates being traversed by an open canal and a towpath. To preserve their amenity, Baird planned to put the canal in a cutting, ten to twenty-five feet deep, along a distance of four hundred yards 'arched over to save objections and opposition'. In fact, the canal was built without any cutting or covering at this point, despite the fact that substantial sums of money had been included in the estimate for the necessary work.

THE RAILWAY NETWORK

Like most major cities, Edinburgh was involved in the railway mania of the 1840s, although not to the same extent as Glasgow, York and Crewe. It did, however, boast a railway as early as 1831, which ran from St Leonard's, in the Pleasance, to Dalkeith, carrying freight and passengers. Initially, it operated with horse-drawn trains only, earning the nickname 'the Innocent Railway', on account of its accident-free record.

In 1842, a much grander scheme, by the Edinburgh and Glasgow Railway Company, linked the two main cities of Scotland by rail, a distance of forty-six miles. The expected revenue from the project assumed that twice as many people would travel by rail as previously travelled by road, and that half of the Union Canal traffic would transfer to the railway. On that basis, the anticipated revenue was over £126,000 annually. To finance the venture, capital of £900,000, in £50 shares, was required, with power to borrow a further £300,000. By 1845, the number of passengers carried in the week ending 26th July was 25,234, which produced an income of £2,637 or £137,124 on a similar 52-week period. At the Edinburgh end, the line began at Haymarket Station, and was not extended to what is now Waverley Station until 1846. The long straight section of track, west of Haymarket, created a northern boundary to the districts of Dalry and Gorgie, and gave access to numerous industrial sidings. The Innocent Railway and the Edinburgh – Glasgow Railway were generally profitable, but bigger prizes were anticipated by linking Edinburgh and Glasgow with London. Although it was thought, in the early stages, that only a single route to Scotland would be commercially viable, in fact both the pro-

*This fairly modest building, erected in 1870, was the second Caledonian Station at
the junction of Lothian Road and Rutland Street. The station was replaced in 1894,
incorporating the present Caledonian Hotel in 1903.*

posed east and west coast routes were built. The North British Railway
route from London, up the east coast to Edinburgh, was opened in
1846, and linked (at the Waverley) with the Edinburgh and Glasgow
Railway, extended from Haymarket. The two companies merged in
1865, retaining the name North British Railway, which became part of
the London and North Eastern Railway in 1923.

The west-coast route to Scotland was first considered in 1836 by the
directors of the Grand Junction Railway, which had just opened a line
between Birmingham and Lancashire. A report by their engineer, Joseph
Locke, proposed a route from London to Glasgow of 417 miles in
twenty-one hours, being twice as fast as the existing mail coach, and
three times as fast as the ordinary coach. His idea was to confine the
route to the west side of Scotland, and to use the proposed Edinburgh
- Glasgow Railway to link with Edinburgh. The directors anticipated
attracting passenger traffic only, as freight transport was already well
established between the western seaports. After long delays, a proposal
to divide the line at Carstairs, and reach Glasgow and Edinburgh separately, was approved in 1844, and work started at Beattock on 11th
August 1845, at an estimated cost of £1.25 million. The new Caledonian Railway was partially opened on 10th September 1847, between
Carlisle and Beattock, and finally opened to Edinburgh on 15th Febru-

ary 1848. From an early date, the Company planned to run a service to Glasgow in direct competition with the Edinburgh and Glasgow Railway. Unfortunately for the Caledonian, it was always at a disadvantage, as its route, via Carstairs, was longer, and the gradient, over Cobbinshaw summit to the south-west of Edinburgh, was much steeper. The entire country was in a state of railway mania, which did not have the universal approval of the community. The celebrated Lord Cockburn of Bonaly, a man seldom without a platform for his caustic wit, signalled his disapproval in uncompromising language: 'Britain is at present an island of lunatics, all railway mad. The patients are raving even in the wildest recesses of the Highlands'.

The Caledonian Railway had a much greater influence on the districts of Dalry and Gorgie than its rival, the North British. The story, with particular emphasis on the branch line to Balerno, is told in fascinating detail in *The Balerno Branch and the Caley in Edinburgh*, by Donald Shaw. Although the foundation stone for a grand station in Lothian Road had been laid in 1847, the building was never started, with the result that passengers had to make do with a long timber shed until about 1870. The line ran westwards from Lothian Road, along what is now the West Approach Road. Engineering problems arose at Morrison Street, where the excavations and bridge foundations threatened the safety of tenement buildings in Gardner's Crescent. The track continued in a straight line, running by the south of Caledonian Crescent, and under the west end of Dundee Street. It continued on the south side of Angle Park Terrace and Slateford Road to Merchiston Station, which had access from Slateford Road and, later, Bonaly Road (renamed Harrison Gardens). From the station, the line curved slightly southwards to avoid the existing properties of Gorgie Mains (east of present-day Primrose Terrace) and Gorgie Cottage (on the corner of present-day Shandon Place and Slateford Road). The next station, named Slateford, was actually at Kingsknowe, to the west of the viaduct spanning the Water of Leith valley. A second Slateford Station was built at the east end of the viaduct in 1853, and the first one retained the name Kingsknowe. The present Slateford Station was opened in 1871. In 1856, the Caledonian entered into negotiations with the Duke of Buccleuch, who owned Granton Harbour, to open a branch line to the harbour. It joined the main line, east of Slateford, in 1861.

Slateford was the location of an avoidable accident on 24th May 1853, in which several people were seriously injured, although none fatally. It involved the 8.00 a.m. Carstairs to Edinburgh passenger train which

*The engine being coaled up at Dalry is believed to be No. 905, one of five magnificent 4-6-0 engines in the '903' class, built by the Caledonian's Locomotive Superintendent, J.F. McIntosh, in 1906. (*Courtesy of Bill Forrest.*)*

was stationary, taking on passengers at the new station, when it was run into from behind, by a mineral train, hauling eighteen fully-laden wagons of coal. Investigation revealed that the safety precautions were primitive, to say the least, and had not been properly implemented. Basically, trains on the same section of track were kept apart by a rough system of time-lag, which was made much rougher by the fact that station masters were not supplied with clocks or watches. The rule was that ten minutes should have separated the two trains, but the station master at Kingsknowe did not have a watch. He merely guessed that sufficient time had elapsed to allow the mineral train to proceed with caution. In fact, only eight minutes had elapsed, and the fully-laden train, with inadequate brakes for the steep downhill gradient, was unable to stop in time. The driver of the mineral train was arrested at the scene of the accident, remanded in custody for two months, but eventually absolved.

The Balerno branch of the Caledonian Railway was first mooted around 1864, when it had the approval of most of the mill owners between Slateford and Balerno. The plan was to construct a single-track line, branching from the main line a few hundred yards west of the Slateford viaduct. The track crossed Lanark Road on a stone bridge, now removed, and followed the valley of the Water of Leith, with stations at Colinton, Juniper Green, Currie and Balerno. The construction presented several engineering problems, including twenty-eight bridges, a tunnel at Colinton, several embankments and cuttings, and a general undertaking not to interfere with any of the lades which served the water-powered mills. After long delays, the line was opened on 1st August 1874, without any formal ceremony. The line was very popular with commuters and mill owners alike, until 1943 when the passenger service was withdrawn. Goods traffic continued until 1967, after which the track was converted to a public walkway.

Meantime, the districts of Gorgie and Dalry attracted other railway developments. The Edinburgh Suburban and Southside Junction Railway, opened in 1884 and operated by the North British Railway, had a station at Gorgie, accessible from Gorgie Road and Slateford Road. Dalry Road Station, on another branch of the Caledonian Railway, was not opened until 1900. Both the Caledonian and the North British made special arrangements for the conveyance of thousands of people to the two big exhibitions held in the west of Edinburgh. The first was the International Industrial Exhibition at Slateford in 1890, and the second was the Scottish National Exhibition at Saughton in 1908.

The Caledonian Station in Lothian Road was always intended to be the flagship of the Caledonian Railway, but it had a chequered career. The first foundation stone was never built upon: the original station was just a timber shed; and the second one, built in 1870, was badly damaged by fire in 1890. The fire was, however, fortuitous as the Company already had plans to build a much grander building, which was completed in 1894, and incorporated into the new hotel, in 1903. The Caledonian Railway became part of the London Midland and Scottish in 1923, and the Caledonian Station was closed in September 1965. Since then, the tracks, west of Lothian Road, have been lifted, and the West Approach Road constructed after several abortive attempts at grander schemes.

DALRY CEMETERY: NORTH MERCHISTON CEMETERY

In 1846 the directors of the Metropolitan Cemetery Association announced 'to the inhabitants of Edinburgh and its vicinity' that their new ground at Dalry, extending to about six acres, was ready to be opened under the name 'The Dalry Necropolis'. It was described as situated at the junction of the Mid Calder and Fountainbridge Roads 'entering from the Mid Calder Road beyond Dalry House, and from

A passenger train at Gorgie Station on the Suburban Line in 1958. (Courtesy of Patricia Scoular.)

the Fountainbridge Road, near the gate to North Merchiston'. The attractively illustrated prospectus stated that the situation, and the beauty of the surrounding scenery, were so well known that it was unnecessary to dwell upon them. What it failed to say was that the line of the Caledonian Railway was scheduled to rumble past within a few feet of its southern boundary. The advertising material, by the lithographer Frederick Schenck of No. 9 Greenside Place, appears to transpose Edinburgh Castle into the position to be occupied by the railway. Nevertheless, the cemetery was laid out by one of the foremost architects of the day, David Cousin, who also designed Dean Cemetery in 1845 and Newington Cemetery in 1848. The prospectus also provided full details of the services available and the charges made. At the higher end of the scale, the total cost of a funeral (including a hearse with four horses, grave digging, watching and recording) was £5:8s (£5.40p), reducing by stages to 'a child in arms' at 6/6d (32 ½p). A single private catacomb for one coffin was £10:10s and a vault, capable of holding four coffins, was £36.

By 1883 Dalry Necropolis was overlooked by several tenements, whose upper windows provided an excellent vantage point to observe certain unusual nocturnal events. It had come to the attention of Dr Henry J.

Littlejohn, Medical Officer of Health for Edinburgh, that all was not well at the burial ground. Apparently 'double' burials were taking place illegally, which were attracting double fees. On receiving a letter from one of the 'evening observers', Dr Littlejohn directed his inspector to visit Dalry Necropolis in the company of the informant. They visited the cemetery by night on several occasions and discovered that some recent interments of children had been made very near the surface. Further observation revealed a most unusual and macabre practice. Bodies of children, recently interred, were being exhumed and removed to nearby vaults, where they were kept in secrecy until another body, usually that of an adult, was buried during a normal funeral in the child's grave. At night the grave was again opened and the body, which had been hidden in the vaults, was re-interred above the more recent corpse. In an endeavour to establish if the 'double burial' practice was widespread, the inspector made various measurements of the depth of graves. Of forty measurements taken in the common ground, the average depth was about two feet, and the depth of the graves ranged from two feet to six inches from the surface. The otherwise impeccable language of the report lapsed slightly in stating that the only qualification to the measurements was that they were taken at night and that 'their rigid accuracy cannot be depended on'. Nevertheless, there was a *prima facie* case to answer. Dr Littlejohn brought the matter to the attention of the Public Health Committee and obtained its authority to conduct a public investigation into several city cemeteries. Dalry was revisited and a further thirty borings were made, of which only one was over three feet; the others ranged from eight inches below the surface to two feet eleven inches. The catacombs and vaults were also inspected but nothing unusual was found 'with the exception of an empty coffin'. From then on the illegal 'double burials' ceased.

In 1863 the number of interments at Dalry Necropolis was 276 which had risen to 820 in 1874. Despite the problems highlighted in Dr Littlejohn's report, Dalry maintained its popularity as the final resting place for many residents of Gorgie and Dalry. A century later, however, Dalry Cemetery (as it was then known) was in a very poor state, with overgrown trees and bushes, and many tombs damaged and overturned. Several attempts at a comprehensive solution were undertaken, notably by the Action for Dalry Cemetery Group, who transformed the appearance of the cemetery in a clean-up campaign in September 1976. In 1978 A.S. Cowper made a detailed study of the tombstones erected over the graves of local worthies, and a few from further afield: General

North Merchiston Cemetery: James Strachan, Decorator, Dalry Road.

North Merchiston Cemetery: books piled high on a square pillar for William MacLeod, Builder, Edinburgh; also in memory of his four children who died in infancy.

Dalry Cemetery: George Cupples, Novelist, Critic and Philologist.

Dalry Cemetery: The Rev. Alexander Lockhart Simpson D.D., of Kirknewton and East Calder Parishes.

eil Douglas, Colonel 78th Highlanders, Commander-in-Chief, Scotland, 1779—1853; Alexander Anderson, foreman mason at Donaldson's Hospital; Charles McIntosh, landscape gardener and author of the *Book of the Garden*; John McNab of Inglis Green; and Edward Mather of the Orwell Engineering Works. Furthest from home was a stranger from America, John Robertson:

> O stranger pause and give one sigh
> For the sake of him who here doth lie
> Beneath this little mound of earth
> Two thousand miles from land of birth.

In 1987 Dalry Cemetery was compulsorily purchased by Edinburgh District Council and in 1991 a further clean-up was organised, this time by the Better Gorgie and Dalry Campaign and others. Dalry Cemetery was 'reopened' at a special ceremony on 14th May 1991 as part of the City's first Festival of the Environment.

North Merchiston Cemetery, to the west of Ardmillan Terrace, was first laid out in 1874 but it has never attracted historians to the same extent as Dalry Cemetery. Initially, it was known as New Dalry Cemetery and was extended to over nine acres in 1883. In the mid-1880s it took the name North Merchiston. No prospectus has been traced but its record books are extant. These provide an alphabetical list of the names of people interred since the cemetery was opened, and details of ground sales. In recent years North Merchiston Cemetery, like many other Edinburgh cemeteries, fell into serious disrepair, to the extent that it was not possible to reach individual tombs. Following compulsory acquisition (along with cemeteries at Comely Bank, Newington, Warriston, Saughton and Corstorphine Hill) by Edinburgh District Council in June 1994, the grounds are being renovated by the Environmental Services Department. When the work is completed it is hoped that a comprehensive study of the tombstones will be made by people interested in the cemeteries.

EDINBURGH MAGDALENE ASYLUM: WESTERN REFORMATORY

In the early 1860s the Edinburgh Magdalene Asylum and the Western Reformatory moved into the emerging districts of Gorgie and Dalry from locations in other parts of the city. At first glance their objectives appear similar but, in fact, they were reluctant bedfellows.

The Edinburgh Magdalene Asylum was established in August 1797 under the control of the Edinburgh Philanthropic Society. Its first homes were in West Bow, and Shoemaker Close in the Canongate, but in 1805 a much more suitable building, designed by the architect John Paterson, was erected at No.181 Canongate. At first, admission to the Asylum was 'confined to such unfortunate females as had attracted the attention of the police and been confined to the Bridewell'—a house of correction which stood on the site of what is now St Andrew's House. This early policy of dealing only with convicted females became unworkable, as most of the inmates were older women, who were judged to be beyond redemption! When the Asylum decided to admit girls on a voluntary basis there were three times as many 'admitted from the street' as came from the Bridewell. The word 'prostitution' seldom, if ever, appeared in the Asylum reports which preferred phrases like 'deviation from the path of virtue' or 'an active career in open and shameless vice'. By admitting females who wanted to give up being prostitutes, the Asylum hoped to help them back into society. The methods used were hard work, firm discipline and religious and moral instruction. Short notes were maintained on the progress of each person admitted; 'E. Tait, 5 months in house, rather indolent, not very active, rather thoughtless, hasty in her temper, in good health, appears willing to do well'. It is clear from other case notes that some of the young females involved in prostitution had not 'volunteered' for that lifestyle in the true sense of the word. Many were young, impressionable country girls who came to the city in the honest belief that they were to be employed as domestic servants. The Asylum was administered by a committee of fifteen directors, three of whom were elected by the Town Council. Its main sources of income were donations, subscriptions, and the income derived from the girls' work which included spinning, washing and sewing.

Almost half a century after the Asylum was established, William Tait, an Edinburgh surgeon, made a particular study of the extent, causes and consequences of prostitution in the city. He concluded that 'Magdalenism' was an effective philosophy, but his assessment of the causes of prostitution was somewhat startling by modern standards. Among many causes listed, he included dancing parties and going to the theatre, and even went so far as to quote another author who maintained that 'the morals of a theatre and the morals of a brothel are identically the same'. By comparison, the case notes appear more mundane: 'Mary Brown, aged 26, daughter of Andrew Brown, late keeper of a Beef and Ham Shop in Carnegie Street in the Pleasance appeared before the sub-committee expressing a desire to be committed to the Asylum; she professed penitence, promised to conform to the rules of the House, and was admitted on Probation'.

In 1862 the Asylum found that its situation in the Canongate was becoming untenable owing to the expansion of its nearest neighbour, the Edinburgh Gas Light Company, which occupied the large area of ground on which New Street Bus Depot was built in later years. The directors decided to put their premises up for sale and to look for a more suitable site, out of town, for a new Asylum. An offer of £2,600 was received, and accepted, from the Edinburgh Gas Light Company payable at Whitsunday 1863, with permission to continue in occupation, rent free, until Whitsunday 1864. By good fortune, the directors learned in December 1862 that the Governors of George Watson's Hospital were prepared to feu ground adjacent to the Western Reformatory at Dalry, at the reduced price of £20 per acre. The architects, Leadbetter and Smith, were instructed to draw up plans for a design, not to exceed £5,000 at the very most. Preparation of the site and laying the foundations were proceeding well when a complaint was received from an unexpected source.

Mrs Swan, secretary to the Western Reformatory, wrote to the Asylum directors expressing regret that the Magdalene was to be next door, and asking if the building could be put as far away from the Reformatory as the land would allow. In Mrs Swan's view, the inmates of the Asylum were likely to have a bad influence on her girls, and the work of her staff in trying to reform them! Whilst the directors dealt with the matter sympathetically, they denied that there would be any adverse influence, and stated that, in any case, the foundations were already laid. The Western Reformatory had moved to its new premises on the corner of Ardmillan Terrace and Gorgie Road in 1862. Formerly it had been at Boroughmuirhead, but when it moved to Dalry the opportunity was taken to amalgamate with Dean Bank Institution at Stockbridge. The Western Reformatory catered for about thirty-five girls, most of whom had been convicted of some criminal offence. They were taught reading, writing, arithmetic, sewing, knitting and laundry work, to enable them to take jobs as domestic helps in the city. The Reformatory remained at Dalry until about 1916 when it was transferred, with most of the staff, to Loanhead, under the name Reformatory for Girls, Dalry House, Loanhead.

Despite the objections raised by the Western Reformatory, the foundation stone of the new Asylum building was laid at 1 p.m. on 10th

April 1863. The stone contained a parchment on which were the words:

On the 10th April 1863 this stone was laid by the Right Hon. Charles Lawson of Borthwick Hall, Lord Provost of the City of Edinburgh as the foundation of a building for the use of the Magdalene Asylum established in 1797. The objects of this Institution are the reformation and industrial training of women who have fallen from the paths of virtue and may God Almighty continue to make it a blessing to this great City and to the Community at large for many generations. Leadbetter and Smith, Architects; Adam Dryden, Mason; Robert Henderson, Wright; A. Peters, Plumber; James Green, Plasterer; Andrew Slater, Slater Contractors.

Copious annual reports suggest that the Asylum quickly settled down in its new surroundings and continued to help females in its care for many years. A gradual change in the reasons for admission took place over the years, resulting in the name being changed, in 1941, to Springwell House formerly the Edinburgh Magdalene Asylum. The 1947 report emphasised that the directors were anxious to dispel the idea that any stigma attached to residence at Springwell House. It was a training school, not a house of correction, for girls who had been involved in minor crimes. By 1950, however, it was found that large institutionalised accommodation was ill-suited to changes in policy, which required smaller, more intimate homes. The building, laundry equipment and the delivery van were sold to Edinburgh Corporation for £17,500 with entry on 11th November 1950. In 1954 the Court approved a scheme for the distribution of the assets which were divided between St Margaret's House for Girls, the Guild of Service for Women, and the Salvation Army.

In 1961 renovations and extensions were completed at the Western Reformatory building, which was reopened on 16th December 1961 by the Rt. Hon J.S. Maclay, Secretary of State for Scotland, as the Edinburgh Civil Defence Headquarters. At the present day the group of buildings are occupied by the Social Work Department of Lothian Regional Council and a Health Centre. Several community education activities also take place there. High up on the front of the main building are several inscriptions confirming the dates, the identity of the architects, and the names of the various people involved in building the Edinburgh Magdalene Asylum in 1863. It is a story which has attracted great interest over the years. In 1986 Donald Campbell used 'the Maggie' as the backcloth to his evocative play, *Victorian Values*. Almost two hundred people, many of them unemployed youngsters, were involved in the ten-week project sponsored by Lothian Regional Council. The first six weeks were spent at various workshops based at Springwell House, and the remaining time was used for performances at George Square Theatre and Springwell House. One of the most interesting features was the songs written in the style of hymns, reminiscent of those which the inmates of the Asylum had sung many years previously. Another play, *The Magdalene*, was written by George Williamson in 1988 and performed at St Bride's Centre in Orwell Terrace. It records life in the Magdalene with all the tensions and jealousies to be expected in such an institution, particularly during admissions and expulsions. In the final scene two inmates come by a gift of money from an unexpected source, sufficient to pay their passage to a new life—in America.

A PLACE TO LIVE: A PLACE TO WORK

The main build-up in the population of Gorgie and Dalry occurred in the latter part of the nineteenth century, notably from the mid-1860s to the end of the century. Sporadic development began along the north side of Dalry Lane (now Dalry Road) nearest to Haymarket, no doubt influenced by the arrival, a decade earlier, of the Caledonian Distillery. By 1868, the Terraces on the south side of Dalry Lane were under construction, and the last remnants of the Dalry House policies were earmarked for the streets around Caledonian Crescent. For the first few years, Caledonian Road was named Caledonian Street, and Orwell Place was called Dalry Place. Nearby, the only person listed at West End Place, in 1870, was John Oman, the builder, but shortly afterwards a terrace of houses was built on the east side of the street.

In the late 1870s, further speculative building began along the south side of Gorgie Road at White Park, near to where the Heart of Midlothian Football Club had their first ground. The triangle formed by Henderson Terrace, Angle Park Terrace and Ardmillan Terrace was also under construction, with the exception of the site on the corner of Ardmillan Terrace and Angle Park Terrace. The corner was still occupied by the iron church belonging to the first congregation of St Michael's Parish Church, and was not moved until the stone church, on the opposite corner, was opened in 1883. The tenement, erected in 1887, has a biblical text *The Lord Reigneth, Let the Earth Rejoice*, set in stone, on the west-facing wall. A few hundred yards to the west of St Michael's Church, another group of Terraces was planned in the late

Mrs Isabella Paterson (née Ronaldson) wife of James Paterson, the joiner, outside her home, Glenlea Cottage, Gorgie Road, in 1890. The house survives, but without its roses, railings and entrance porch. (Courtesy of Jack Paterson.)

1870s, on ground between Gorgie Mains and Gorgie Cottage. Both properties had previously been saved from demolition by a slight deviation in the line of the Caledonian Railway. Gorgie Mains lay between St Michael's Church and Primrose Terrace. It was a substantial property, surveyed in 1897 by Thomson & Wright. Entry was gained from Slateford Road by a long driveway on the east side. The eight-roomed house was set back from the road behind a large ornamental garden, and was flanked by a paddock along the west boundary. Behind the house were the farm steadings, arranged around an inner courtyard. The buildings on the north side included a byre, hay shed, stable, straw barn and corn barn; on the south side were the harness room, mash room, pig house and cart shed. The sheep dippers were in the south-east corner, and the south boundary abutted the platform of Merchiston Station on the Caledonian line. At the time of the survey, Gorgie Mains was occupied by Walter Amos, a farmer, his wife Mary, and one housekeeper. The nearby property, Gorgie Cottage, was eventually demolished also and replaced by a tenement in 1895.

In the 1880s, tenement houses were erected on both sides of Gorgie Road, immediately west of McLeod Street. When Hearts moved their ground to the north side of Gorgie Road in 1886, the vacated ground,

Dalry Meadows - Tynecastle.
One and Two-roomed Dwellings.

Public Works Office.
City Chambers, Edin? 29ᵗʰ Feb,1896.

R. Morham
Architect

*In 1896 Robert Morham, the City Architect, drew up plans for one- and two-roomed
dwellings at Dalry Meadows, Tynecastle. One of the blocks was demolished c.1980
and the other was renovated and modernised by Gorgie Dalry Housing Association,
now Canmore Housing Association. (Courtesy of Canmore Housing Association.)*

on the south side, was used for the construction of Wardlaw Street and
Wardlaw Place. The houses in and around Murieston Road were completed around 1888. For reasons which are not now known, the remaining parts of Cathcart Place, Springwell Place and Downfield Place
were not completed until the late 1880s. The mason's progress, in
Downfield Place, is recorded in date stones, 1887 at Nos. 17, 20 and
22; 1888 at No.12; and 1903 at No.26 on the corner with Duff Street.
Towards the close of the century, Smithfield Street and Wheatfield Street
were built, along with Wheatfield Road (1897-98), and the remaining
parts of the north side of Gorgie Road (1896-98).

A study of the Census returns for 1851 and 1891 shows how the
population altered from mainly groups of families in fairly isolated farms
and cottages to the greater density of tenement life. In the process, of
course, the occupations also changed. The 1851 Census lists all the
outlying farms, which have now been absorbed into the district. At
Gorgie Farm (near Robb's Loan) the farm house was occupied by James
Robb, who farmed 216 acres, with 7 to 150 labourers, depending upon
the season. The permanent farm labourers lived nearby, usually a husband and wife, and at least four children. Much the same pattern is

Gorgie Crescent, in 1904, between Alexander Drive and Westfield Road. Originally it was reached directly from Gorgie Road but this entrance was discontinued when the flats and shops (with projecting canopies) were built on Gorgie Road in the 1920s. (Courtesy of Wilfred Grubb.)

recorded at Damhead Farm to the north of Westfield Road. Gorgie Mains (at Primrose Terrace) was occupied, before the Amos family, by William Todd, a farmer, his wife, two sons, three daughters, a nephew, an aunt, and Biddy, the servant girl from Ireland. Farther west, at Gorgie Park (near Moat Drive) there were nine families, mostly involved on the land, or in domestic service. The Henderson family, with two daughters and a son of their own, looked after a nine-year-old boy, Charles, described as 'a pauper scholar from the Poor House'. Not everyone was employed on the land: at 'Gorgie' several persons are listed as skinners, glue workers and gelatine finishers, either at Saughton Leather Works or Cox's Glue Works; and, at Tynecastle, James Waldie and James Muirhead are described as toll keepers.

A different social mix is evident in the Census of 1891, conducted at a time when most of the tenement buildings of Gorgie and Dalry had been built. In Gorgie Road, the occupations included mason, french polisher, quarryman, sweep, rubber worker, railway worker, carver, sculptor, and brewer, most of which reflected the arrival of mass employers in the district. In houses with only two rooms, six persons or more were commonplace. Facilities were basic: no bath; frequently a shared toilet on the landing; and all hot water and cooking done on the coal-fired range in the main room. One three-roomed house had a mother, a father and eight children, all to be fed off a joiner's wage. It is also interesting to note that a high percentage of the adults were born outside Edinburgh: Sutherland, Inverness, Aberdeen, Fife, Peebles, Lauder and Dumfries. Many families in Gorgie Square (at one time nearly opposite Telephone House but long since demolished) had at least one member of the family working in Cox's. In stark contrast to the other dwellings was Gorgie House (where the Poole's Roxy Picture House was built) which had twenty-three rooms and was occupied by Finlay Dun, the secretary to a public company in Edinburgh. He lived there with his two unmarried daughters, a son who was studying to be a doctor, and a staff consisting of a cook, a tablemaid and a housemaid. At Saughton Hall Asylum, all the patients are listed with their occupations, which included a solicitor, a warehouseman, a landed proprietor, an advocate and a retired lieutenant in the Indian Army. At Ardmillan Terrace, the Western Reformatory or the Girls' House of Refuge lists several females between the ages of 12 and 22, many of them born outside Edinburgh. They were all described as scholars. In the Magdalene Asylum next door, most of the inmates were older, in their 20s, and described as either seamstresses or laundresses.

Some of the main employers of the district are dealt with in detail in Chapters 6 and 7. Cox was in Gorgie from 1798, but the main batch of industrialists did not arrive until the second part of the nineteenth century. The Caledonian Distillery was first in 1855, followed by the Caledonian Brewery and Scott Morton, the cabinetmakers, in the 1860s. The North British Distillery arrived in 1885 and Mather, the Engineers, in 1896. There were many others, too numerous to mention, and the trend continued into the twentieth century, with Henshaw (metal sculptors) in 1904; T. & H. Smith (chemicals) in 1906; and Macandrew (public works' contractor) in 1919.

4

Churches and Mission Halls

Gorgie and Dalry, like other established parts of Edinburgh, contain churches of many different beliefs and denominations. Most of them were established in the district towards the end of the nineteenth century when the population was beginning to grow quite rapidly. Some churches were offshoots of those already in the Old Town of Edinburgh, whereas others grew more slowly from humble beginnings. It was quite common for small groups to meet in houses, halls and later in iron churches, which were temporary, prefabricated buildings frequently sold on to other emerging congregations.

The presence of so many churches is inexorably linked to the wider history of the Church in Scotland. The Disruption, in 1843, created a major division in the established Church of Scotland, partly over the issue of whether or not members of the congregations should be allowed a say in the selection of their own minister. The 'Disruptionists' broke away from the established Church and formed the Free Church of Scotland. Most of the Free Church of Scotland joined with the United Presbyterian Church in 1900 to form the United Free Church of Scotland, and in 1929 a further union between the Church of Scotland and the United Free Church of Scotland formed the Church of Scotland as it is known today.

Gorgie and Dalry also have a significant involvement with other churches and missions including: the Congregational Church; the Episcopal Church; the Church of God; the Gorgie Mission; the Church of the Nazarene; the Roman Catholic Church; the Salvation Army; and the United Free Church of Scotland Continuing. Those which no longer have a direct presence include the Baptist Church, the Evangelical Union Church, the Jewish Synagogue, and a small Episcopal Mission Hall, St Luke's, in Caledonian Crescent. St Luke's Mission was under the control of St Mary's Cathedral in Palmerston Place. It had quite a narrow frontage on the south side of Caledonian Crescent, a few hundred yards west of Dalry Swim Centre. On the ground floor there was a large hall at the east front, and a small hall at the back. The main church and vestry were on the first floor with the caretaker's flat to the rear. All the furnishings were of light-coloured pine and were dispersed to various churches when St Luke's closed around 1967.

ST DAVID'S PARISH CHURCH

The story of St David's is closely linked with that part of the Lands of Dalry which in recent years has been more commonly known as Fountainbridge. In 1826 Gardner's Hall Church was built at the south end of Gardner's Crescent for the United Associate Secession Church. Their first minister, the Rev. David Marr, lived at No.8 Gardner's Crescent. The Secession congregation moved in 1831 to Lothian Road Chapel (now the Filmhouse) and Gardner's Hall Church was acquired by St Cuthbert's Parish Church and renamed St David's. In those days Gardner's Crescent did not communicate directly with Fountainbridge, which may have been the origin of a rather quaint legend concerning a right of way from the south end of Gardner's Crescent to a short lane running north from Fountainbridge. It is said that the right of way ran through the church building and that on at least one occasion it was used by a milkmaid who walked through the church one Sunday morning, rested her milk pails for a moment whilst she listened to the minister, and then made her way along 'the milky way'.

The real Disruption occurred in 1843. The Rev. Robert Fergusson, who had been at St David's for only two days, 'came out' and joined the Free Church with most of the congregation. In the following year a new church was built for them in Morrison Street almost opposite Dewar Place. In 1859 that church was rebuilt and two halls were added at the rear. The church became St David's United Free in 1900 and then St David's Morrison Street at the Union with the Church of Scotland in 1929. Finally in 1961 St David's Morrison Street amalgamated with Broomhouse and the Morrison Street building was sold and demolished. The site is now occupied by a suite of offices, St David's House.

Meantime St David's at Gardner's Crescent began to look for a more suitable site for a new church in the first decade of the twentieth century. A site was obtained on the west side of Viewforth near the junction with Dundee Street. The land, purchased for £1,500, had previously belonged to the Scottish Vulcanite Works and had recently been acquired by the North British Rubber Company. The church endowment fund was enhanced by a conditional gift in the will of the late minister, the Rev. Alexander Webster, who bequeathed £2,500 pro-

*Laying the foundation stone at St David's Church, Viewforth on 27th May 1911.
The congregation was first established in 1831 at Gardner's Hall, at the south end of
Gardner's Crescent.*

vided the new church was opened, free of debt, not later than one year
after the death of his widow. An appeal was launched in April 1909 and
plans were drawn by the architect James D. Cairns. Work started in
April 1911 for a church to seat 970, and it was built by Scott and
Brown using Dumfriesshire red sandstone for the dressings and Hailes
rubble for the infill. The foundation stone was laid on 27th May 1911
by Lord Glenconner of Glen, Lord High Commissioner, and the church
was dedicated on 29th December 1912. Unfortunately the completed
building was never really seen to best advantage as it was designed to sit
at right angles to Viewforth, the idea being that it would face onto a
new street to be built between Viewforth and Gibson Terrace. When
the new street never materialised, the church was left with its main
entrance facing onto a narrow passageway.

St David's amalgamated with Viewforth St Oswald's in 1973, leaving
the St David's building surplus to requirements. When the church building was demolished a few years later, care was taken to locate the glass
casket known to have been placed under the foundation stone at the
base of the pulpit. It was found to contain the usual assortment of
newspapers of the day, coins of the realm, communion tokens, a list of

people involved in the construction of the church, and a small card from Peter Stevenson of Forrest Road, Edinburgh advertising glass caskets 'to be deposited in the foundation stones of buildings'.

DALRY CONGREGATIONAL CHURCH

Dalry Congregational Church, at the junction of Caledonian Road and Caledonian Crescent, was built in 1872, much earlier than many of the other churches in the growing district of Dalry. Its origins lie at the beginning of the nineteenth century.

In 1802 the Rev. John Aikman built a church at his own expense in Argyle Square in the Old Town of Edinburgh. He remained the unpaid minister until his death on 6th February 1834. His burial chamber inside the church building was marked by a marble memorial tablet giving details of his ministry. By 1855 substantial changes were planned for the area around Argyle Square, necessitating its complete demolition for the construction of the National Museum of Industry (later the Royal Museum of Scotland) in Chambers Street. On 3rd July 1861 the Rev. Aikman's remains were re-interred in Greyfriars Churchyard near the gate at the north end, and a monument was erected by the congregation in the following year. The old church was demolished, but the marble memorial tablet was saved, along with the £2,000 compensation paid for the loss of the church building. Most of the congregation transferred to Queen Street Hall and later to Augustine Congregational Church in George IV Bridge.

By 1870 there was serious talk of using the £2,000 fund to build a new church in Dalry. The architect, Alexander Heron, was asked to draw up plans and the completed structure, in the Gothic style, was opened in 1872. A hall in a similar style was built to the south of the church in 1878. The original marble tablet in memory of the Rev. Aikman was incorporated in the vestry of the new building with an additional explanatory wooden notice placed below it. The building has one or two other interesting features. On the east wall is a stained-glass window erected by James L. Mack, S.S.C., a former treasurer of the church, in memory of one of his family. To the right-hand side of the pulpit (as viewed by the congregation) is a small organ rebuilt by H. King, organ builder, of Edinburgh in 1892, twenty years after the church was opened.

Dalry Congregational Church celebrated its centenary in 1972 and the present minister is the Rev. Robert Patton.

ST COLM'S PARISH CHURCH

St Colm's, on the corner of Dalry Road and Cathcart Place, has roots which go back more than a century. The present building, with the original clock saved from Dalry Free Church, was built in 1988, creating a new church and sheltered housing in one complex. The story, however, goes back to at least 1871 and includes the different denominational churches of Haymarket, Dalry and St Bride's.

Haymarket United Presbyterian Church began on 5th November 1871 under its first minister the Rev. Thomas Kirk, in an iron church on the east corner of Caledonian Place and Dalry Road. The prefabricated building came from Woolwich, cost £400, seated 300, and was completely demolished on 21st October 1874 when the gable end of a partially completed tenement was blown on top of it. A new stone church designed in the Romanesque style by the architect John Paterson was built on the north side of Dalry Road, nearer to Haymarket. This church, seating 840, was opened on 17th December 1875 by the Rev. Dr McGavin of Dundee. Its central, triple doorway had embellished stonework, above which was an arrangement of long elegant windows with rounded tops. There were flanking square towers on each side, the west one having a miniature belfry on each corner: the east tower belfries were never completed. Haymarket United Presbyterian became Haymarket United Free in 1900 and Haymarket Parish Church in 1929. The last service held at Haymarket was on 31st January 1960, after which it was united with Dalry Parish Church on 7th February 1960 to form Dalry Haymarket Parish Church. Haymarket Church was demolished and the site was sold to Woolworths, a change of use which attracted a lot of comment at the time. Perhaps influenced more by nostalgia than a knowledge of the architect's plans, one elderly parishioner was heard to say: 'Aye, I was baptised just over there at the Haberdashery counter'. Prior to demolition of Haymarket Church the various memorials were transferred to Dalry Parish Church which was then used for worship by the joint congregation. At the time of closure, Haymarket's minister was the Rev. D.C. Murray.

Dalry Parish Church had been in existence for many years before the union with Haymarket. It began as Dalry Free Church in 1878 under its first minister, the Rev. Alexander Rodger. For the first few years the congregation held services in the church hall built at the expense of St George's Free Church, Shandwick Place. On 8th January 1881 the foundation stone of the new church on the corner of Cathcart Place and Dalry Road was laid by Dr Benjamin Bell, physician, and office-bearer at St George's. The architect, Robert Raeburn, gifted a stained-glass window behind the pulpit in memory of Dr Candlish, and the church was opened on 11th December 1881. The building was a prominent Edinburgh landmark for many years with a clock situated midway between the square base tower and the long slender spire.

By the early 1920s the original hall accommodation had been inadequate for many years. To finance an extension a bazaar was held in the Music Hall in George Street (now the Assembly Rooms) on 4th, 5th and 6th December 1924, which raised over £3,000. The 84-page brochure lists various entertainments, including piano recitals, gramophone selections, wireless demonstrations, and one which no longer has current appeal: 'the Electric Coil one penny per shock'. The method of constructing the hall extension was equally bizarre: the roof of the old hall was cut from the wallhead and jacked up twelve feet. A new floor was inserted and the walls were extended to create a two-storey building with a separate hall on each level.

Dalry Free Church changed its name to Dalry United Free Church in 1900, Dalry Parish Church in 1929, Dalry Haymarket Parish Church in 1960, and finally St Colm's Parish Church in 1973. At the time of the union with Haymarket in 1960 the minister at Dalry Parish Church was the Rev. Dr D. McDougall.

The third piece in the jigsaw is St Bride's Parish Church in Orwell Terrace. Its history falls into three separate eras: firstly there was the mission; then there was the chapel of ease; and finally the parish church. The original parishes of the Church of Scotland to the west of Edinburgh were St Cuthbert's and Corstorphine. In 1870 West Coates was disjoined from St Cuthbert's and became a separate parish. Under its minister, the Rev. Robert Gibb Forrest, it set up Dalry Mission around 1880. In 1898 a hall was built in Orwell Terrace and a separate minister was appointed independent of West Coates. The foundation stone of a new stone church was laid in 1908 on a site adjacent to the hall in Orwell Terrace. On 22nd May 1909 the new building, costing £7,000, was dedicated as St Bride's Chapel of Ease under the guidance of West Coates. Among the donors to the building fund were the Misses Walker of Dalry House. In 1923 St Bride's was made a separate parish independent of West Coates and in 1929 it became part of the re-united Church of Scotland. St Bride's last minister was the Rev. J.S. Forbes MacDonald whose death in July 1971 led to negotiations for a union between St Bride's and Dalry Haymarket.

*St Colm's Parish Church in Dalry Road in 1984. The building dates from 1881 when it was Dalry Free Church. It was demolished in 1988 and replaced with a new church and housing by Canmore Housing Association. (*Crown Copyright: RCAHMS.*)*

For some months after the death of the Rev. J.S. Forbes MacDonald, combined services were held on alternate Sundays at Dalry Haymarket and St Bride's whilst details of the union were being worked out. The Rev. Ian P. Renton (previously minister at Dalry Haymarket) was appointed to the combined congregation, which took the name St Colm's. The Dalry Haymarket church building was used as the place of worship and St Bride's was sold and later became a Community Centre.

When St Colm's was established on 7th June 1973, it already had a history of change stretching back to 1871 — and there was more to follow. In September 1983 a feasibility study was undertaken on the possible redevelopment of St Colm's Parish Church. There were several factors to consider: the church congregation was increasingly being drawn from an ageing population; the former St Bride's Church building had become a flourishing Community Centre; and the cost of maintaining the fabric of the old church had become very onerous. There was an underlying feeling that if these problems were not tackled quickly there would be no church at all. The proposals, carried into effect in 1988, required the complete demolition of the old church and its replacement by a new building containing a new church on the corner site, and housing to the north and east. Units of family housing and sheltered housing are entered from a pend off Dalry Road and there are two special houses for the disabled entered from Cathcart Place. The church is much smaller than the original Dalry Church, but what it lacks in size it makes up for by a much more comfortable and friendly atmosphere. There is no pulpit, but other furnishings such as the baptismal font and some stained-glass windows maintain a link with the earlier building. The present minister at St Colm's is the Rev. Stewart McPherson.

DALRY SYNAGOGUE

The section of the *Ordnance Survey Map*, 1893, showing Caledonian Crescent, provides an interesting clue to a small congregation of which very little information has survived. On the south side of the road, immediately east of St Luke's Episcopal Church, a small rectangular building is shown: 'Synagogue—Seats for 100'. At the end of the twentieth century the Edinburgh Hebrew Congregation owned, and worshipped in, a synagogue in Graham Street (now part of Keir Street), off Lauriston Place. Surviving minutes of the Edinburgh Hebrew Congregation disclose that around 1880 a group of Jews from Manchester arrived in the Dalry area to work for William Currie & Co. at their

Caledonian Rubber Works, on the north side of Dalry Road between Washington Street and West Park Place. In establishing the Dalry Synagogue, the group caused a certain amount of controversy as the existing Hebrew Congregation was inclined to look upon the newcomers as a branch synagogue only. The group leaders, most of whom lived in the Gorgie and Dalry area and carried out the communal duties, included D. Levenson, L. Raddin, P. Phin, T. Levenson, H. Franks and S. Kleinblatt. In 1890 they asked the Graham Street Synagogue for assistance in securing a separate butcher shop in Dalry and a Jewish teacher to teach their children. Whilst the Chief Rabbi, Dr H. Adler, was sympathetic to these requests, the granting of them again caused concern to the main congregation. In 1911 the subject of co-ordination with Graham Street and other small branches was mooted but dismissed by the communities themselves as 'impracticable'. It is not known when the Dalry Synagogue closed but it is likely to have been before the outbreak of the First World War: certainly the last listed minister was M. Abrahams in 1909. In 1932 the Graham Street Synagogue and two others joined forces when the Salisbury Road Synagogue was opened. The site of the former synagogue in Caledonian Crescent is now occupied by modern flats between Dalry Swim Centre and Telfer Subway.

DALRY EVANGELICAL UNION

The Evangelical Union Church was established in Edinburgh following a public meeting on 4th July 1845 of seventy-five people led by the Revs. John Kirk, Ebenezer Kennedy and James Morison. Many of those who attended at Waterloo Rooms had previously been Congregationalists. Services were held at Calton Convening Rooms until 1874 when the venue was changed to Grindlay Street Hall, to coincide with the appointment of the Rev. John Kirk Jnr. as minister. There were problems with Grindlay Street Hall, however, as it had been built for one thousand people and was far too big for a religious gathering of less than one hundred. A decision was taken to leave 'the howling wilderness full of draughts rather than people' and build a new chapel more in keeping with the congregation's needs. The new church, opened in 1877 at East Fountainbridge, attracted one hundred members from Brighton Street Church who followed their previous minister, Professor Kirk, in his decision to transfer to his son's church at East Fountainbridge.

In the early years at East Fountainbridge, J.H. Fordham of London took an active interest in the church. He proposed that if the congregation could raise £600 he would advance a loan of £1,000, free of interest, on the understanding that the anticipated saving in interest on an existing loan should be applied to improve the minister's stipend. The £600 was raised at a bazaar held in the Literary Institute and the deal was concluded. Some years later, in 1891, the same commercial expediency was not so evident. Another benefactor offered the church £40 per year for four years on condition that a fixed sum should be raised by the church itself, either by collection or seat rents. The gift was, however, declined by the church managers on the basis that 'to name conditions in such circumstances was unscriptural'. In fact the decision masked deep-rooted misgivings among the congregation about the church's poor financial position. One faction took the view that this was the fault of the minister who did not 'by his preaching draw the wealthy class of people who would be able to contribute more liberally'. The minister's displeasure was all the greater when he learned the following year that his salary was to be reduced. Mr Kirk replied that if that happened he would resign, not because of the decrease in salary but because of the reflection on his work. The motion to reduce was carried and he resigned in 1891.

Despite these setbacks the work of acquiring a new and bigger church building continued. After much deliberation a site on the west corner of Dalry Road and Murieston Crescent was secured. The church, designed in the Gothic style by Simon and Tweedie, was finished in 1894, with a buttressed tower and spire on the south-east corner. The total cost was just less than £6,000 including the hall which was used for worship whilst the main church was under construction.

In 1915 the building was sold to Gorgie Baptist Church who remained there until 1982. In the late 1980s, when the triangle of ground bounded by East Fountainbridge, Earl Grey Street and High Riggs was being cleared for development, the old shell of Mr Kirk's Evangelical Union Church was visible for a few weeks until the complete demolition of the surrounding S.M.T. garage. When the Evangelical Union Church moved from Dalry Road in 1916, they relocated at the west end of Gorgie Road between Westfield Road and Westfield Street in the building vacated by Gorgie Baptist Church.

GORGIE BAPTIST CHURCH

The early history of the Baptist Church in Gorgie and Dalry is described in the *History of Baptists in Scotland* edited by the Rev. George

Yuille. At the Annual General Meeting of the Edinburgh Association of Baptist Churches on 24th February 1904 the retiring president, George W. Emslie, made reference to the opportunity the Association had for 'Extension Work in Edinburgh'. Following a number of other meetings, it was decided that any new church should be in the thickly populated districts of Gorgie and Dalry. It was not until 1907, however, that real progress was made when a building belonging to the Reformed Presbyterian Church at Gorgie came up for sale. This was probably the building known as the 'Little Church in the Field' which had been used by various church denominations over the years. On 9th December 1907 Gorgie Baptist Church was officially constituted with forty members. The first minister was the Rev. Donald McNicol, followed in 1911 by the Rev. George Harper. Extensions were made to the church in 1909 but within five years the improved accommodation was again inadequate. At the end of 1915 the Evangelical Union Church in Dalry Road was offered for sale and the two churches decided to exchange buildings. Removal to the new church took place in January 1916 and the opening service conducted by Rev. Principal Jervis Coats was held on 13th February 1916.

Gorgie Baptist Church flourished in its new building until the 1960s, but thereafter there was a slow but steady decline in membership. In 1982 the church building was sold to St Martin of Tours Episcopal Church, and the Baptist congregation worshipped temporarily in Gorgie City Mission in Wheatfield Terrace. The following year a formal union was concluded with the church at Stenhouse Cross which then took the name Stenhouse Gorgie. Around the same time a new church was begun at Colinton Mains to which some of the Gorgie congregation transferred. The former minister at Gorgie, the Rev. Alan Montgomery, took joint charge of Stenhouse Gorgie and Colinton Mains, with the Rev. Ambrose Else as Associate.

ST MARTIN OF TOURS EPISCOPAL CHURCH

The Episcopal Church of St Martin of Tours has been established in the districts of Gorgie and Dalry since 1883. Its origins were humble. A small mission building was opened at White Park on the south side of Gorgie Road under the care of the Rev. N. W. Usher, one of the chaplains from St Mary's Cathedral. Early services were taken by Charles Pressley-Smith, at that time still a student at Edinburgh Theological College. It is recorded that the first congregation consisted of one man and a few children, with a collection amounting to 1½d. From such acorns great oaks seldom grow. However, by the end of 1884 a group had been formed to run the Tynecastle Working Men's Club in a shop on the corner of Newton Street and Dalry Road. The baptismal records give an interesting insight into the everyday occupations of the fathers—causeway layers, lath splitters, skinners, tanners, a ploughman from White Park and a farmer from Newton Street.

By 1887 the size of the congregation was such that new accommodation was urgently required. An iron church was proposed for the bottom of Ardmillan Terrace (on the corner of Gorgie Road and Murieston Road, described as 'the most valuable site in the district'. Pressley-Smith went off to Northampton to look at an iron church which was for sale, and secured it with a loan of £500 from the National Bank of Scotland. No sooner was the purchase made than all manner of disputes arose about its transfer to Edinburgh. There was a row with the architect over his fee, trouble with the contractor (who also happened to be a member of the church), and criticism from the Northampton congregation about what they saw as needless damage to the rose window.

During the 1890s many changes took place at St Martin's. In 1893, the church purchased for £1,700 the feu on which the iron church stood, possibly in anticipation of a stone church being built in the years ahead. The Rev. Charles Pressley-Smith transferred to Oban in October 1895 and was replaced at Ardmillan by the Rev. Norman Gourlie in February 1896. It was not a particularly happy transfer, however, as Mr Gourlie, who tended towards the evangelical style, refused to wear the vestments and demanded the removal of four of the six candlesticks in the church. On a more positive note, however, a chancel was added to the iron church and the school rooms were enlarged.

Shortly after Mr Gourlie's transfer to Ardmillan the question of a permanent stone church came up for discussion again. A site in Bonaly Road (later renamed Harrison Road) was rejected in favour of Ardmillan, and John Robertson of Inverness was instructed to draw up plans. His first idea 'in the early French Gothic style' was very elaborate and, being three times longer than what was eventually built, was thought to be over-ambitious. The building costs were defrayed, to some extent, by selling a portion of the ground to the National Bank of Scotland for £700 and selling part of the old iron church for £100. An appeal for funds was launched under the title 'Grand Concert and Dramatic Entertainment in aid of the Building Fund of St Martin's Episcopal

St. Martin's Church.   Edinburgh.

St Martin of Tours Episcopal Church, c. 1905. John Robertson's French Gothic edifice in red and white stone was a landmark on the corner of Gorgie Road and Murieston Road from 1900 until the church was demolished in the early 1980s.

Church, Gorgie Road', held in St Cuthbert's Hall, King's Stables Road on Shrove Tuesday 14th February 1899 at 8 p.m. The programme consisted of songs, recitations and violin solos under the direction of the stage manager, Henry O'Conner. The foundation stone for the new church was laid on 15th July 1899, and the first service was held on 14th July 1900.

John Robertson's French Gothic edifice in red and white stone was a landmark on the corner of Gorgie Road and Murieston Road from around 1900 to the early 1980s when it was demolished. It was particularly arresting from Ardmillan Terrace, which looked directly towards the ornate doorway. The church was constructed at a time when most buildings of religious or public importance were built of good-quality stone, cut, shaped and bedded by local tradesmen. Robertson's entire plan was never carried out, but documents preserved at West Register House in Edinburgh provide a glimpse at the methods of construction and the use of terms and materials no longer seen in building contracts. It was the responsibility of the surveyor to draw up a schedule of measurements for each of the main trades and to pass copies of the schedule to the contractors who wished to tender. The schedules for 1st February 1899 make interesting reading. For the plumbing work, 'the lead to be of the best soft English milled kind and to be clinked at joinings where necessary'. The schedule for masonry ran to twenty-three pages with numerous sketches of window tracery and other features. The rubble walls were to be made from Hailes quarry rubble with 'at least 2 cross bonded headers in every superficial yard', and the dressings were to be 'carefully droved diagonally six strokes to the inch'. Internally, the plasterwork had a local flavour, 'plaster to be composed of best Burdie's House Midlothian lime and clean sharp river or pit sand with a due proportion of long fresh bullock's hair all well mixed and soured at least three weeks before being used'. Finally, the glazing work referred to 'Pilkington's best quality Cathedral tinted glass, wedged into groove in stone work, bedded and pointed with mastic and oil outside and inside'.

Of the seven bays intended for the nave, only four were completed, and the south-east tower was stopped below the level of the main roof. At a later date, a brick chancel was grafted onto the north end of the truncated nave but the bond was not a happy one. The nave and the chancel went their separate ways, opening up a dangerous gap between the two structures, which eventually led to their demolition around 1983. When the Rev. W.J.T. Brockie came to St Martin's in 1976,

Robertson's unfinished building had been in use for three-quarters of a century. In 1982 St Martin's moved to the church building vacated by Gorgie Baptist Church on the corner of Dalry Road and Murieston Crescent. The pipe organ was brought from the previous building and rebuilt by R.C. Goldsmith. Also transferred were the reredos given by Mr Pressley-Smith and the lecturn resented by Mr Gourlie. A service of celebration was held on 28th April 1991 to mark the successful cleaning of St Martin's warm pink Doddington stonework.

CHURCH OF THE NAZARENE

The Church of the Nazarene, in Henderson Terrace, is part of a much wider organisation which began in Britain, Canada and the United States of America. Eleven small denominations, all sharing the Wesleyan heritage, came together in a series of unions between 1896 and 1958. The 1908 union is generally taken to be the official beginning of the church. Of the original eleven denominations, three were British: the first, led by the Rev. George Sharpe at Parkhead, Glasgow, joined in 1915; the second, led by David Thomas of London, joined in 1952; and the third, led by the Rev. Maynard G. James in Lancashire, completed the trio in 1955. At the present day there are over one hundred churches in the British Isles.

The Church of the Nazarene first came to Edinburgh in 1953 when the congregation took over an existing church building, previously used by the Congregational Church in Albany Street. The Nazarene congregation remained at Albany Street until October 1973, after which it moved to the present building in Henderson Terrace. Edinburgh has one other Church of the Nazarene, at Clermiston, which was established in 1963.

Worldwide the church is a very extensive organisation with 10,000 separate church buildings, 11,000 ministers and 1,000,000 members. There is a substantial commitment to three hospitals (India, Swaziland and Papua New Guinea), and to numerous schools and colleges. The first Nazarene Theological College in the British Isles was established in 1943 at Hurlet, Nitshill, but later transferred to its present location in Manchester. The Nazarenes have two main assemblies. The British Isles is divided into two Districts, each of which holds a District Assembly each year, usually near to Easter. In addition to the District Assemblies there is a General Assembly, held once every four years, usually in the United States of America, which attracts 18,000 delegates from all over the world.

THE CHURCH OF GOD IN EDINBURGH

The Meeting Place of the Church of God has been at No.5 Ardmillan Terrace since moving from Morrison Street in 1971. In earlier years it was at Nicolson Square, Marshall Street, Jamaica Street, Buccleuch district and Haymarket. It is linked to other Churches of God in a Fellowship throughout the world. Although the present Fellowship takes its origin as the year 1892, the Brethren movement was active in Edinburgh and other parts of the country for many years before that. Early pioneers in Edinburgh included J.A. Boswell, who was related to James Boswell, biographer of Dr Samuel Johnson. J.A. Boswell was involved in evangelical work with the then Brethren movement in the north of Scotland from c.1859, until he separated to be linked with the Churches of God. Another pioneer was Ludovic Alexander who became co-editor of the Fellowship's teaching magazine *Needed Truth*.

The Fellowship does not have ordained ministers, although each church has elders who take an active (but not exclusive) role at assembly meetings. The elders represent the various churches worldwide at an elders' meeting, normally held once per year at Nottingham University. District meetings are also held once every two months of elders from the East of Scotland district, which includes Musselburgh, Innerleithen, Bathgate, Buckhaven and Cowdenbeath, as well as Edinburgh.

ST MICHAEL'S PARISH CHURCH

The building of St Michael's Parish Church on the corner of Slateford Road and Harrison Road was begun in 1881, to designs by the Glasgow architect John Honeyman. The congregation had, however, been in existence for several years before being able to afford such a grand edifice.

In the mid-1870s three people in particular were interested in church extension work in the new districts of Dalry, Tynecastle and North Merchiston. They were James Hope of Belmont at Murrayfield, James Adams Wenley, Treasurer of the Bank of Scotland, and John Hope Finlay W.S., whose efforts were given a great deal of support from St Cuthbert's Parish Church at the West End of Edinburgh. In 1877 an iron church, 'North Merchiston', to seat 500, was erected for the sum of £1,575 at the junction of Ardmillan Terrace and Angle Park Terrace. The Rev. Dr James MacGregor and the Rev. Dr James Barclay shared the Sunday services until a permanent minister was found. By 1882 membership was 748, rising to over 800 in the following year, many more than the capacity of the church built only five years previously. In 1879 a building fund for a new church was started and the triangular piece of ground on the corner of Harrison Road and Slateford Road was bought for £1,176. The estimated cost of the new building was £15,000 to seat 1000 persons. Building work began in January 1881 on a very grand building, measuring internally 130 feet long, 62½ feet wide and 70 feet high. The architect's insistence that twenty inches per person was adequate ensured that all future expansion was tightly controlled!

The first minister was the Rev. George Wilson of Cramond and the completed building was opened at 3 p.m. on Wednesday 28th November 1883. As the iron church was no longer required, it was sold on 30th April 1884 for £406 to the authorities of West House, Morningside, and is currently in use in the grounds of the Royal Edinburgh Hospital. In addition to his early work at St Michael's, Dr Wilson was active in mission work which eventually led to the erection of Tynecastle Church in Gorgie Road.

According to the Edinburgh volume of *The Buildings of Scotland*, St Michael's is a 'large and very perfect example of Early English—an historical division of English Gothic architecture covering the period 1200-1250'. The church sits on an east-west axis with a high square tower on the north-west corner, containing the main entrance, but still lacking the intended broach spire which would have greatly enhanced its external appearance. The nave, with a rear gallery, has a central aisle flanked by two side aisles: the clerestories have triple groups of windows, and the roof is timbered. The pulpit in the north-east corner has decorated panels by Gertrude Hope, and the original organ of 1895 is by Brindley and Forster. There are several commemorative stained-glass windows. In 1886 two windows by James Ballantyne in the south aisle were gifted by David A. Carnegie, M.D. The window at the east end is divided into seven sections each of which has a separate theme, and that at the west end depicts Jairus's daughter. The three chancel windows completed by A. Ballantine and Gardiner in 1895 were a gift by James Hope of Belmont in memory of his wife the Hon. Mrs Gertrude Hope. Finally two south lancet windows were completed in 1925 by Douglas Strachan in memory of John Campbell and his wife.

The present minister is the Rev. Margaret Rae Forrester, appointed in 1980.

NORTH MERCHISTON PARISH CHURCH

North Merchiston Parish Church stood in Slateford Road immediately to the west of Shandon Bridge, almost opposite the top of Robertson Avenue. The congregation was dissolved in 1986 and the building was demolished shortly thereafter. Its origins can, however, be traced back to the middle of the nineteenth century in the old village of Gorgie.

David T. Lyon wrote his book, *Memorials of Gorgie Mission and Free Church*, in 1899. He records that in 1860 Mrs Wilkie and Walter Clark led a small religious group which met twice a week in the Old School building beside Cox's Glue Works. The villagers were alerted to the service 'by reliable boys' who were sent round the village ringing a bell fifteen minutes before the start. Most services were taken by lay persons from the village but the Rev. Dr J. Hood Wilson of Barclay Free Church frequently travelled out to Gorgie to take the Sunday services. The accommodation was always a problem, alleviated to some extent in 1872 when John Cox (uncle of Robert Cox M.P.) agreed to build an extension to the Old School building.

In the mid-1880s a decision was taken to build a new Free church on ground opposite the recently constructed Gorgie Board School. Plans were drawn by David Robertson for a hall to seat 250, with a vestry, session room and small gallery above the pulpit. It was named the 'Little Church in the Field' and was opened as a Territorial Mission Station on 15th October 1887 by the Rev. J.M. Sloan of Chalmers Memorial Free Church in the Grange. Assistance in setting up various supporting organisations was provided by Morningside Free Church and Barclay Free Church. In subsequent years the Little Church in the Field was used by other denominations and later renamed Gorgie War Memorial Hall. It is currently used as a Community Centre.

In 1891 Gorgie was made a regular charge under its first minister, the Rev. William Kilpatrick, whose first task was to secure a new church building. The original intention was to use the ground in front of the old church, but after much deliberation the Slateford Road site was chosen. The feu charter was signed with Simon Henderson on 6th March 1894 and work began early in 1895, following plans by McArthy and Watson. The foundation stone was laid on 25th May 1895 by the Rev. Dr J. Hood Wilson, Moderator of the Free Church General Assembly that year. The mason work, using dressed stone from Corncockle Quarry, Dumfriesshire, and rubble work from Ravelston Quarry, was done by W. & J. Kirkwood of Annandale Street Lane and the joinerwork

North Merchiston Parish Church, Slateford Road, c.1904. The congregation, which could trace its origins to the middle of the nineteenth century in the old village of Gorgie, was dissolved in 1986. The building was demolished shortly thereafter. (Courtesy of the Rev. A. Ian Dunlop.)

by W. Beattie & Son of Fountainbridge. The completed church was opened on Thursday 14th May 1896 at 3 p.m. It had a wide central nave with two aisles, the nave terminating at the pulpit end in a semi-octagon measuring 86 feet by 51. The gallery at the north end over the vestibule increased the total seating capacity to 760. After the church had been in use for a few months it was found necessary to reduce the height of the pulpit. The total cost to construct the church was £5,883, reduced by £575 when the Little Church in the Field was sold to the Original Secession Church.

Gorgie Free Church became Gorgie United Free Church in 1900 and North Merchiston in 1929. When the church was demolished in 1988 the pulpit and pews were transported to a new Free Presbyterian church at Leverburgh in the Outer Hebrides and a stone cross from the roof was repositioned in the garden ground of St Michael's Parish Church. The last minister was the Rev. Keith S.P. Robinson who came to North Merchiston from Walkerburn on 6th September 1966 and retired in 1986.

ST CUTHBERT'S ROMAN CATHOLIC CHURCH

St Cuthbert's Roman Catholic Church stands at the east corner of Hutchison Crossway and Slateford Road. It is a very prominent landmark, particularly for people travelling into the city from the west of Edinburgh. The building, designed by J.B. Bennett in 1894 in a chunky geometric style, lies on a north–south axis, but lacks the intended southeast spire.

St Cuthbert's parish, originally known as Gorgie, was established in September 1889, its first priest being Father John Forsyth, ordained at St Mary's Cathedral in June 1888. Initially the parish boundaries were very wide, stretching from the Pentland Hills to the Firth of Forth, and as far west as Gogarburn. In the following decade additional parishes were formed: St Columba's, Upper Gray Street in 1889; St Andrew's, Ravelston Place in 1901; and St Peter's, Falcon Avenue in 1906. St Cuthbert's School Chapel to the north of the present church was opened on 27th July 1890, and the parish presbytery was occupied later the same year. The commissioning and building of the main church took place in the early 1890s, a substantial part of the funding coming from private individuals. The completed church was opened on 31st May 1896 by the Most Rev. Angus MacDonald, Archbishop of St Andrews and Edinburgh.

During the whole of St Cuthbert's first century (reviewed in *St Cuthbert's Parish Centenary, 1889-1989*) the parish was served by only three parish priests, and a number of assistant priests. By far the longest-serving was Father John Forsyth who came to St Cuthbert's as a recently ordained priest in 1889 and held the position until his death in 1942. In 1930 when Father Forsyth was almost seventy years of age he was elevated to the status of Monsignor, and celebrated his golden jubilee in 1938. The second priest was Father Peter Connolly (later Monsignor), from 1943 until 1969, after which he moved to St Mary's, Haddington. During his stay at St Cuthbert's a new organ was installed in 1950, and two years later the church was completely renovated and a new altar was built. The church was consecrated on 30th May 1956 by Archbishop Gray of St Andrews and Edinburgh (later Cardinal), the rule at that time being that a Roman Catholic church could not be consecrated until it was free of debt. When Monsignor Connolly left the parish in 1969, his position was taken by Father Laurence Davison, who returned to Edinburgh from having been parish priest at Lochgelly. One of his early tasks was to implement the necessary alterations to the

The consecration of St Cuthbert's Roman Catholic Church in Slateford Road took place on 30th May 1956. On the left is Archbishop Gordon Joseph Gray (later Cardinal), and in the centre is Father Laurence Davison (later Canon), parish priest of St Cuthbert's from 1969 to 1989. The church was first opened on 31st May 1896. (Courtesy of Monsignor Tony Duffy, parish priest of St Cuthbert's.)

sanctuary as envisaged by the Second Vatican Council. These were part of several changes implemented by the Roman Catholic Church over a five-year period in the late 1960s, to emphasise that the saying of Mass should be a public and social act in which the laity participate fully. The altar was brought forward, the saying of Mass in Latin was discontinued, and the priest faced the congregation throughout the service. The alterations to St Cuthbert's were done under the guidance of the architect Peter Whiston, using existing furniture and materials. Two tapestries, designed by Archie Brennan and woven at Dovecot Studios in Edinburgh, were added, and first shown at an exhibition during the 1971 Edinburgh International Festival. The tapestries, each measuring 14 feet by 3 feet 5 inches, are framed between pairs of oak columns. Two additional tapestries, the Baptismal Tapestry and the Tabernacle Tapestry, designed by Fiona Matheson and woven at the same studios, were added in 1979.

At the present day, the priest at St Cuthbert's is Monsignor Tony Duffy, who came to the parish on the retirement of Father Davison in 1989.

GORGIE PARISH CHURCH

Gorgie Parish Church was created on 5th August 1979 by the amalgamation of two previous congregations, both in Gorgie Road, namely Tynecastle and Cairns Memorial. A panel of arbiters decided that the building previously used by Cairns Memorial Church, opposite the end of Wardlaw Street, should be used by the new congregation. A new minister, the Rev. Charles M. Stewart, was appointed and in 1984 the old Tynecastle building was demolished. Its former position on the north side of Gorgie Road, to the west of Gorgie Parish Church, is easily located where the gap in the tenement buildings is now filled by a two-storey retail shop. Up to this point the previous congregations of Tynecastle and Cairns Memorial had developed quite separately from one another.

The Tynecastle congregation was the older of the two. In 1885 the recently appointed minister at St Michael's, the Rev. George Wilson, involved himself in mission work in Tynecastle. A room was first rented at No. 6 Newton Street followed by larger premises at No. 4 White Park in 1886. Eventually a hall to seat 250 was acquired on the north side of Gorgie Road opposite White Park, around the time that Mr Wilson's assistant, the Rev. J. Bell Nicoll, began his work in the district. By 1891 the need for a permanent church building was evident. Before the tenement buildings on the north side of Gorgie Road were completed the church acquired a feu set quite far back from the line of Gorgie Road. On this feu the new church was built to seat 530 at a cost of £2,000; it was opened in May 1891. Within four years a plan was put forward to double the size of the existing church but the idea was abandoned in favour of a completely new church which could be built for only £500 more. This was built with its façade in line with Gorgie Road, and the old church at the back was retained as hall accommodation. The foundation stone was laid by the Rev. Dr Scott of St George's, Edinburgh on 3rd November 1900 and the official opening was on 9th November 1901.

The Cairns Memorial Church congregation can trace its roots back to 1896 when students from the United Presbyterian Divinity College at the Synod Hall in Castle Street began mission work in the district. They used the 'Little Church in the Field', vacated by Gorgie Free Church when they moved to Slateford Road at the top of Robertson Avenue. A year later the students opened Stewart Hall and lived in a commune beside the hall at No. 198 Gorgie Road. When the first minister, the Rev. J. Aitken Clark, was appointed, the roll was 150. On

Gorgie Parish Church was created on 5th August 1979 by the amalgamation of Tynecastle Church and Cairns Memorial Church. The Cairns Memorial Church building (seen here) was retained for worship and Tynecastle Church, to the west, was demolished. (Crown Copyright: RCAHMS.)

a feu adjoining Stewart Hall the foundation stone for the present church building was laid on 15th December 1900 by the Rev. Principal Rainy D.D., the first Moderator of the new United Free Church of Scotland. The church, opened on 3rd May 1902, was named after Principal John Cairns D.D., the last head of the United Presbyterian College prior to the Union of the United Presbyterian Church and Free Church in 1900. When Cairns Memorial Church opened it was fortunate to receive a number of gifts: the pulpit was given by Palmerston Place Church; the communion table came from Wallace Green Church in Berwick-upon-Tweed; the silver communion plate was presented by Robert W. Wallace of Broughton Place Church; and the first organ was installed by Robert McVitie of the famous biscuit-making family. At the union with the Church of Scotland in 1929 several members of Cairns Memorial left the congregation and formed the nucleus of the United Free Church of Scotland (Continuing), Edinburgh West.

The surviving church has therefore had a few names over its long history. It started life as Gorgie United Presbyterian Church, became

Cairns Memorial United Free Church in 1900, Cairns Memorial in 1929, and Gorgie Parish Church at the time of the union with Tynecastle in 1979. The present minister is the Rev. Peter I. Barber who succeeded the Rev. David J.B. Anderson on 22nd January 1995.

GORGIE MISSION

Gorgie Mission in Wheatfield Terrace can trace its history to 1887 when Miss Emily Pearce began her missionary work in the lobby of the Booking Hall of Haymarket Station. Seventeen railwaymen attended the first meeting of the Gorgie Railway Mission, part of the Railway Mission founded in Scotland in 1882. Early meetings took place at a Mission Hall belonging to one of the churches nearby but this hall closed in March 1888. Fortunately the Mission was able to transfer to the hall of Haymarket United Free Church in Dalry Road, where it remained for several years. At the beginning of the twentieth century the Mission moved to Wheatfield Street Hall and then to a purpose built hall seating 400 in Wheatfield Terrace, which was opened on 29th February 1908. The work of the Mission was characterised by visits to local factories, yards, railway works, and further afield to hospitals and poorhouses.

Gorgie Railway Mission altered its name to Gorgie Gospel Mission in 1965, by which time the direct influence of the railwaymen had diminished. In 1978 it formed part of Edinburgh City Mission but regained its independence again in 1992 when it took its present title of Gorgie Mission. At the centenary in 1987 a small booklet was published giving details of the Mission since inception, from which it is clear that the Gorgie missionary tradition is kept alive even by persons no longer residing in the district. One of the early stalwarts, who must have known the founder, was James Maxton Stevenson, O.B.E., president of the Mission for twenty-three years until his death in 1922. After the death of Mr Stevenson, his wife took over the leadership until 1929. Even more remarkable was the presidency of Robert Johnston from 1936 to 1976. Gorgie Mission also had the benefit of support from another husband-and-wife team, the Sandersons. Mr Sanderson was very active in encouraging young people to join the organisation and also served as secretary and treasurer. When he died in 1947 Mrs Sanderson continued, and held the position of treasurer for twenty-five years.

In more recent years the position of president has been held for much shorter periods, the present incumbent being Gordon Forbes. At the present day Gorgie Mission continues its work with a small group of about thirty dedicated followers. Services are held twice each Sunday and there are numerous midweek activities.

UNITED FREE CHURCH OF SCOTLAND, EDINBURGH WEST

On the south side of Gorgie Road, a few hundred yards east of the junction with Hutchison Crossway, is the United Free Church of Scotland Edinburgh West church. Its very existence is historically important. When the United Free Church of Scotland merged with the Church of Scotland in 1929, there were several congregations, ministers, elders and members who did not agree with the merger. This dissenting group, known as the United Free Church (Continuing), found themselves with no church in which to worship and no manse in which to house their minister. Their position was very similar to that of the congregations who broke away from the established church at the time of the Disruption in 1843.

At Gorgie, the United Free congregation met firstly in Ardmillan Hall from 1929 and later moved to Westfield Hall. Within a few years, however, a building fund was started with a view to completing a permanent church in the Gorgie area. A feu was secured from Edinburgh Corporation in 1934 with a feu duty of £5: 10s., to be doubled in the event of the ground or buildings being used for non-religious purposes. The south boundary of the plot was marked by the mill lade running from the Water of Leith to Cox's Glue Works to the east of the church ground. On Saturday 6th June 1936 the site was dedicated in a short ceremony by the Moderator of the General Assembly of the United Free Church, the Rev. A. Merriweather, assisted by the congregation's interim Moderator, Chas. B. Boog Watson. Work commenced on the construction of the church halls positioned towards the rear of the available ground. The builder was Stellmacs Ltd. of Glasgow whose total costs were £1,260 plus £190 for boundary fencing. The opening ceremony was performed by Mrs Mills, the oldest lady member of the congregation, with Chas. B. Boog Watson presiding.

In 1929 the Gorgie group did not exceed thirty people, but by the time the church halls were opened the congregation had risen to over two hundred. The intention was to use the halls as a place of worship to begin with and then to construct a bigger church on the front portion of the ground. Unfortunately, funds never became available for the more expensive building programme and over the years the halls have been progressively adapted as the main place of worship. As viewed from Gorgie Road the front porch leads directly into the nave which has a centre aisle flanked by removable wooden pews. At the south end there is a raised platform with the pulpit on the left and the small Italian organ on the right. On the west wall there is a memorial to the renowned Edinburgh historian Chas. B. Boog Watson who made a substantial contribution towards the building of the church.

Perhaps the congregation's best remembered figure was the late Rev. R.K. MacDonald who first came to Gorgie as a probationer in charge in December 1937. He later moved to Montrose and Glasgow before returning to Edinburgh West in 1957. After his death on 29th January 1990 the congregation placed a commemorative seat in Saughton Park Rose Garden.

The present pastor is Mr David Dunn who spent a number of years as a missionary in Taiwan before taking up his appointment in September 1993. The present congregation is in the region of seventy. The United Free Church of Scotland's other Edinburgh congregations are in Leith, Corstorphine, Portobello and Blackhall, and a General Assembly is held in alternate years in Edinburgh and Glasgow.

THE SALVATION ARMY

The Salvation Army has had such a visual and spiritual impact on the Gorgie and Dalry scene for so long that it would be difficult to imagine the district without it. When the Gorgie Corps was first established in 1891 that impact was less obvious. In fact the Army's own newspaper, *The War Cry*, devoted only a six-line entry on 12th December to the birth of Edinburgh IV (later referred to as Gorgie Corps) under the command of Captain Maggie Liddle and Lieutenant Cameron.

In the early days the 'barracks' was a small brick building standing in a field adjoining the Gorgie Road entrance to Tynecastle Park. Its proximity to one of Gorgie's other great attractions ensured that its perimeter fence was used as an unofficial grandstand on Saturday afternoons. Around 1897 the Corps' second home was built in Murieston Road, a purpose-built citadel of three storeys including officers' living accommodation. During its seventy years of use the building was gradually developed to accommodate all aspects of the Corps' work. Further working space was obtained by moving the officers' quarters out, and acquiring the adjacent Ardmillan Hall. By the 1960s, however, it was clear that new and improved premises were required. The site of Cairns Cottage on the south side of Gorgie Road, near its junction with Hutchison Crossway, was chosen for the new citadel, designed by Mat-

Dedication of the site of Edinburgh West United Free Church (Continuing), at Gorgie Road on 6th June 1936. (Courtesy of the Kirk Session.)

thew, Hamilton, McLean of Edinburgh. The new building was opened by General Coutts in December 1967, and extended and renovated in May 1990 in time for the centenary celebrations.

There can be little doubt that the Salvation Army's distinctive uniform and lively band have contributed to the public's awareness of their existence. The band, formed in 1898, has completed almost one hundred years of continuous service. Whilst operating basically to accompany the singing at both indoor and outdoor services, its range and sphere of activity is enlarged through regular visits to hospitals, nursing homes, concert halls and establishments like Saughton Prison. One of the band's most prestigious engagements was to play on the forecourt of Holyrood Palace for Her Majesty Queen Elizabeth and H.R.H. The Duke of Edinburgh on the occasion of the band's Diamond Jubilee in July 1958. In 1968 Alex Thain was presented with the Order of the Founder on completing forty years as bandmaster at Gorgie.

Over the years Gorgie Corps has introduced a great number of separate activities, many of them having junior counterparts to ensure continuity of commitment. The Songster Brigade, formed in 1911 to fulfil the equivalent function of a church choir, carry out many local engagements as well as travelling throughout Britain. Closely associated with the Songsters are the Miriams, a group of skilled timbrellists formed in the 1970s. Other groups include: the Home League (ladies' meeting) whose four aims are Worship, Education, Fellowship and Service; the Home League Singers; the Men's Fellowship begun in 1982; the Over 60s Fellowship; and the League of Mercy, started in 1989, to undertake home and hospital visits to the elderly and infirm. The Corps, however, owes a great deal to the work of its Young People's section. This includes the JAM club (Jesus and Me), the Singing Company and Junior Timbrels, the Junior Band, the Corps Cadets, Wednesday Clubs, Brownies and Guides, a Mother and Toddler group and—most recent of all—a pre-school play group.

STENHOUSE ST AIDAN'S PARISH CHURCH

The congregation of Stenhouse St Aidan's was created on 6th June 1993 by the union of two churches, Stenhouse Saughton and St Aidan's, each of which has its own distinct history.

St Aidan's was established at Bread Street, Tollcross before it moved out to Stenhouse. As early as 1831 a church known as Bread Street Relief was erected on the south side of Bread Street, on ground later occupied by St Cuthbert's Co-operative Association. The church cost £2,600 to build, seated 1050, and was in use by the United Presbyterian congregation until it moved in 1883 to its new home in Leamington Terrace. The Bread Street building was purchased by St Cuthbert's Parish Church in 1885 and used by St Aidan's until it moved to a new church in Stenhouse Drive. The new St Aidan's, designed in 1933 by the architect J. Inch Morrison, is cruciform in shape with a deep chancel, walls of red brick, and a copper roof. The organ was brought from St John's in Galashiels and the font from the old Bread Street church. The foundation stone was laid on 20th December 1933 and the completed church was ready for worship on 28th December 1934.

In contrast with St Aidan's, Stenhouse Saughton has always been in the Gorgie/Stenhouse/Saughton area. Its early history is told in a small publication, *Stenhouse Saughton Parish Church, Semi Jubilee 1928-1953*. In the 1880s George Gilray, an elder at Morningside United Presbyterian Church, opened a Sunday School at his own expense at Stenhouse Mills. Following financial assistance from the Morningside U.P. congregation, a missionary assistant, George F. Nicol, was appointed in 1894. Ground for a new hall was secured on the west corner of Chesser Avenue and Gorgie Road in 1902, but it was not until 1912 that any real progress was made in the building programme. This was financed by Mrs Meikle (sister of Robert Edgar, an elder at North Morningside

The Salvation Army Band c. 1898, outside the Citadel in Murieston Road. (Courtesy of the Salvation Army and Charlotte I. Potter.)

United Free Church) who, on the death of Mr Edgar, gave his house to the new church at Chesser. Mr Edgar's house was sold and the proceeds were used to build the first hall, still known as the Edgar Hall. The United Free Synod of Lothian authorised a Church Extension Charge and the first minister, the Rev. William Downie, was appointed on 21st June 1928. The following year, Stenhouse United Free Church became Stenhouse Saughton Church at the reunion with the Church of Scotland. In 1935 the Duke of Kent, Lord High Commissioner, laid the foundation stone of the present church, designed by T. Aikman Swan, and built to the west of the Edgar Hall.

The congregation of Stenhouse Saughton was linked with St Aidan's on 15th December 1983. This was precipitated by the death in 1982 of St Aidan's minister, the Rev. A.S. Currie, and the retirement of the Rev. William Maxwell from Stenhouse Saughton. The Rev. S.E.P. Beveridge was appointed to the linked charge in 1983 which was maintained until 1993, when a full union of the two congregations took place. On 12th January 1994 a new minister was appointed to Stenhouse St Aidan's, the Rev. Mary Morrison from the joint charge of Carmichael, Covington, Pettinain and Upper Clydesdale.

5
Schools

In Gorgie and Dalry eight schools were built between 1871 and 1934, only one of which has subsequently been closed—Gorgie in 1952. The growth of these schools, and later the decline in the attendance rolls, reproduced the pattern in other parts of Edinburgh. Four schools were established in the nineteenth century, namely: Gorgie (1871); Dalry (1875); St Cuthbert's (1876); and Orwell (1881). The other four belong to the twentieth century: Tynecastle (1912); Willowpark (1914); St Nicholas (1930); and Balgreen (1934). Dalry was one of many Board schools, set up under the first Education Act of 1872, which required that all children, between the ages of five and thirteen, should be educated in the 'three R's'—reading, writing and arithmetic.

There is clear evidence that some of these schools emerged from being village schools, i.e. Gorgie, Dalry and St Cuthbert's, and two began with strong denominational connections. St Cuthbert's Roman Catholic School still has strong links with St Cuthbert's Roman Catholic Church, but Orwell no longer has any direct connection with the Episcopal Church. At the present day, all seven schools are acutely aware of their history and have strong ties with the community around them.

There are also several nursery schools for pre-school-age children, most of which are based at the school buildings already mentioned.

GORGIE SCHOOL

David T. Lyon, author of *Memorials of Gorgie Mission and Free Church*, (1899), gives an interesting account of the schoolhouse in Gorgie village during the nineteenth century. He describes it as a small, low-roofed building in the centre of the village adjoining Messrs Cox's Works. The schoolmistress lived under the same roof in a single apartment used as a parlour, bedroom and kitchen. He refers to the last occupant, Miss Macdonald, as 'rather eccentric', but unfortunately does not elaborate. In addition to its educational functions this small school was also the meeting place of the Gorgie Mission and Free Church, an early

Gorgie School was in the centre of the old village, adjoining Cox's Glue Works. It was eventually replaced by Gorgie Public School which was built in 1871 on the south side of Gorgie Road, near Robertson Avenue. (Memorials of Gorgie Mission and Free Church, 1899.)

progenitor of North Merchiston Church.

The new Gorgie Public School was built in 1871 on a site immediately west of the railway bridge at the junction of Robertson Avenue and Gorgie Road. The earliest logbook entry makes it clear that the new school was adjacent to 'the old school' and communicated with it, but 'the old school' referred to cannot be the one described by Mr Lyon. The headmaster's daily log was sometimes written in a rather terse style: 25.12.1872 (Christmas Day) nothing new to remark; 1.9.1873 roll 41; 2.9.1873 parents complaining that they cannot pay fees quarterly; 12.9.1873 many children without slates. Early problems in setting up the new school had obviously not been fully addressed by the time I. Samuel, Her Majesty's School Inspector, completed his 1874 report: 'My Lords will look for a better report next year. More time and attention should be devoted to sewing. Should H.M. Inspector report so unfavourably on this branch next year the whole grant will be endangered'. Fortunately the 1875 report observed that the school was efficiently run by the head teacher who had been there for three months only.

By 1901 the total roll had risen to 1596 pupils from only 41 in 1873. Four separate entries during the years of the First World War give a reminder of the effects of world conflict: 4.9.1914 some male teachers absent as territorials are called up for active service; 22.1.1915 Mr Ramage left yesterday having joined Kitchener's army; 18.6.1915 Miss McRury absent all week her brother being amongst those killed at the Dardanelles; 5.9.1916 Mr Ramage resumed duty having been discharged from the army. A more cheerful note was struck on 11th July 1923 during a gathering by Edinburgh schoolchildren which took place in Holyrood Park in honour of King George V's visit to the city. Children from Gorgie Public School were 'entrained' at Gorgie Station (adjacent to the school) in the morning and conveyed to Abbeyhill Station. The children were lined up along with other schoolchildren on both sides of the Drive 'as the royal carriage with the King and Queen drove slowly down the line'. By 1939 the country was again in the midst of conflict and most children had been evacuated to Dalkeith and Newtongrange. The remainder were taught in groups of not more than twelve pupils in bowling-green clubhouses, church halls, a shelter beneath the Roxy Picture House and several private houses. Immediately to the west of Gorgie Public School, the 'tin' building occupied by Gorgie Special School was taken over by the Auxiliary Fire Service. In January 1940 children began to return to Gorgie after air-raid shelters were built in the school playground, and a double shift system was introduced for teaching. Later the same year medical examinations were carried out of children being registered for overseas evacuation but no reasons are recorded for this procedure. Early in 1941 air raid warnings began in earnest.

At its height Gorgie Public School had a roll of over 1500 pupils but there were several occasions when pupils were lost to other schools. As early as 1878 Gorgie's intake was greatly reduced when the main Dalry School was opened, and again in 1910 when Dalry Annexe was opened in McLeod Street. Even greater losses occurred, firstly in 1930 when Stenhouse School was opened and, secondly, in 1934 on the opening of Balgreen School. The eventual transfer of several classes to Broomhouse School in 1952 heralded the end for Gorgie. Despite angry protests by parents the school was closed on 31st October 1952. For many years after, the building was used as Tynecastle School Annexe before being demolished in 1993.

Surviving records also give an insight into the early days of Gorgie Evening School, later renamed Gorgie Continuation School. The first term in 1895 included chemistry, magnetism and electricity, 'well fitted

A class of forty at Gorgie School in 1936, most of whom were evacuated a few years later at the start of the Second World War. (Courtesy of Mrs Jeanette Berg, née Wilson.)

to train the reasoning faculties of the lads'. The first mention of classes for females was in 1914 when dressmaking, cooking and sick nursing were added to the curriculum. There are several references to the Evening School's involvement with local employers. In 1923 Mr Taylor, the veterinary surgeon, ran a course of twelve lessons for van boys and van drivers on the care and management of horses and ponies. Two years later overall attendances declined, due mainly to a change in the system of guaranteed fees to the employees of St Cuthbert's Co-operative Association. Further losses occurred when several butchers' message boys claimed the right to attend Tollcross Butchers' Classes where they were required to attend two nights per week instead of three as at Gorgie. The records indicate that Gorgie Continuation School closed on 24th March 1939 despite the fact that the roll reached over three hundred. Post-war requirements were met by the introduction of night-school classes.

DALRY PRIMARY SCHOOL

It is well documented that Dalry School, on the west corner of Dalry Road and Cathcart Place, was opened on 18th February 1878. What is probably less well known is that a much smaller Dalry School existed nearby in Washington Lane, between 1875 and 1878. It was run by Dr Thomas W.E. Robson, a teacher of English, who also had teaching rooms in the New Town of Edinburgh. Unfortunately no records of Dr Robson's school at Dalry have survived other than listings, which show it as a public school, not under the control of the Edinburgh School Board. In 1889 the Edinburgh School Board controlled approximately twenty-three schools including the second Dalry School. The next nearest schools were at North Merchiston and Torphichen Street, but Gorgie School was just outside the Edinburgh jurisdiction. They were all subject to the same rules and regulations, covering duties, responsibilities, conditions of service and salaries. The 1889 salary scale for headmasters (which had not been increased since 1886) varied according to the number of pupils on the roll. With 400 pupils the salary commenced at £230 per annum, and 'could' rise to £300 per annum; and with 1,200 pupils the range was £350 to £420. Mr Martin, the headmaster at Dalry, earned £410 per annum in 1889: his first assistant earned less than half of that at £175; the infant mistress earned £192; and the teachers 'struggled' at between £65 and £120 per annum. Evidence of inequality between the sexes was not hard to find: male pupil-teachers were paid just over £17 per annum and female pupil-teachers just over £12 during their first year of apprenticeship. Fees were also charged: infants paid 2d per week (less than 1p); juveniles paid between 3d and 7d per week, depending upon age; and a standard fee of 4d per week was paid by the Parochial Boards for those children whose parents could not afford to pay. It was the responsibility of the headmaster to collect the fees, which totalled nearly £800, and, guided by a battery of regulations, to deal with resultant problems: 'while the child is not to be sent from School because he has not the fees, he should be told to bring his fees next day, failing which, the Janitor should be sent to inquire and report to the Head Master upon the case'.

Unfortunately no record now exists of how many pupils enrolled at Dalry School in the first decade or so, but by 1897 the total was a staggering 1,884, divided into 959 juveniles and 925 infants. The main subjects were Drawing, English, History, Geography, Arithmetic and Sewing. Additional subjects included Domestic Economy, Drill, French, Gymnastics and Calisthenics, Latin, Mathematics, Religious Instruction and Singing. In the sewing class, the Board supplied the necessary material, but parents could order specific articles of clothing to be made, for purchase when finished. The 1882 regulations on discipline remained unaltered up to 1889, and probably for many years after that. The Board

DALRY SCHOOL.

Dalry Primary School, on the west corner of Dalry Road and Cathcart Place, was opened on 18th February 1878. By 1897 the school role was 1,884.

left decisions on punishment to the headmaster, but stipulated that no child should be punished for not bringing fees or for irregular attendance 'unless it is clear that the fault is not entirely that of the Parents'. Equally confusing signals appear to have been sent by the Board's desire 'that as far as possible, the infliction of corporal punishment should be avoided during the time set apart for Religious Instruction'.

Many of Dalry School's logbooks have survived giving us a day-to-day picture of the main events occurring in the school. Two unrelated items, in 1905, make interesting reading. In March, members of the Town Council Committee visited the school to assess the level of noise in the classrooms caused by cart wheels rumbling over the granite setts in Dalry Road. The Committee members were trying to decide whether or not to go to the expense of replacing the granite setts with wooden ones which would be much quieter. Secondly in October 1905 mention is made of the death of Flora Stevenson, chairman of the School Board, and one-time School Visitor to Dalry School. On Saturday 30th September 1905, 87 pupils and several teachers met at the school at 1p.m. and walked to the north side of the Dean Bridge where they lined the route of the funeral cortège, as it made its way from Miss Stevenson's home at No.13 Randolph Crescent to the Dean Cemetery.

The years of the First World War, 1914-1919, brought different problems, many of them not directly attributable to hostilities. In June 1917 an acute shortage of accommodation and equipment forced the head-master to have four classes taught in the open air—two in the boys' playground and two in the girls' playground. The following year, some of the boys were involved in offences under the Children Act, 1908. These related to theft, malicious mischief, hanging onto cable cars and playing football in the street. The sentence was usually an admonishment for a first offence and a fine of one shilling (5p) for a subsequent offence. Very few direct references are made in the logs to the War, until the end, when the children were given a half holiday to go to see Sir Douglas Haig. Whether they all took the opportunity is doubtful but they did attend the celebrations in July 1919 at Merchiston Castle Cricket Ground (the site of which is now occupied by George Watson's School in Colinton Road), where they received a bag of cakes, a bag of rock and two bars of chocolate.

Milk was first provided at Dalry School in 1931. Those on the 'free food' list also received free milk, whereas the others were charged 1d per day. Only about 200 pupils received milk on the first day, which might have been an indication that the school roll had fallen drastically from the very high levels of 1897. By 1935 the school population of the area had decreased so much that more than one third of the accommodation was vacant. The pupils were all evacuated to Bathgate and Armadale at the outbreak of the Second World War. The problems, which were common to all the schools in the area, are discussed elsewhere in this chapter. Post-war events included the Coronation celebrations in 1953 and an increase in the number and variety of visits, outside the school, to museums, galleries and even the Waverley Station.

At the present day, Dalry School has just over two hundred pupils in the main school and sixty children in the nursery. The staff of ten teachers was led by the head teacher, Mrs Agnes M.M. Sturgeon and the deputy head teacher, David Fleming. On the retirement of Mrs Sturgeon at the end of 1994 David Fleming was appointed to the position of head teacher. In addition to the class teachers there are visiting specialist teachers for Home Economics, Music, Physical Education, German, English as a Second Language, and Learning Support.

ST CUTHBERT'S ROMAN CATHOLIC SCHOOL

St Cuthbert's Roman Catholic School predates St Cuthbert's Roman Catholic Church by about thirteen years. It was established in 1876 by Sister Mary Aloysius in two converted cottages in Longstone village.

Dalry Primary School basketball team, winners of the Edinburgh Primary Schools Sports Association Trophy, in 1988, photographed with Mrs Nancy Sturgeon, headteacher and John McDonald, class teacher. (Courtesy of Dalry Primary School.)

She remained there for the first six years, but by 1882 increased numbers necessitated a move to larger premises in Gorgie. Unfortunately no details survive of the Gorgie school, which was in use until 1896 when a purpose-built school was opened in Hutchison Crossway at the same time as the new church.

It is not known how long Sister Aloysius remained in charge of the school but it is possible that she knew the legendary Miss Boland, who joined the staff in 1901 and served as head teacher from 1912 to 1951. In the latter half of Miss Boland's remarkable half-century, accommodation at the school was becoming very overcrowded. Her Majesty's Inspector's report for 1937-38 stated that three infant classes occupied a hall and that four classes were still taught in the hut. A very different picture emerged in September 1939 when most of the children were evacuated to Kincardine, Saline and Blairhall, leaving the school building available for the Civil Defence Authorities. The traumatic effect upon children evacuated during the Second World War is a study in itself. Many children from St Cuthbert's were taken by train from Gorgie Station to Blairhall, where they were billeted mainly with mining families and attended the local Blairhall School. Parents did not generally accompany their children, who had to rely on brothers and sisters, friends or teachers for comfort and encouragement. A few families were accompanied by their mothers and were given accommodation at farmhouses within reach of Blairhall School. When this occurred, the whole tenor of evacuation was more like an adventure or even a holiday.

Following the retiral of Miss Boland in 1951, Mr Howie was appointed head teacher until 1960. During this time the school Annexe, on the west side of Hutchison Crossway, was extensively damaged by fire on 20th March 1955. For the next two years several classes were taught at St Mary's School in York Lane until the new St Cuthbert's School was built on the site of the old Annexe. The school, designed by the architects, Fairbrother, Hall and Hedges of Edinburgh and built by William Arnott McLeod & Co. Ltd., of Russell Road, was opened on 30th September 1957 by the Court of Session judge, the Right Honourable Lord Wheatley. The school brochure produced in time for the opening stated that 'in planning the school an effort has been made to provide accommodation of an intimate and friendly nature'. After the new school opened, the opportunity was taken to upgrade Sighthill Annexe, which became St Joseph's School in 1958. A further Annexe was opened at Oxgangs in 1961, renamed St Mark's School in 1967. For a time the Convent School at Colinton was also run as an Annexe of St Cuthbert's.

At the present day St Cuthbert's School has a roll of 157 and a staff of nine led by the head teacher Mrs Rosemary Crichton, who was appointed in October 1993. The school maintains close links with St Cuthbert's Church, forming an important centre of Catholic education on the west side of the city. The original school building on the east side of Hutchison Crossway has not been owned by the Council for many years. It was used as a postal Sorting Office until 1993, after which the entire site was acquired by the People's Dispensary for Sick Animals for redevelopment as a Veterinary Centre. When the old building was demolished in 1995 the time capsule and the apex stone, bearing the initials S.C.S., were recovered.

ORWELL PRIMARY SCHOOL

Orwell Primary School has a roll of just over one hundred pupils in a small building adjoining Dalry House in Orwell Terrace. Although the school has been under the control of the local authority since the 1930s, its roots are historically different. The Episcopal Training College for

*During the Anti-Litter Campaign organised by Edinburgh District Council in 1994,
St Cuthbert's R.C. Primary School received an Award of Merit and a cheque for
£100. The children are, left to right, Nicola, Clare, Fabio, Angela, Angela and
Christopher. The adults are Mrs Crichton, headteacher, Councillor Robin Slack, and
Mrs Girvan, parent helper. (Courtesy of St Cuthbert's R.C. Primary School.)*

teachers was established in Dalry House around 1877. A few years later,
in 1881, the Episcopal Church opened the Edinburgh Episcopal Normal School in the adjacent building, to the south. This rather unusual
name has not always been quoted in the same style: initially it was
referred to as the Normal School; then in 1900 it was called the Practising School; and in 1936 it combined the titles to become the Normal Practising Episcopal School. It retained this designation in theory,
if not in practice, until 1975 when the name was changed to Orwell
Primary School. According to the school log for 16th May 1975, the
head teacher asked that the name be changed because 'the old name of
Normal Practising Episcopal School was proving to be an embarrassment to both staff and pupils'.

When the school began in 1881 there were separate Infant and Upper Departments, each controlled by its own headmistress. On the first
day there were only nineteen children in the Infant Department and
eleven in the Upper Department, with two students to assist with teaching. The presence of the two students was significant, as the school was
established specifically to give young teachers practice in dealing with a

class of pupils. Indeed, within the first few months the headmistress reported that she could not keep to the timetable without the assistance of the students. The Episcopal Church kept fairly tight control over the school by frequent visits from the Diocesan Inspector, who examined the children in Religious Knowledge. The students were also subject to examination, usually in nine separate subjects. The results in 1899 gave high marks in Dictation and School Management but, rather ominously for their chosen profession, much lower marks in English. The number of students employed at any one time probably varied greatly as the school roll did not remain constant. In the late 1880s many children left the school to attend one of the Free Board Schools: Dalry, Gorgie or North Merchiston. The total fees at the Episcopal School Infant Department in 1884 were £13 :1:10d from a roll of 125 pupils. When the Episcopal School lost more than half of its pupils to the Free Board Schools, the governing committee announced that no fees would be charged after the summer term of 1892. Almost immediately the roll returned to its previous level. With just a hint of self-satisfaction the Diocesan Inspector was able to report: 'The Church has in this school a valuable asset, and as most of the staff have been trained in Dalry House, there is here proof also of the value of that institution to Nation, to Church and to these children fortunate enough to come under such influence'.

When the school was established in 1881, the premises were probably quite modest, but as numbers increased, so too did the need for more space. The first reconstruction was in 1900 and provided seven classrooms, each with accommodation for fifty pupils. This was followed in 1902 by the addition of cloakroom facilities and a new room for the headmistress. Major reconstruction was again carried out in the mid-1920s to create an assembly hall and other facilities on the ground floor. On this occasion it was necessary to transfer pupils temporarily to Dalry School, North Merchiston School and St Luke's Church Hall in Caledonian Crescent. All classes returned to the reconstructed school on 14th March 1927.

Like most schools, Orwell has had its high days and holidays, all carefully recorded over the years: 6th June 1900, half holiday given this afternoon in connection with the City's rejoicings on the Fall of Pretoria; 5th July 1937, children go to Princes Street to see the State entry of King George VI and Queen Elizabeth; 15th May 1950, Commonwealth Gift Scheme—eight cases of apples arrive from British Columbia; 29th May 1953, Coronation celebrations; 16th October 1962, chil-

Children, from each of the classes at Orwell Primary School, at the Harvest Festival in the school, 1994. (Courtesy of Orwell Primary School.)

dren go by train from Haymarket to Waverley to see King Olav. The greatest event of all, however, was on 17th October 1967 when Queen Elizabeth II and the Duke of Edinburgh spoke to the children in the playground on the occasion of the opening of Dalry House.

In 1982 a proposal was put forward to amalgamate Orwell, Dalry and Tollcross Schools, but after widespread opposition the plan was abandoned. At the present day Orwell School has five class teachers, one nursery teacher and visiting specialist teachers. The head teacher, Mrs Marion B. Fortune, was appointed in April 1993.

TYNECASTLE HIGH SCHOOL

Tynecastle High School, in McLeod Street, was opened as Tynecastle Supplementary School on 3rd September 1912 with fifteen teachers recruited from various Edinburgh schools including Dalry, Gorgie and North Merchiston. More than five hundred pupils enrolled, mainly from Craiglockhart School, Dalry School and Gorgie School, but there was insufficient furniture for such a large intake, and only twelve classrooms were ready for occupation. Despite these initial setbacks the formal opening by the Right Hon. Alexander Ure, Lord Advocate, went ahead as planned on 16th November 1912. By 1914 there were twenty-five classes with an average roll of 790 pupils. From the beginning, Tynecastle was a new venture for the Edinburgh School Board, concentrating on technical subjects, and equipped with all the latest machinery in a range of workshops beside the main building. Subjects included joinery, plumbing, cobbling, hair-cutting, engineering, plastering, laundering, sewing, cooking and housewifery. The academic subjects were taught in the main building, where the boys and girls were strictly segregated up to the leaving age of fourteen. On leaving the school, each pupil was issued with a Juvenile Employment Scholar's Card giving brief details of academic achievement to show to the Youth Employment Department in Cornwall Street.

This early leaving age was probably one of the reasons for the hugely successful Tynecastle Continuation (Evening) Classes, which also began in September 1912. On the opening night, five hundred pupils and thirty-three teachers were present, which meant that the workshops had to be opened five nights per week. The number and diversity of the subjects taught reflected Gorgie's importance as an industrial area: motor body building, engineering, joinery, moulding, cabinet making, tinsmithing, tailoring, pattern making, dressmaking, cookery, shoemaking and upholstery. Later, classes for coopers and railwaymen were added and several local firms were involved in particular subjects, including McVitie & Price, the North British Rubber Co., and Allan's Shoeshop. By 1913 the roll for the Continuation Classes had reached 1335 pupils.

During the first World War several members of staff were called up for war service. The Juvenile Labour Bureau was set up to assist pupils to obtain suitable employment, and an additional class was added for Physical Exercises, taken by Lt. Walker of Craiglockhart Military Hospital. That was not the only link which Tynecastle had with the famous wartime hospital, 'Dottyville', now occupied by Napier University, near Firrhill. One of its most famous patients, Wilfred Owen, the wartime poet, taught English at Tynecastle School during his stay at the hospital after being wounded at Picardy. Owen went back to the front line in November 1917 and was killed in action a week before the Armistice. At the end of the war Tynecastle School helped to train soldiers returning to 'civvy street' so that they could find full employment.

In the 1920s and 1930s the school changed its name on more than one occasion. In the early 1920s it became Tynecastle Higher Grade School and at the end of the decade it was Tynecastle Intermediate Technical and Commercial School. By 1939 it was simply Tynecastle

LAUNDRY CLASS

A few problems to be ironed out in the laundry class at Tynecastle School. (Tynecastle School Magazine, 1912-1972.)

The casting workshop in full swing at Tynecastle School. (Tynecastle School Magazine, 1912-1972.)

Secondary School. Overcrowding had also become a serious problem. In 1936 H.M. Inspector of Schools stated that 'the prospect of early relief through the diversion of pupils to a new post-primary school is . . . welcome', but it was not until 1939 that Tynecastle's roll of around 1,399 pupils fell to 900 after the opening of Saughton Junior Secondary School.

Tynecastle was subject to the same disruption as other schools during the Second World War. Many male teachers were called up, some of the pupils were evacuated, and the curriculum included some hitherto unknown subjects: 'Economic Use of Food and Clothing', and 'Education under the Nazis' by a German refugee. A decision was taken in 1947 to erect a War Memorial in the school to former pupils and teachers who had been killed in action. The Memorial was unveiled by Lord Provost Sir John I. Falconer, at a ceremony attended by many of the friends and relatives. The school still retains a small file of letters, usually

from mothers or sisters, but strangely seldom from fathers, responding
to an appeal for the names of those who had fallen. A letter dated 27th
August 1947 reads:

> I wonder if you could put my son's name on the Memorial among
> his chum's names. I have been away for a long while for my health
> after I got word about my son. I completely broke down and I don't
> feel right yet. I have always been thinking he would turn up again as
> the only word I got from the War Office he was supposed to have
> drowned.
>
>> And Oblige
>> Yours Trustfully

The War Memorial, inside the main entrance to the school, contains
over fifty names, headed by that of Corporal Thomas Peck Hunter,
Royal Marines, who was posthumously awarded the Victoria Cross for
bravery during the Italian campaign.

After the war, the school became Tynecastle Senior Secondary School,
gaining a high reputation in commercial subjects and providing well-
trained pupils for such employers as Nuclear Enterprises Ltd. On closure of Gorgie Primary School in 1952, the building was used as
Tynecastle Annexe. In 1972 the main school was renamed Tynecastle
High School, providing a six-year comprehensive education. In 1982
the school celebrated its 70th anniversary and its 75th anniversary in
1987. On both occasions open days were held at the school when staff
and pupils met many former pupils and staff. A display of school photographs and other memorabilia was put on by the History Department.

At the present day Tynecastle High School has 900 pupils. The head
teacher is Michael J. Hay, who was appointed in 1987, and the deputy
head teacher is Joe Smith, appointed in 1994.

WILLOWPARK SCHOOL

Willowpark School is housed in a range of low-rise buildings set back
from the south side of Gorgie Road, near its junction with Westfield
Road. The buildings were first constructed with open verandahs to the
rear (rather like those at East Fortune Hospital and the Astley Ainslie
Hospital) but they were enclosed in the 1960s to form corridors. The
school provides for pupils whose special educational needs are associated with some degree of physical disablement, and as such is adminis-

Willowpark School, 1984. The Social and Vocational Skills class prepare a feast for the wedding of class teacher, Kate Hart, to Richard Filleul at St Mary's Cathedral. (Courtesy of The Scotsman Publications Ltd.)

tered by the School Support Services Division of the Education Department. Willowpark shares a few of the facilities of St Nicholas School, which is immediately adjacent to it.

Willowpark School was opened on 25th May 1914 as Gorgie Special School for Physically Defective Children, under its headmistress Jane S. Murray, assisted by Annie Sharp. The first building, affectionately known as 'the tin school', lay much nearer to Gorgie Road and immediately west of Gorgie Public School. Only sixteen pupils were enrolled but numbers quickly increased to forty. Within a very short time the headmistress demonstrated her commitment to every aspect of the pupils' health and welfare—whether it was welcome or not: three couches, plus rugs and pillows, were supplied for those children who needed to rest after dinner; a system was introduced for all children to brush their teeth regularly under the teachers' supervision; and Cod Liver Oil Emulsion was provided, firstly for the most delicate children, and later, by popular demand, for everyone! One of the few references in the school log books to the First World War was on 24th May 1915, which was celebrated as Empire Day. In 1926, during the General Strike, no fires were allowed in school unless for cooking or laundry work; and in

1929 St Cuthbert's Co-operative Society was distributing boots to 'necessitous and deserving pupils'. Specific health problems required specific action. In October 1920 a pupil was sent home immediately when it was discovered that she was suffering from Scarlet Fever. The room in which she had been working was scrubbed and sprayed with disinfectant, and her books were burned.

From 1936 the school logs contain several references to national events: 21.1.1936, the death of His Majesty the King; 28.1.1936, school closed for the funeral of the late King; 29.4.1937, children line the route to cheer the Duke and Duchess of Gloucester. By May 1939 Air Raid Wardens were fitting respirators for the children, and the staff were having emergency meetings to learn about evacuation procedures. Later, the Education Committee approved a scheme for the re-opening of some of the Special Schools in Edinburgh, but as Gorgie Special School could not be protected satisfactorily the pupils were transferred to the new annexe of St Nicholas School. To mark the end of war in Europe in May 1945, the pupils stood on the west side of Westfield Road 'to see their Gracious Majesties King George and Queen Elizabeth accompanied by Princess Elizabeth and Princess Margaret Rose on their Victory tour of the city'.

The post-war years brought some new and challenging ideas. In June 1947 all pupils born in 1936 were given a group intelligence test arranged by the Scottish Council for Research in Education. The object of the survey was to secure evidence for the Population Investigation Committee to determine whether or not there had been a decline in intelligence since the previous survey in 1932. The wording does not appear to have anticipated an *increase* in intelligence, but unfortunately the result was never entered in the record. Following the dropping of the word 'Special' in school names, Gorgie Special School was renamed West Park School on 22nd August 1960. In 1972 various discussions took place with the Education Department concerning the proposed new school for physically handicapped children at Graysmill. In August 1973, when Willowbrae School was closed, some of the pupils were transferred to West Park School and some to the new Graysmill School. In recognition of the merger with the former Willowbrae School, West Park School was renamed Willowpark School in 1974. During the 1970s Willowpark's increased involvement in extra-curricular activities achieved considerable success. In March 1975 a group of children, trained by Miss Neilson, won the trophy for the highest award in Music and Drama presented by Simon Square Centre during Scottish Disability

Week, and in the following year the junior swimmers won a cup at the Portobello Swimming Baths Gala. In 1991 Willowpark received the Scotvec Annual Award when the Scottish Vocational Education Council recognised the school's work on the integration of National Certificate Modules into its curriculum. In many ways this was the culmination of many years of dedicated work towards certification, first achieved in 1963 when West Park School (as it was then) entered pupils for the Edinburgh School Certificate.

At the present day Willowpark is staffed for a maximum of eighty-four pupils between the ages of five and sixteen. Each class has a maximum of eight pupils and all the classwork is as similar to mainstream education as is possible having regard to the physical abilities of the child concerned. The head teacher of Willowpark, presently Mrs Jean Moffat, is also responsible for running Lothian Region's Hospital/Home Teaching Service. The service is based at Willowpark but entails travel by the staff throughout Lothian to locations where pupils are unable to attend school because of accident or illness.

ST NICHOLAS SCHOOL

St Nicholas School is adjacent to Willowpark School and shares with it the playground area and other facilities. The school makes special provision primarily for pupils with learning difficulties between the ages of five and seventeen. As such it is administered by the School Support Services Division of the Education Department.

The school was formally opened on Wednesday 30th April 1930 by W.W. McKechnie, Secretary to the Scottish Education Department, at a ceremony presided over by Councillor P.H. Allan. A lengthy report appeared in *The Scotsman* for 1st May 1930 giving details of the new school. The single-storey building of five main classrooms was built around an inner courtyard with the doors opening onto verandahs. The cost was £12,000 excluding acquisition of the two and a half acre site. The school opened for pupils on 16th June 1930 with a roll of 51, which had doubled by October 1931. The first headmistress was Miss Margaret Helen Annal, assisted by Miss Elizabeth McKay and Miss Mary McLennan. Most of the first pupils were transferred from special classes previously at Bruntsfield School and Dalry School.

At an early stage in its development the school decided to celebrate St Nicholas Day (6th December) by a gift service, first held on Monday 7th December 1931. Almost thirty visitors, interested in the work of the school, were treated to a rather solemn ceremony at which the Very Rev. J. Harry Miller dedicated the school flag 'with due impressiveness'. One of the other early visitors to the school was Mr Bruce of the East of Scotland College of Agriculture who supervised the plans for the garden. Gardening was (and still is) a most important vocational subject on the curriculum, which also included cookery, laundry, woodwork, cobbling, swimming, netball and football. The emphasis on some of these subjects was also put to practical use by the head teacher who contacted several local employers, notably Waverley Rubber Company and McVitie & Price, in the hope of securing employment for some of the senior pupils. One employer, whom the headmistress found difficult to ignore, was J.G. Cox who manufactured glue on an extensive site to the west of the school. When the smell became unbearable she was forced to complain to Dr Boog-Watson who promised to look into the problem! The pupils and staff of St Nicholas appeared in a film specially commissioned for the Edinburgh Education Week in June 1936. In May of the following year there were numerous celebrations in Edinburgh and throughout the country for the Coronation of George VI. The pupils of St Nicholas made their own decorations of shields, crowns, the St Andrew's Cross and the Lion Rampant on each of the seventeen pillars of the verandahs. Red, white and blue bands were fitted to the tables outside, where the children sat for cakes and lemonade. The atmosphere was very different, however, in 1939 when the pupils faced the same wartime difficulties as Willowpark next door.

The school celebrated its fiftieth anniversary on 12th June 1980. An open day was arranged for parents and visitors who included two former head teachers, Miss Earsman and Miss Rennie. Part of the entertainment was a film of schools in Edinburgh in 1929 entitled *Men and Women of Tomorrow*. Also in 1980 St Nicholas increased its roll by taking some pupils from St Christopher's School when it closed. In 1994 the head teacher of St Nicholas is Mrs C. McLaren, assisted by Mrs J. Eales and a staff of nine full-time teachers, five part-time teachers, plus auxiliary staff.

BALGREEN PRIMARY SCHOOL

Balgreen Primary School is situated on the east side of Balgreen Road, opposite the junction with Stevenson Drive. It is the youngest school in the group, dating from 1934 when the houses at Whitson were built to accommodate people from the Bristo area of the city. Many of Balgreen's first pupils had previously been at Bristo School in Marshall

The staff and pupils of St Nicholas School photographed in September 1993 at the retirement presentation to the school janitor, George Hay. (Courtesy of St Nicholas School.)

Street. The new school was built on a very historic site, namely Balgreen House, occupied for many years by Sir John Batty Tuke, already discussed in connection with Saughton Hall Mansion. After Sir John died in 1913, Balgreen House was used by Edinburgh Corporation as a children's home until around 1930 when it was demolished.

Balgreen School was opened on 4th September 1934 under its first headmaster, John J. Atkinson, assisted by eleven members of staff and a janitor. The total roll was 491, divided into 243 boys and 248 girls. The school was formally opened on 5th October 1934 by Baillie Laurence Raithby, Senior Magistrate, at a ceremony presided over by Councillor Taylor, Chairman of the Education Committee. The following afternoon three hundred parents attended an open day to allow pupils and parents to meet the staff and to inspect the new building. When the school was first opened, Balgreen was considered to be quite far out of town but that did not, in any way, inhibit out-of-school activities. Swimming lessons were started immediately at Dalry Baths in Caledonian Crescent and in January 1935 forty pupils attended the Lord Provost's Treat at the King's Theatre. A few weeks later eighty-six pupils were taken one Saturday morning to the Rutland Picture House (later renamed the Gaumont) to see *S.O.S. Iceberg*. No doubt the morning was greatly enjoyed by the children but the headmaster's judgment was more reserved: 'really too sensational to be suitable for children, but many parts of it were excellent for giving the scholars a good knowledge of Arctic conditions'. Presumably he was not referring to the cinema's heating system.

During its first decade, the school was involved in the celebrations of several events of national importance. On 3rd May 1935 a special service was held in the hall 'to impress the importance of the King's Silver Jubilee on the pupils'. The Rev. J. Brown made a speech on the King's reign and the Empire, five verses of *Land of our Birth* were sung, and the rest of the time was taken up with the serious business of distributing boxes of Ferguson's Edinburgh rock to the pupils. Festivities continued a few days later when Balgreen School staged a tableau representing Canada at the Schools' Pageant. Unfortunately, George V survived his jubilee by only a few months and died on 20th January 1936. On 22nd January senior pupils listened on the wireless to the proclamation of King Edward VIII from St James's Palace, London, and on the following day from the Mercat Cross in Edinburgh. The dust had hardly settled, however, when King Edward VIII abdicated on 11th December 1936. Three days later, the same pupils were back at the wireless set listening to the proclamation from the Mercat Cross of King George VI's accession. When further holidays and treats accompanied the Coronation celebrations in May 1937, the children must have thought that school life had its attractions. The mood changed dramatically, however, on the outbreak of the Second World War. In September 1939 pupils were evacuated to various locations in East Lothian and Berwickshire, air-raid shelters were later erected in the playground, and a double-shift system of teaching was introduced over the following months.

Shortly after the end of hostilities in 1945, a nursery school was set up at Balgreen but was separated from the main school in October 1951. A year later the closure of Gorgie School was announced and implemented at very short notice. Several pupils from Gorgie were transferred to Balgreen on 3rd November 1952. In the following year the enlarged school sent three hundred pupils by train from Balgreen Halt to Waverley Station to see Queen Elizabeth at her ceremonial entry to Edinburgh after her Coronation on 2nd June 1953.

In 1984 Balgreen School celebrated its own Golden Jubilee. It was a very grand affair, the main events being held on 4th September exactly fifty years after the school had been opened. The morning events at

The staff and pupils of Balgreen Primary School in the school playground at the time of the fiftieth anniversary in 1984. (Courtesy of The Scotsman Publications Ltd.)

Saughton Enclosure included a puppet theatre, a mini marathon and the Pilton Circus, with clowns, jugglers and stilt walkers. In the afternoon the children returned to the school where they were entertained by their own fashion parade, a display of gymnastics and the Army Motor Bike Display Team. Music, at various times in the afternoon, was provided by the Edinburgh Police Pipe Band, the Drums and Bugles of the Royal Marines, and Tynecastle School Orchestra.

In 1994, at its sixtieth anniversary, Balgreen School has 405 pupils, divided almost exactly between boys and girls. The head teacher is Miss Catherine S. Douglas and the deputy is Mrs Ella Tollervey. Over the years the basic structure of the building has not been altered greatly except that the open verandahs were enclosed during the 1970s, allowing more comfortable passage from one classroom to another. The playground area has also been fitted with an astroturf section which is shared with Tynecastle Club. In recent years, the curriculum, in keeping with educational trends, has been extended to include a much wider range of subjects including Environmental Studies, Information Technology, and Social and Personal Safety Programmes.

6

Commercial and Industrial Development, 1:
Builders, Cabinetmakers, Engineers
and Others

Until the mid-nineteenth century, the districts of Gorgie and Dalry were mainly rural in character, but there were clear signs that the districts would attract significant industrial development: for several reasons. When the line of the Union Canal was being considered in the early nineteenth century, different routes were proposed, all of which contributed to an uncertain future for residential properties along the line of Dundee Street. In addition, the complex system of railways, west of Princes Street, provided an ideal focus for firms which required sidings for the transport of materials and finished products, to and from the works. The main Edinburgh-Glasgow railway line had sidings, west of Haymarket, for the Caledonian Distillery, and for various firms on the north side of Duff Street; and the Caledonian Railway line (now the West Approach Road) served Alexander Mather & Sons, Engineers, Colin Macandrew & Partners Ltd., Public Works Contractors, and several others along the route.

In Dalry many building-related trades were established. Joiners and cabinetmakers abounded: Watherston & Sons, West Park Place; Nathaniel Grieve, Washington Lane; A. & J. Cameron, Duff Street; Heggie & Aitchison, Duff Street; Scott Morton & Co., Murieston Road; David Wilkie, Murieston Road; and Jack Paterson, Glenlea, Gorgie Road. Often working on the same contracts as the joiners were the builders and contractors: Colin Macandrew & Partners Ltd., of West End Place; Stuart's Granolithic Stone Co. Ltd., Duff Street; and James Gerard, Wheatfield Street. The other big employers were the engineers: West End Engine Works, Dundee Street; Alexander Mather & Son, Orwell Terrace; and James Carrick & Sons, Dalry Iron Works.

ALEXANDER MATHER & SON

Alexander Mather & Son, engineers, were at Orwell Terrace from 1896 until 1972 when the firm was sold. The origin of the firm, however,

Alexander Mather & Son's Orwell Works in Orwell Terrace in 1921, where they made a variety of oatmeal and barley milling machines. (Courtesy of Ian Mather.)

goes back to 1844 when Alexander Mather started in business, as a millwright, at No.28 Bread Street. By 1850 Mather's address was given as No.162 Fountainbridge which lay on the north side of the road now known as East Fountainbridge. It is possible that the two addresses related to the same site which was later redeveloped by St Cuthbert's Cooperative Association Ltd. From 1857 Mather was operating from No.121 (renumbered from 63), which lay on the south side of the street near to what was the Palais Dance Hall. By the 1870s Mather was trading as Alexander Mather & Son and he had extended his activities to millwrights, engineers and ironfounders. The move to the Orwell Works in Orwell Terrace in 1896 gave the firm the opportunity of expanding further and developing new markets.

The main contracts at Fountainbridge and Orwell Terrace were for the construction and supply of oatmeal and barley milling machines, conveyor and elevator equipment, cutting and stacking machines for paper mills, and printing ink manufacturing plant. The main customers were A. & R. Scott (makers of porridge oats), Imperial Chemical Industries, Distillers Company Ltd., Scottish Malt Distillers, A.B. Fleming & Co., and a host of firms in Australia, New Zealand, South Africa,

Norway and Sweden. One of the most difficult jobs to manoeuvre out of the works at Orwell Terrace and onto the adjacent railway track was the supply of steel girders for the Murrayfield Bridge of the Caledonian Railway in 1900. A photograph in the Mather family archive shows the girders loaded onto ten waggons near Dalry Station, ready for the journey.

In the opening years of the twentieth century Mathers entered the new and challenging age of the motor car. As appointed agents for Clement Delivery Vans, Mathers announced in their advertising material that 'almost every make of car in general use in this country has passed through the works, in many cases having been entirely rebuilt'. The business was sufficiently prosperous to open a motor car showroom in 1906 at Nos. 79-81 Shandwick Place, and to have a stand at the Kelvin Hall Motor Show in the following years. Well before the time when the internal combustion engine was commonplace, Mathers designed and built a steam-powered tractor in 1870, which was on show at the International Exhibition of Industry, Science and Art, 1886, in the Meadows. It was a short, stocky, three-wheeled vehicle with massive rear wheels supporting the steam boiler and funnel. Two men were required to operate it: the driver sat perched at the front in an open cab; and at the back a second person was stationed, presumably to fire the boiler.

During the Second World War many of Mather's usual contracts were suspended and replaced by contracts associated with the war effort. These included aircraft engine mountings and part of the catapult mechanism on aircraft carriers. Despite the austerity of the times there was, however, sufficient time and money for a modest celebration of the firm's centenary on 7th April 1944, when a dinner/dance was held at the Silver Wing Roadhouse at Sighthill.

Post-war contracts tended to concentrate more on printing and inking machines and less on the traditional business of cereal milling. During the 1960s, despite their long independent history, Mathers found themselves increasingly unable to compete with the new larger engineering concerns, as a result of which the business was sold in 1972.

SCOTT MORTON LTD.

William Scott Morton was born in Carluke, Lanarkshire on 16th May 1840, the son of Robert Morton, joiner and wheelwright, and Ann Scott. In his teens, William was apprenticed to a Glasgow architect, James Smith, father of Madeleine Smith of the famous poisoning trial.

Alexander Mather started in business in 1844. This steam-driven tractor was built at the Fountainbridge Works around 1870. It was demonstrated at the International Exhibition of Industry, Science and Art held in the Meadows in 1886. (Courtesy of Ian Mather.)

Around 1860 William went to London where he was employed by Johnston and Jeans, a high-class furnishing house in the city. He also augmented his earnings by drawing the architectural backgrounds of paintings by Frith and Landseer. In the late 1860s, he came to Edinburgh and started a business as a cabinetmaker with his brother John, who was a qualified engineer. There is doubt as to the location of their first premises, but in 1874 they were at Dalry Park, and in 1877 they were on the south side of Caledonian Crescent, adjacent to Telfer Subway. For a short while, William and his wife and young family lived nearby, in Dalry House. By 1880 the brothers were operating as Morton & Co., furniture and interior decoration manufacturers at Wester Dalry. It is likely that this last address was the extensive Albert Works in Murieston Road (now Linton Court), designed by William Scott Morton, which they occupied until the firm closed in 1966. The works were named after Albert, the Prince Consort, who took a great interest in the development of British industry before his premature death, from typhoid, in 1861. From a fairly early stage, the firm operated two main divisions: the Scott Morton Company undertook cabinetmaking and carving; and the Tynecastle Company made a wide range of plaster mouldings and embossed canvas wallcoverings. The cabinetmaking and carving side of the business was by far the larger part, at one time employing well over one hundred men as carvers, cabinetmakers, joiners and machinemen.

In the early years at Murieston Road, Morton & Co. was involved, principally, in the design and manufacture of furniture, but soon William branched out into interior decoration, and the firm began to stock oriental carpets and all kinds of upholstery. They also designed and built mantelpieces in a variety of styles, as well as individually for particular clients. From 1890 to 1916, the interiors, of private houses, designed by several eminent Scottish architects, formed a large part of Scott Morton's work, including carving, panelling, library shelves, staircases and furniture. The lengthy list, covering many parts of the country, included No.6 Heriot Row, Edinburgh, for Alexander Maitland, by Sir Robert Lorimer; Harmeny, Balerno, for W.J. Younger, also by Lorimer; the restoration of Falkland Palace for the Marquess of Bute, by John Kinross; and Manderston House, Duns, for Sir James Millar, Bart., also by Kinross. Morton & Co. were equally prolific in their contribution to the interiors of public buildings. The list of contracts reads like an inventory of notable buildings in Edinburgh and beyond: Reid Memorial Church; St Giles Cathedral; St Mary's Cathedral, Palmerston Place; Holyrood Palace; Thistle Chapel, St Giles Cathedral; Scottish National War Memorial, at Edinburgh Castle; St Andrew's House; the Sheriff Court; National Library of Scotland; St Michael's Church, Linlithgow; oak bookcases for the Bodleian Library, Oxford; and innumerable banks and insurance companies throughout the country. Scott Morton also built consuls for Ingram, the organ builders in Gorgie Road. Another main source of business was fitting out luxury apartments for the ocean-going liners of the day, the *Queen Mary* and the *Queen Elizabeth*, and building the interiors of 'railway cars' for the London North Eastern Railway and the London Midland and Scottish Railway. The firm probably reached its heyday between the First and Second World Wars. William Scott Morton's two sons had been running the firm since the death of their father in 1903: William Stewart Morton became managing director, and Alec Morton toured the country building up remunerative contracts from many of the stately homes. It

Prince George visiting the carving shop of Scott Morton & Co., cabinetmakers, in Murieston Road in 1933. William Stewart Morton is on the extreme left and Bob Young, the foreman carver, is on the right. (Courtesy of Mrs Jessie Miller.)

was a time (the early 1930s) when a first-year apprentice earned 7/4d (37p) for a forty-four hour week, which included a Saturday morning. One of the first jobs to be mastered was transferring the design drawings onto blocks of wood using carbon paper and a tracer. The block would then be shaded blue or red to assist the machineman, and later the carver. Drawing-office apprentices who wished to become skilled craftsmen attended Edinburgh College of Art on a daily basis at the beginning of the working day, and again in the early evening, before going to Heriot-Watt College (now University) at night. The skilled draughtsmanship and the formal education obtained in architecture resulted in all such apprentices becoming prominent architects in the city and throughout the country.

The other main, but smaller, division of the firm was Tynecastle Tapestry, which specialised in high-grade wallcoverings. This side of the business was advanced with great enthusiasm by William Scott Morton's son, William Stewart Morton. He established contacts in the main cities of the United Kingdom, and in 1889 he went to America to set up additional agencies. Detailed research done by Elspeth Hardie (daughter of William Stewart Morton) in 1976 traced his progress and correspondence with his father back in Edinburgh. Although Stewart Morton was only twenty-one years of age, his business acumen, and youthful zeal, enabled him to make substantial progress, but unfortunately his father did not agree with the idea of manufacturing Tynecastle Tapestry in America. When the small office in New York was closed in December 1890, Stewart returned to Edinburgh, leaving behind him a network of agencies which produced good business for the Tynecastle Company for many years to follow. An article in *The Art Journal* in 1900 provides a fascinating glimpse of the highly unusual skill of tapestry making:

> In the first long, well lighted workshop you find dozens of men and boys engaged in embossing the canvas. Large sheets of metal, many bigger than a good-sized door, are laid flat upon specially prepared steam chests, which are heated and cooled at the operator's pleasure by a most ingenious method invented by Mr Scott Morton. On this heated plate of metal, with the design cut deeply into its substance, the operators spread canvas which has been boiled so that it presents a limp, pliant fabric, which can be accommodated to the various planes of the intaglio mould.

Thereafter, the limp canvas was coaxed into the recesses of the mould using a light brush. It was then backed up with layers of paper and special cement from which a perfect cast was obtained. The canvases were then set in panels for a simple screw assembly and passed to the finishing room, where about twenty-five female employees began the job of picking out the background colours of the various patterns. Numerous lineal and corner mouldings were also made, including a range of friezes, one of which reproduced the design of the Elgin Marbles from the Parthenon. Scott Morton's sales pamphlet and travellers' samples of the Parthenon frieze provide an interesting insight into this aspect of the business. Full-size casts of the original slabs in the British Museum were made and reduced in size by a special machine invented by John Morton, the engineer. The sets came in two sizes 'in fine hardened plaster and for decorative purposes . . . supplied in any tone of scumbled gold or oxidised silver'. The price varied from 20/-(£1) per yard for the small size in plain plaster to 37/6d (£1.88p) per yard for the larger size in toned gilding.

Considerable disruption to the firm occurred in 1939 on the outbreak of the Second World War. Many employees were called up for military service, most high-grade work was suspended, and the remainder of the workforce were employed making munition boxes, battery cases for submarines and lens boxes for the Royal Air Force. In 1941, due to lack of space at Murieston Road, the Tynecastle wallcoverings part of the business separated from the parent company by mutual agreement and amalgamated with Lothian Kinross at No.17 Greenside Place. At the end of the Second World War, Scott Morton began to re-establish its main lines of business, but it is probably true to say that the demand for such skilled work never fully returned. A notable post-war contract, designed and started before the war, was the National Library of Scotland on George IV Bridge, in which Scott Morton was involved with the Dalry building contractors, Colin Macandrew & Partners Ltd. A further reduction in demand in the 1960s, and crippling independent financial constraints, led to the closure of the firm in 1966: the goodwill of the business was acquired by Whytock & Reid of Belford Mews. Over a period of almost a century, Scott Morton built a reputation of producing many of Scotland's foremost craftsmen and designers whose work has reached far beyond Edinburgh. The firm's impact on architecture cannot be over-emphasised. The last managing director, who succeeded James Lochead in 1960, was Peter Miller, who joined the firm as a young man in 1931, and trained under David Ramsay, chief designer with the firm for almost fifty years from 1905. Peter Miller spent many years designing and perfecting new techniques in the same way as William Scott Morton had done several years before.

COLIN MACANDREW & PARTNERS LTD.

Colin Macandrew was a native of Perthshire who came to Edinburgh as a young man and started his own business as a joiner in 1882. His first premises were at No.45 Candlemaker Row, a few doors down from the junction with Merchant Street. A watercolour painting shows the original shop front in an old dilapidated tenement with tiny windows and a pantiled roof. For a very short time Colin Macandrew had a partner, Mr Swinton, but by 1884 the business had been moved to No.18 Chapel Street, and there was no mention of Mr Swinton. In 1889 Macandrew moved again to larger premises at No.13 Lauriston Gardens where he remained as a mason and joiner until 1919. When he moved to West End Place, off Dalry Road, his former premises in Lauriston Gardens were taken over by his son Gordon C. Macandrew, the motor engineer.

From an early stage Colin Macandrew decided that his firm would tender for works of major importance, many of which are photographed in a commemorative brochure entitled *Colin Macandrew & Partners Ltd.—A Story of Achievement, 1882-1955*. Prior to the First World War the main contracts included several public buildings: Morningside Free Church (now Church Hill Theatre) was designed in 1892 by Hippolyte Blanc and built of Corsehill sandstone; the Royal Infirmary of Edinburgh Diamond Jubilee Pavilion was built of red sandstone in 1897; and, perhaps the biggest contract ever undertaken by Macandrews, Redford Barracks was begun in 1909. The Cavalry Barracks and the Infantry Barracks were built between 1909 and 1915 to designs by Harry B. Measures, Director of Barrack Construction. Before work was started a light railway was built from Slateford to Colinton Road to transport the vast quantity of stone, timber and other materials required for the job. During the entire Barracks contract Macandrews were operating from the Lauriston Gardens premises.

In the period between the two World Wars the firm consolidated its position as one of Scotland's leading public works contractors. Colin Macandrew's son Percy joined the firm and took control after the retirement of his father. In 1933 Colin Macandrew Ltd. became the holding company for twin companies formed to run the joinery and masonry sides of the business. Between 1918 and 1939 a number of important Edinburgh buildings were completed, among them the Royal Bank of Scotland, Hope Street; George Heriot's Junior School; George Watson's Junior School; Princess Margaret Rose Hospital; and the John Menzies headquarters in Rose Street. The building programme also included several places of entertainment: Blue Halls Picture House; Regent Picture House; part of the New Victoria Picture House (now the Odeon Film Centre); and the rebuilding, in 1927, of the Empire Theatre, now the Festival Theatre, in Nicolson Street.

At the outbreak of the Second World War in 1939 the firm made several organisational changes. The two separate companies were amalgamated as Colin Macandrew & Partners Ltd., with Percy Macandrew as Governing Director. G.L. Orchard who came to the firm in 1926 as a surveyor also joined the board. When Percy retired in 1940, G.L. Orchard acquired his interest in the company. Immediately after the Second World War G.L. Orchard's son Ronald R. Orchard joined the firm and was Managing Director when it closed. Post-war contracts included the first 'prefabs' in Edinburgh (detached prefabricated structures intended as temporary family accommodation); Fountainbridge Telephone Exchange; the Robin Chapel in the Thistle Foundation Settlement; and the most prestigious of all, the National Library of

The workforce of Colin Macandrew & Partners Ltd., Public Works Contractors, at West End Place in the mid-1930s. The firm built Redford Barracks and the National Library of Scotland, among many other public and private buildings. (Courtesy of Phyllis Margaret Cant, née Robson.)

Scotland on George IV Bridge. The National Library building was designed by Reginald Fairlie in 1934, but only the steelwork had been completed by 1939 when the whole contract was suspended during the Second World War. The Library was not completed until 1955. Later contracts included the School of Architecture at the Edinburgh College of Art, the Teachers' Training College at the Convent of the Sacred Heart, the Rose Street extension to Jenners of Princes Street, and the Control Building for the new Lock Gate at Leith Docks.

The recollections of a young apprentice (later journeyman) joiner employed by Macandrews in the 1940s and 1950s are worth recording. The working week, as in most other trades, was forty-four hours: 8a.m. to 4.30p.m. Monday to Friday with half an hour for lunch, and 8a.m. to 12 noon on Saturdays. After 1945 a five-minute break was given in the morning which lengthened the day to 4.35p.m. Apprentices were given a thorough training but were also expected to watch the glue pots and 'bile the cans'—2lb. syrup tins with the rim cut off and a wire handle added, which the men used as a practical alternative to cups. Learning the trade meant undertaking the simpler jobs, such as preparing and assembling small chests of drawers for the Land Army, and making engine crates. As experience was gained, more responsible work was allocated associated with the main contracts at St George's Church, George Heriot's School, Edinburgh University and the Royal Dick Veterinary College. The guiding light was Jimmy Watt, the chargehand setter-out whose experience of managing men and timber was legend. Whilst rates of pay were not high (in 1946 tradesmen were paid two shillings and six pence per hour or 12½p, and labourers, two shillings per hour or 10p), they were in keeping with those of other firms and there was the added bonus of four shillings (20p) per night for fire-watching duties during the Second World War. There were, of course, lighter moments. On the occasion of the retirement of a long-serving foreman the management decided to mark the occasion with a dinner and presentation in the Freemasons' Hall in George Street. Perhaps in anticipation of mildly raucous behaviour, selected employees were al-located to different tables to maintain law and order. The brickies and labourers all sat together in perfect formation, watched by their reluc-tant 'chaperon', until the starter was served—'a saucer with a wee sar-dine on a lettuce leaf'. Order was eventually restored, occasionally chal-lenged during the lengthy speeches, until the moment arrived for the evening's entertainment. A well-proportioned female singer in long flowing robes appeared and severely depleted the attendance with the first few bars of *Cherry Ripe*. Despite a thorough search of the building the brickies were never located. It was always said that they had made a move to the first few bars in Rose Street.

Macandrews remained at West End Place until 1967 when they were forced to vacate their site after failing to purchase it from the Railway Board. After considerable upheaval, and discarding 'treasured', but non-essential, equipment, Macandrews settled at a much smaller site in Bowl-ing Green Street, Leith. Sadly, as a result of this and the effects of infla-tion, the firm's financial position deteriorated around this time and Macandrews went into liquidation in 1971.

Of the various addresses at which Macandrews operated, West End Place will always be considered the home base, for a period of almost fifty years. Many memories still linger of the times when Macandrews' men made a significant contribution to the face of Edinburgh. The site, extending to about one and a half acres, lay between Dalry Road and the railway line from the Caledonian Station to the south and west. Immediately adjacent to the track was the covered timber yard, leading to the joiners' bench shop and machine shop, and the kiln where the

Colin Macandrew, founder of Colin Macandrew Ltd. (A Story of Achievement, 1882-1955.)

G.L. Orchard, O.B.E., F.R.I.C.S., F.R.I.A.S. (Hon.), Managing Director of Colin Macandrew & Partners Ltd. (A Story of Achievement, 1882-1955.)

Robert Tully who founded the interior decorator's business in 1906 at No. 240 Dalry Road (Courtesy of his great-grandson James Tully.)

William Scott Morton, founder of Scott Morton Ltd., Cabinetmakers, Murieston Road. (Courtesy of Mrs Elspeth Hardie.)

timber was dried. To the east of the timber yard was the masons' yard where a centrally positioned crane could lift blocks of stone off the railway waggons ready for sawing and dressing in the semi-open sheds. The machines included frame saws, carborundum disc saws, a small saw with diamond impregnated teeth, and planing machines. Macandrews also had their own forge and blacksmith's machine shop for wrought iron work and steelwork.

The administrative offices and the board room were located in two terraced houses at the south end of West End Place. It was here, some years ago, that the Managing Director, Ronald R. Orchard, received an unusual enquiry from railway enthusiasts in England. They had recently acquired a small working steam engine covered in dirt and grease. When they began to renovate it Macandrews' name appeared under several layers of paint. It was quickly established that the engine was one of two 'pugs' bought by Macandrews to work on the special railway track leading from Slateford to Redford Barracks. The engine had been built by Andrew Barclay of Kilmarnock and supplied to Macandrews in 1911. After being bought and sold several times, it was acquired in 1966 by the Midland Group of the Railway Preservation Society. The working engine is now on show at Chasewater Light Railway & Museum, Chasewater Pleasure Park in the Midlands. In Edinburgh the railway line has long since been lifted but its position is shown in the *Ordnance Survey Map* of 1914. It started from the sidings near Slateford Station and headed towards Redford Barracks in a large S-shape, crossing the Union Canal on a bridge which now carries water pipes near Allan Park Road. The track crossed Craiglockhart Avenue slightly south of the church and took the line of present-day Craiglockhart Road to emerge into Colinton Road near the junction with Elliot Road.

CHARLES HENSHAW & SONS LTD

At the beginning of the twentieth century, Charles Henshaw, artist and sculptor, was living and working in the Birmingham area, but for reasons not now known he came north to Edinburgh around 1904. His business was first recorded as Henshaw and McIntyre at No.42 Gorgie Road, the partnership lasting for one year only. Charles Henshaw remained at No.42 until 1907 when he moved to No.29 Murieston Crescent. He felt sufficiently confident about the future of his business, as a decorative metal worker, to advertise in the illustrated catalogue of the

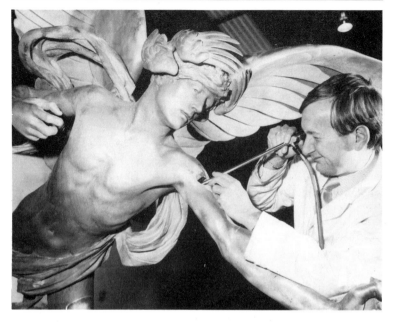

The statue of Eros, from Piccadily Circus in London, was brought to Charles Henshaw & Sons Ltd., Russell Road, Edinburgh for repair in 1985. The photograph shows scientific examination of the original 'Roman joint' of Eros's arm. (Courtesy of Charles Henshaw & Sons Ltd.)

Edinburgh Architectural Association Exhibition held in the National Portrait Gallery, Queen Street, in 1905. He described his occupation as 'brassfounder and smith, designer and modeller, chaser and repoussé workers, and went on to list twenty separate buildings where specimens of his work could be seen. These included a ship in wrought sheet copper as a finial for the Sir William Pearce Memorial Institute in Govan; a bronze medallion and festoons for the Christie Memorial, Stirling; bronze switch plates for Minto House, Roxburgh; a wrought-iron stair railing, grilles, door furniture and bronze standards for Century House, Charlotte Square, Edinburgh; and the very latest fashion—electric light fittings—for Gorgie United Free Church and Tolbooth Church (Highland Tolbooth St John's), Edinburgh. In contrast, Corstorphine Parish Church decided on fittings for the 'Inverted Incandescent Gas Light'.

In common with many other firms, Henshaw was required to enter the munitions business during the First World War and again during the Second World War. Between the two World Wars Charles's three sons entered the business which became a limited company around 1940. Charles Henshaw & Sons Ltd. then moved to their present address in Russell Road in 1946. Until the 1960s the greater part of the business was foundry work but in more recent years there has been considerable diversification into new markets and new uses for traditional materials. This has undoubtedly been stimulated by architectural trends towards the use of brass and bronze in doors and glazing systems. Much of the present-day work is for doors, screens, canopies and staircases using stainless and mild steel, brass, cast aluminium and bronze. There is also a specialised glazing division which includes the manufacture of bullet resistant and fire resistant screens. Some of the most prestigious contracts have included ornamental brass balustrading at Birchan Lane, London; glazing and feature metalwork at St Enoch Square, Glasgow; entrance screens at Halford's, Dunfermline; and curtain walling and staircases at Saltire Court, Castle Terrace, Edinburgh. The contract which caught the public's attention in 1985 was, of course, the repair and refurbishment of the statue of Eros (in Piccadily Circus, London), which was brought all the way to Russell Road in Edinburgh to renew its youth.

SOLAGLAS

Solaglas has operated from No.26 Orwell Terrace since 1976 but its history, through the previous firm Cunningham, Dickson & Walker Ltd., can be traced to the late eighteenth century. Individually the detailed links may appear mundane, but taken together they represent a remarkable degree of continuity and commitment to the glazing trade in Edinburgh.

In 1780 John Baxter was a glazier in the Old Town of Edinburgh. A decade later he moved to Leith Street where his address was described either as No.18 Leith Street or No.18 Low Terrace. Surviving documentation confirms that in 1840 the firm was quoting for the glasswork in Donaldson's Hospital at '11d per foot for ornamental pattern in iron astragale and ½d per foot for diamond shaped square in lead'. Baxter's business was taken over by John Russell around 1850 and then by Andrew Cunningham & Co. in 1867. Cunningham & Co were still at No.18 Leith Street in 1932 when they amalgamated with another long-established company, Dickson & Walker of No.31 Frederick Street.

The other link is equally interesting but not quite so old. In 1804 George Bookless was a glazier in Rose Street. His business was acquired by William Musgrove in 1842, who moved to larger premises at

No.33 Frederick Street in 1856. That business was acquired by Dickson & Walker in 1860, who moved to No. 31 in 1866, and amalgamated with Andrew Cunningham & Co. in 1932.

With two such long pedigrees it is hardly surprising that the combined firm, Cunningham Dickson & Walker, became Edinburgh's foremost glazing company with branches in several Scottish cities. Their advertisements for 1933 announced that they were glazing contractors for 'North British Station Hotel, Caledonian Station Hotel, New Fever Hospital, Extension Royal Infirmary, North Bridge Buildings, Usher Hall, Etc., Etc.' At the time of the amalgamation the firm had retail outlets in Frederick Street, Leith Street and Home Street. Frederick Street became the Head Office with adjacent workshops at Rose Street North Lane where consignments of glass were received. It was here that a lot of the specialised leadwork and stained glass work was done for churches and staircase windows. Polishing, sandblasting and embossing were undertaken at workshops in Greenside Place and later at Sunnybank, Abbeyhill. One of the largest contracts, in 1971, was with the Bank of Scotland for alteration of the logo on the doors and windows of six hundred branches following the absorption of the British Linen Bank.

In 1956 difficulty with access at Frederick Street forced the firm to move to No.26 Duff Street where a hand-operated crane was available to lift heavy sheets of glass directly into the works. Although the Duff Street premises were modernised, it was eventually found that they were not large enough to carry sufficient stock for the expanding business. Two Glasgow-based glaziers were taken over, City Glass Co. Ltd., and George G. Kirk, including its Aberdeen subsidiary Hugh Dow and the Falkirk operation of O'May. In 1976 Cunningham Dickson & Walker moved to larger premises at No.26 Orwell Terrace, previously occupied by Alexander Mather & Son Ltd., where up-to-date equipment and office services were installed.

In 1968 Cunningham, Dickson & Walker were taken over by Standard Industrial Group (SIG) who were a public company established by S. Pearson & Son Ltd.—later S. Pearson PLC. Pearson, in 1971, acquired Doulton & Co. (Royal Doulton), and the glass interests of SIG (which included Cunningham, Dickson & Walker) were transferred to Doulton & Co. Later these same interests were sold to a South African Group, Plate Glass & Shatterpruffe Industries (PGSI). Then in 1990 the glass interests in the building industry were sold to St Gobain SA, the French Group, whilst PGSI retained the automotive interests. It was during the South African ownership that C.D.W. changed its name to Solaglas.

At the present day, Solaglas has retail and wholesale outlets for glass and double glazing units throughout Scotland, England and Northern Ireland—more than two hundred years after the first link in the chain was established by John Baxter, the glazier, in the Old Town of Edinburgh.

ROBERT TULLY

Robert Tully was born in Kelso in 1875 where he completed an apprenticeship as a painter and decorator. In the late 1890s he moved to Edinburgh, working with James Clark & Co., painters at No.124 George Street, Edinburgh until 1906 when he decided to set up his own business at No.240 Dalry Road. The business, now in the fourth generation of the family, has remained at the same address in Dalry since it was established. The founder, Robert Tully, brought his son James into the business around 1920. Subsequently James introduced his son, Robert, in 1955, who in turn brought in his son, James, in 1981.

In the early days of the firm much of the business was done in houses in and around Dalry and Gorgie. This practice was based almost entirely on the absence of motorised transport to reach other parts of the town. Whilst a contract to decorate a Marchmont or Bruntsfield parlour was a good job to get, a lot of the working day was wasted pushing a handbarrow, full of materials and equipment, all the way there and back. The first vehicle used by the firm was in the early 1930s when an old Morris 8 saloon was bought, and later converted to something resembling a shooting brake.

The public's use of professional decorators has also changed greatly over the years. When Robert Tully first established his business, DIY shops were non-existent, and having rooms decorated by professional tradesmen was very much higher up the list of family priorities than it is nowadays. In addition, materials used by the professional were not so easily managed by the amateur. Rolls of wallpaper were made with a narrow protective edge, which had to be removed before the pattern could be matched. In the early days this was done, rather laboriously, by cutting with scissors, but later the job was done mechanically. The first machine used by the Tullys at Dalry was hand-operated, later replaced by an electric model. With the advent of the DIY trade many new varieties of wallpaper, trimmed, wrapped and ready pasted, have been introduced. The introduction of paint rollers has reduced the need for extra ladders and planks for the amateur and professional alike. Even basic materials like wallpaper paste have greatly improved from the days when it was one employee's job to mix up a large tub of paste in the back shop. The hard skin which formed on the top of the paste had to be carefully skimmed off to ensure that particles did not get stuck behind the wallpaper on the finished job.

As Tully nears its centenary the basic skills remain constant, but the materials used, and the wide-ranging customer base, have changed out of all recognition from 1906 when the business was first established.

DIDCOCK BROS

Didcock Bros., the upholsterers and furniture makers, have operated from No. 410 Gorgie Road since 1936 when they took over part of the premises then occupied by Cox's Glue Works. Prior to 1936 Didcock Bros. were in business for several years at Dowie's Mill, Cramond. Ernest Didcock Senior, born in 1880, worked with John Weller who had come north from High Wycombe to Edinburgh in 1894. Initially Weller worked from No.13 Duke Street Lane before moving to Dowie's Mill around 1896. Ernest Didcock became a skilled craftsman and took over the business in 1920 when John Weller went to America. Unfortunately John Weller was not able to settle in America and returned to Dowie's Mill hoping to start up again where he had left off. When he discovered that that was not possible, he set up in opposition at Peggy's Mill further downstream.

In 1920 Dowie's Mill was a very isolated spot on the River Almond where the water wheel was still capable of driving the machinery and also powering a small dynamo to generate electricity. The water was taken from the weir along a short lade, through a bypass, to a wheel mounted on the side of the mill building. This arrangement meant that the 'spent' water from the bypass re-entered the Almond directly, thereby reducing the main supply going on to Peggy's Mill. Most of the time there was an adequate volume of water and also a good supply of hardwood timber, beech, oak, elm and ash, taken from the neighbouring estates. The felled, rough timber was hauled by horse to the sawmill where it was cut into lengths before being sawn into planks of various thicknesses ready for seasoning. Timber was not kiln-dried at Cramond. It was stacked horizontally in the open with one-inch thick slats, or pins, separating each plank. The rule of thumb measurement for seasoning was one year for every one-inch thickness of timber.

The second generation of Didcocks, Ernest and William, entered the firm in the late 1920s when it was still operating at Dowie's Mill. In

1936 the firm moved to its present site in Gorgie Road, maintaining contracts with the main furniture retailers of the day, Underwoods in Antigua Street, Scottish Furniture Warehouse in the High Street and Brown's Furniture Store in Leith Walk. Edward, younger brother of Ernest and William, joined the firm in 1939 and remained with Didcock's all his working life. During the Second World War, when the firm closed temporarily owing to shortage of skilled labour, the premises were used by C. & J. Brown. At the end of the War the Didcocks, like their competitors, were subject to the Government's restrictions on furniture manufacturers, which specified the quality and design of what was to be produced. Each piece of furniture bore the utility mark, and a number identifying the workshop in which the item had been made. Contacts had to be re-established with the retailers of the day: C. & J. Brown of Newington; Binns of the West End; Patrick Thomson's of North Bridge; Findlater Smith of Lothian Road; and Lorimer & Beetham of Church Hill.

Since the 1960s the third generation of Didcocks, John, Michael and Charles, has entered the business, maintaining the family traditions, but acutely aware of the competition from large furniture warehouses. Adjusting to new markets and a degree of specialisation has enabled the firm to prosper, albeit with a reduced workforce. Much of the present work comes from the refitting of pubs, restaurants and private function rooms, and diversification of skills, for example, fitting the wall drapes for several art galleries in Edinburgh.

Over the years Didcock Bros. have maintained a close family business with the respective wives also playing their part at various times: Sylvia (wife of Ernest) was a machine sewer for over twenty-five years; Nancy (wife of William) undertook office administration in the 1960s; and Irene (wife of John) continues that work at the present day.

PATERSON THE JOINER

The Paterson family, joiners in Gorgie, can trace their involvement in the district as far back as 1820, that being the year in which Robert Paterson was born. The 1871 Census describes Robert as head of the household, married to Elizabeth, with five sons and three daughters. The eldest son, James, established a joiner's business, c. 1868, at the rear of the cottage known as Glenlea, in Gorgie Road. The cottage still remains, on the south side of the road, a few yards east of the United Free Church, but its small front garden and entrance porch have been

*Tommy Scoon and John Didcock working on a section of bar seating for an Edinburgh public house, at the Gorgie premises of Didcock Bros., c.1975. (*Courtesy of Ernest Didcock.*)*

removed during road widening schemes. James's son David started in the business c.1893 and in turn was succeeded by his two sons, David Jnr., in 1922, and Jack in 1927. The business was moved in 1934 to much larger premises previously owned by Thomas Forrest, the joiner, on the east corner of Gorgie Road and Hutchison Crossway.

In the early part of the twentieth century much of the work coming to Patersons was either through one of the many house factors or on houses built locally, including villas at Kingsknowe and bungalows in Robb's Loan. Good-quality timber was supplied by either Park, Dobson & Co. of Easter Road or D.W. Beattie & Co. of Baltic Street who sold timber 'off the wharf' at Leith. Another source of business was the specialised job of making cart wheels. The hub, or knave as it was called, was invariably made of elm. The spokes were of oak and the felloes (forming the outer circumference) were made of either ash or elm. It was a skilled job to fit the spokes and shape the felloes using a trainer, or measuring device, taken from the centre of the hub. Once assembled,

Workers and visitors at the premises of Paterson, the joiner, at No. 437 Gorgie Road in 1934. Third from the right is David Paterson Snr., flanked by two of his sons. On his right is David and on his left is Jack. (Courtesy of Jack Paterson.)

the wheel was taken along to McDougall the blacksmith to have the iron rim fitted. The timber joints were all, of course, held tightly with dowels. In that era joinery fitments were put together with Cox's glue, manufactured only a few doors away from Paterson's workshop. The glue was bought in cakes or slabs measuring nine inches by five and a half inches. A slab would be put in a sack, broken up with a hammer, and the pieces put into a pail of water for a day or two until the mixture was the consistency of jelly. At that stage it was ready to be put into the glue pot and heated until it was liquid.

In the days before Patersons had motorised transport it was the responsibility of the apprentice to fetch supplies in a two-wheeled handcart. Jack Paterson recalls pushing the cart, every Saturday morning, all the way to Brownlie, the home-grown timber merchants, in East Silvermills Lane, Stockbridge to load up with a selection of Scotch fir boards, knaves and felloes, and to push the loaded cart back to Gorgie. The handcart was later replaced by a motor cycle and sidecar, then by an open Austin Tourer and finally by more orthodox vans.

In 1977, after a lifetime in the joinery business, Jack Paterson retired and the premises were sold to Farley the window manufacturers. In 1981 the premises were converted into a restaurant.

ANDREW MCDOUGALL, BLACKSMITHS

In 1876 Andrew McDougall established his business as a blacksmith at 'Gorgie damside' in the village of Delhaig, to the west of Gorgie Mills. The postal address was listed in the *Edinburgh and Leith Post Office Directory* for 1877-78 under 'Murrayfield'. At that time there were a few dozen houses at Gorgie Mills and at Delhaig, but otherwise the area was one of open farmland. Immediate neighbours were David Bower, physician at Saughton Hall; Thomas Clark, gluemaker at Gorgie Mills; the famous J. & G. Cox, glue and gelatine makers, also at Gorgie Mills; and another blacksmith, William Henderson, at Cairns Cottage. In that rural setting much of the work coming to Andrew McDougall would be related to milling and agriculture—repairing farm implements, shoeing horses and re-fitting iron rims on cart wheels. The traditional blacksmith's business, centred around the forge and the anvil, continued, uninterrupted until the 1950s when there was a gradual reduction in agricultural work, and a corresponding increase in work on gates, railings, balustrades, fire escapes and security grilles. The traditional material, wrought iron, was gradually replaced by steel supplied in long strips, rounded or flat.

The business, still operating from the same premises, is now numbered 469 Gorgie Road. It is managed by two brothers, Stuart and Graeme McDougall, great-grandsons of Andrew McDougall who started the firm in 1876. In the early 1970s, when the stonework on the adjacent dwelling house was being restored, the original sign was discovered under the old harling: ANDREW McDOUGALL, GENERAL BLACKSMITH. The dwelling, known as Etive House, takes its name from Glen Etive in Argyllshire where the McDougall family originated.

7

Commercial and Industrial Development, 2: Beer, Biscuits, Glue and Others

Gorgie and Dalry attracted significant industrial development in addition to the building-related trades already discussed. The same economic and logistical factors were operating, which included unlimited space and efficient railway transport. A good supply of water, either from the Union Canal (for cooling purposes) or from deep wells (for processing) was also of paramount importance to the brewing and distilling industries. The first firm to appear was the Caledonian Distillery, at Haymarket, built in 1855 by Graham Menzies & Co., who already owned Sunbury Distillery, near the Dean village. The other great distillery, The North British, was established in Wheatfield Road in 1885. The main brewing companies were Bernard's at Slateford Road and Wheatfield, and the Caledonian Brewery established in Slateford Road in 1869.

A host of other trades and businesses existed, or still exist, many of them doing quite specialised work: manufacturers of rubber (Currie & Co.); glue (J.G. Cox); chemicals (Macfarlan Smith); biscuit makers (McVitie & Price); oven builders (James Cruikshanks); organ builders (Ingram); gas meter manufacturers (Alder & Mackay); and printers (Waddie's and Annan's).

COX'S GLUE WORKS

Cox's Glue Works was established at Linlithgow in 1725 but moved within a relatively short time to Bell's Mills at the Dean Village. The firm settled at Gorgie in 1798 where it remained until 1969. For almost two and a half centuries Cox's presence was keenly felt by everyone who lived within breathing space of its processes. In 1969 Cox's ceased production of its high-grade glue, gelatine and other related products, a victim of changed markets and different economic considerations. But for the efforts of John Cox, the firm would have ceased production more than a century earlier for reasons which were quite unforeseeable.

*This aerial view of Dalry shows the Edinburgh-Glasgow railway with sidings serving the Caledonian Distillery and premises in Duff Street. At the top right-hand corner, part of the Caledonian line can be seen which had sidings for Mather, the engineer, and Macandrew, the public works contractors. (*Courtesy of Patricia Scoular.*)*

A group of Caledonian railway workers at Dalry Sheds beside Dalry Road Station. (Courtesy of Bill Forrest.*)*

Cox's Glue Works were based at Gorgie Mills, which straddled a
slight bend in the road to the Calders, a few hundred yards west of
Westfield Road. The major part of the works was on the south side of
the road, on a site now occupied by Telephone House and the modern
houses of Coxfield. Much of the ground area was laid out in open
tanning pits where the scrows (scrapings from hides and skins) were
immersed in water for several weeks at a time. On the north side of
Gorgie Road the flour mill was also used to power some of Cox's other
processes. The pits and the mill wheel were fed from a long lade which
was constructed to take water from the Water of Leith near Saughtonhall
(now Saughton Rose Gardens). The whole process of glue and gelatine
manufacture relied on a steady flow of good clean water from the Water
of Leith. Unfortunately for Cox, in the middle of the nineteenth century their natural water supply was threatened by Edinburgh's need to
increase the quantity of water coming into the city for domestic and
industrial use. The Edinburgh Water Company obtained statutory control of springs at Bavelaw to feed the city supply, but in doing so they
reduced the amount of spring water going into the Water of Leith. To
compensate for this loss Harlaw Reservoir was constructed to act as a
feeder to the Water of Leith. The peaty nature of the soil around Harlaw
meant that the water entering the Water of Leith was discoloured and
caused havoc with industrial processes farther downstream. Particularly
affected was Cox's Glue Works whose products and reputation were
seriously threatened. Mr Cox introduced changes in his processes to
counteract the effects of the impure water but they were neither practical nor economic. In desperation he went to law and appeared per-
sonally before the Select Committee of the House of Lords on the
Edinburgh Water Bill, June 1856. The evidence led was lengthy, including interesting comments on the nature of the business, its processes, and how the firm was in danger of being ruined if an adequate
supply of clean water was not restored quickly. Mr Cox explained to
the Select Committee that the basic process was to soak the scrows in
clean water to wash out the impurities. Counsel was intrigued to know
more about the process and the origin of the skins and hides, but Cox
appears to have been equal to him in caustic wit.

> COUNSEL: We have been told that you use dead cat skins and dead
> dog skins. Are these articles of common use?

> MR COX: I have never heard of them. I have heard of them going
> to pie shops but that is all.

Animal skins and hides were soaked in open pits for several weeks at Cox's Glue Works in Gorgie Road, before being lifted out and moved to the washers where the impurities were removed. (Courtesy of Stanley Jamieson.)

When the 1856 Act was passed it contained several provisos which greatly assisted Cox's Glue Works. An extra reservoir was constructed at Harperrig to augment the flow of water into the Water of Leith, and a committee was set up from among the mill owners to regulate the discharge of water from Harperrig. In addition, a separate piped supply of spring water was guaranteed for named mills along the banks of the Water of Leith. The allocation for Cox's Glue Works was 72,000 gallons per day for eight months of the year or 48,000 gallons per day for a full year.

With the water restored, Cox and his glue went from strength to strength. A review of the firm in 1913 confirmed that it was foremost in its field with increased products and worldwide markets. Among its many products were Cox's 'Elfin Jellies' and gelatine in its distinctive red, white and blue packaging. A further report in 1931 from *The Cabinet Maker and Complete House Furnisher* also placed Cox's glue at the forefront of the industry, with products such as Long Scotch Glue, Liquid Scotch Glue and Cock Brand. A special non-frothing glue was also introduced for use in the veneering and joint-making trades. The industry was clearly bubbling with confidence—'No reliable synthetic substitute for it [Cox's glue] has yet been discovered, and Messrs. Cox are confident that whatever may transpire during the coming years the improved British glue products of today fear comparison with no other makes in the world'.

Whilst the various glue processes have varied in detail over the years, the basic treatment of the skins and hides has remained fairly constant. The recollections of several ex-employees paint an interesting picture of an unglamorous industry. The skins and hides arrived by road or by rail from abattoirs throughout Scotland and from abroad. They were stored in a dry warehouse before being taken to one of the pits, which occupied the centre area of the works. Water and lime were added to soften the skins and make them more pliable. To ensure a thorough preparation, the skins were turned from time to time before being lifted out about one week later by a small mobile crane. The softened skins were then put through a series of washers (water running over revolving blades) to remove the impurities. The clean skins were then taken into the works where they were boiled in large vats until the mixture was somewhere between liquid and solid. This jelly composition was then run off, cooled and sliced, before being put into shallow trays or pallets stacked on bogies. The bogies were then placed, either in an oven for the glue to dry, or at one time in a series of half-open structures to be air-dried. Once dry, some of the slabs of glue were put into a hopper to be ground into powder, bagged and taken away by road or rail. The gelatine process was similar except that more detailed checks were carried out by the laboratory staff, who also had responsibility for the glue strength-testing procedures. The finest glue was No.7, used almost exclusively for the match industry. Unfortunately the industry found more economic ways of producing the glue used for match heads, which was a serious blow to Cox's business. Synthetic glue, such as PVA (polyvinyl acetate), had been introduced in the mid-1960s but the volume of business from that source was insufficient to prevent J. & G. Cox from closing in 1969. At the time of closure the managing director was Dr T. Shedden who had been with the firm for many years. A former managing director, Major Robert Bruce, joined Cox's in 1908 as a young chemist and remained on the Board of Directors after he retired in 1959. He was one of the assistant Masters of the Merchant Company of Edinburgh. Robert Cox W. S., of Gorgie, is remembered for his generous bequest to Edinburgh University which enabled the intended dome to be completed in 1887 at a cost of £3,700. A commemorative plaque in the dome room of the Old Quad states that Robert Cox of Gorgie was 'a just and generous man, a learned author,

No self-respecting cook was ever without Cox's Manual of Gelatine Cookery. *A leaflet of 'delightful recipes' was enclosed in every packet of gelatine. (*Courtesy of Mrs Jean Moffat.*)*

an enemy of ignorance and superstition, who bequeathed the fund for the erection of this dome, a feature in the original design by Robert Adam, now built from the plans of R. Rowand Anderson, LL.D.' Further details and an excellent photograph by Joe Rock appear in Dr Andrew G. Fraser's book *The Building of Old College*, published in 1989.

CALEDONIAN DISTILLERY

The Caledonian Distillery at Haymarket was built in 1855 by Graham Menzies & Co., who owned Sunbury Distillery near the Dean village. It was one of the first firms to move into the Dalry area which, at that time, was a greenfield site with ample space for expansion. There were other important factors which influenced the decision to move. The Dalry site lay between the Caledonian Railway and the Edinburgh—Glasgow Railway, both of which had branch lines, which led into the centre of the works. In addition, the Union Canal was relatively close, providing a gravity-fed supply of water along an underground pipe nearly a mile long. The distillery was designed to produce the lighter grain whisky as opposed to malt whisky.

The original distillery buildings included the granary or principal grain store; the mash house, containing the mash tun, in which the cooked grains and malted barley were mixed with heated water to extract fermentable sugars; the tunroom, containing the washbacks (large fermenting vessels), where the liquor from the mash had yeast added and was left to ferment; and the still house, with the Coffey still, in which continuous distillation took place. Alfred Barnard, author of *The Whisky Distillers of the United Kingdom* (1887), described the Caledonian as 'the model distillery of Europe'. It was designed in such a way as to reduce, as far as possible, the labour-intensive tasks of moving bulk ingredients about the works. Deliveries of grain arrived every twelve hours in railway waggons fitted with special trap doors. When opened, the grain poured out into a continuous screw which carried the grain up to the top floors and to other parts of the distillery. The motive power was provided by steam which also required constant trainloads of coal to feed the boilers. This basic organisation is clearly shown in *Goad's Plans* of 1906. The site was more or less rectangular in shape, lying along the south side of the Edinburgh—Glasgow Railway line. The entrance was at the east end, via Distillery Lane, where there was a gatehouse and adjacent rope store. To the south-east of the gatehouse were offices, a loading shed and duty-free warehouse No.3. The rail-

*The interior of the new spirit store at the Caledonian Distillery at Distillery Lane.
The Caledonian was opened in 1855 and closed in 1987. (*Courtesy of United
Distillers.*)*

way track came in on the north side of the works and ran parallel to the
mainline tracks until it reached the gatehouse where the waggons could
be turned at right angles and led into other parts of the distillery. To the
west of the offices was the main production plant which included the
mash house, tank rooms, grain mill, malt mill, still house and numerous
grain stores. Further west were the coopers' shop, cask shed, smithy,
stables, and finally the barrel yard. To the south of the barrel yard were
duty-free warehouses and a malt house which abutted Dalry Road,
opposite Orwell Terrace.

The 1906 layout had probably not altered very much from the original in 1855, but after the First World War the distillery was re-equipped
with a new power house, a mechanical coal-handling plant, and grain
silos. Steam used for water heating and distillation was also used for
power, being produced by seven Lancashire boilers. During the Second World War extensive damage was caused by a bomb falling on a
warehouse in Duff Street, as a result of which more than a million
gallons of whisky were lost. Full-time production of grain whisky spirit

did not restart until after 1945, when home-grown barley was the main unmalted raw material, followed by maize. Canadian barley was malted in the 1950s. After the Second World War, the plant was extensively modernised. A new copper column replaced the wooden analyser (one of the two columns of the Coffey still) in 1948, and Colclad washbacks (having a stainless steel lining to reduce the likelihood of bacteria entering the wash) gradually replaced the old wooden ones. Coal-fired boilers were installed in 1957 and converted to oil in 1967. Electric power was gradually transferred to the public mains supply.

In addition to the main product, grain whisky, the Caledonian Distillery was involved in recovery of two by-products. Carbon dioxide gas was collected from the fermentation process at Haymarket and also brought in by pipeline from the North British Distillery in Wheatfield Road. It was then purified and compressed into either liquid or solid form. By a reciprocal agreement, the spent wash from the Caledonian stills was pumped along another pipeline to the North British Distillery where it was used, along with their own spent liquor, in the manufacture of cattlefeed under the brand name North British Golden Grains.

Although the Caledonian Distillery had moved to Dalry, in 1855, to gain the advantage of greater space, the passage of time removed that asset completely. In recent years the Distillery became very cramped for space, was difficult of access for lorries, and offered no opportunity for expansion. Following a process of rationalisation in the production of grain whisky, the owners, United Distillers, closed the plant in 1987. Parts of the remaining buildings, including the tall chimney, have since been listed.

THE NORTH BRITISH DISTILLERY COMPANY LTD.

During the first half of the nineteenth century the whisky trade in Scotland was dominated by the production of malts, but revolutionary changes lay ahead. In the 1860s Andrew Usher was experimenting with whisky blending by the skilful mixing of two or three malts with two or three grain spirits. It was a development which brought the consumption of whisky to a much wider public in Scotland, England and overseas. Two other well-established names in the whisky trade, John M. Crabbie of Leith and William Sanderson of Leith, joined Andrew Usher to form the nucleus of a new whisky distillery, intended to serve the existing wholesale trade in Edinburgh, and beyond. A phenomenal growth in trade took place: during the first half of the nineteenth century the average annual production in Scotland was less than one million gallons, whereas in the last quarter of the same century duty was paid annually on about thirty-five million gallons. In 1885 Andrew Usher was appointed as the provisional chairman of a committee set up to find a place to build the new distillery. After various proposals were considered a site at the north end of Wheatfield Road was chosen, with good access to railways, water and sewers. The name 'The North British Distillery Company Limited' was chosen and the company was incorporated on 24th October 1885. The first premises at Gorgie were built in record time by the Glasgow engineers, Russell & Spence, for the sum of £142,000. By 20th September 1887 the first managing director, William Sanderson, was able to send out samples of grain whisky to the trade, commenting that 'in no circumstances whatever shall we admit within the gates of this distillery any inferior materials'.

The scene was set for a long and eventful involvement in the whisky trade. At that time Edinburgh had three other main distilleries: the Edinburgh, in Sciennes Road; the Dean, beside the Water of Leith; and the Caledonian, off Dalry Road. The Caledonian was the largest, producing 40,000 gallons of spirit per week, whereas the North British was designed to produce 25,000 gallons. Competition was keen and industrial espionage was by no means unheard of. Although parties of visitors were allowed to tour the distillery, sensitive areas were screened off and no brewers or distillers were allowed in the visiting groups. Up to the end of the nineteenth century production and expansion were the order of the day, with strong balance sheets and good dividends for the hand-picked shareholders. The surging energy which had characterised the early years was, however, temporarily checked in 1898 by the retirement and premature death of the first chairman, Andrew Usher. In the following years production levelled off and then went into decline, the first time since the company had been incorporated. Further problems lay ahead. In November 1905 the North London Magistrates Court was asked to hear a case under the Sale of Food and Drugs Act 1875, the allegation being that a *blend* of whisky was not of the 'nature substance and quality' of the liquor legally described as 'whisky', i.e. malted barley put through a pot still. Not to put too fine a point on it, the magistrates were being invited to say that what the North British produced was not whisky. The threat of an adverse ruling caused great consternation and uncertainty at Gorgie. Legal wrangles ensued followed by a Royal Commission set up in February 1908 under Lord James of Hereford. The commissioners toured the plant at Gorgie in

April 1908 and two months later issued their interim report, which was in favour of the blenders. Confidence was restored only to be dented again when the whole issue was challenged in the United States of America. It was eventually resolved in favour of the blenders.

During the First World War the company faced other problems, many of which were shared by competitors. Grain was in very short supply which had an immediate effect upon production. Then early in 1916 the chairman was summoned to London by Lloyd George to be told that the Gorgie works had been earmarked for the manufacture of acetone, an explosive used in munitions. In the following year all dis-tilling ceased, putting the coopers and labourers at Gorgie out of a job for several years to come. Full production was not achieved until early in 1920. As the men flooded back after the war they were met with the final irony—the acetone factory lay unused in the centre of the works, never having made any contribution to the war effort. During the post-war period the North British spent time and money modernising the distillery and replacing worn-out machinery, so that they would be in a strong position when the recovery came. The company's fortunes im-proved considerably from 1935, the year of the golden jubilee: the staff received handsome bonuses; a further programme of modernisation was announced, to include electric light; an extension to the railway sidings was needed to cope with increased production; and new ware-houses were built at Westfield. In the last accounting year before the outbreak of the Second World War the North British sold three million gallons of spirit at 2/3d (11p) per gallon, a price which had remained unaltered for the previous eight years. In contrast, by December 1939 the whole works were closed owing to lack of raw materials and man-power, most of the employees having been called up to the armed services. For the duration of the war years (until 1945) the company had no option but to concentrate on developing its by-products de-partment, particularly with the introduction of North British Golden Grains, a nutritious form of cattle feed.

The post-war era was described by the chairman J.A.R. Macphail as 'a very challenging and progressive time'. It was characterised by a huge expansion of buildings to house the ever-increasing stock. Further ware-houses were built at Westfield; the former Edinburgh Corporation tram depot was acquired; and brewing premises in Slateford Road were con-verted for storage. By then the North British had the capacity to store twenty-one million gallons of spirit, equivalent to seven years' supply. During the 1960s the total staff rose to almost four hundred in the

The grain intake and store at The North British Distillery, Wheatfield Road in 1993. The distillery was established in 1885. (Crown Copyright: RCAHMS.)

wake of Scotch whisky's ever-increasing popularity in almost every corner of the globe. Land was purchased at Muirhall, West Lothian for the construction of more warehouses, on the site of the defunct mineral-oil firm founded by James 'Paraffin' Young. On 12th November 1970 at 2.15p.m. exactly, the 250,000,000th gallon of North British proof whisky was distilled and sealed up in a commemorative keg at Wheatfield Road.

In 1985 The North British Distillery Company Limited celebrated its first hundred years at Wheatfield Road, when a handsome centenary history was produced, *The N.B.—The First Hundred Years*, written by Leslie Gardiner. It reviews in great detail the formative years of the company, the early problems, and the subsequent blossoming of a company which was established on sound economic judgment and an intimate knowledge of the whisky trade. Following a period of destocking by the industry in the early and mid-80s production started climbing again and reached an all-time record in 1990. In 1993 the 'N.B.' was acquired by a new joint venture company, Lothian Distillers Ltd., owned by its two largest customers Robertson and Baxter Ltd., and International Distillers and Vintners Ltd.

CALEDONIAN BREWERY

The Caledonian Brewery is situated within the wedge of ground bounded by Slateford Road, North Merchiston Cemetery and the railway. It owes its existence to a partnership between two young men in the middle of the nineteenth century. In 1865, George Lorimer, then aged only eighteen, was working in London as a tea broker when he received news that his father, the Dean of Guild in Edinburgh, had died tragically in a fire in the city's Theatre Royal. Young George came north to Edinburgh to support his widowed mother who had several other children to look after. He entered the brewing business where he met Robert Clark, twelve years his senior, who was already an experienced brewer with Alexander Melvin of Boroughloch Brewery. Lorimer and Clark formed a partnership in 1869 and bought an acre of ground at Shandon, where the brewery was built. The partnership did not, however, last long as Robert Clark died very suddenly at the brewery in 1874 when only forty years of age. George Lorimer continued to use the partnership name, and brought his brother John into the business shortly thereafter. George retired in 1918 after nearly fifty years as a brewer and died in 1939, aged ninety-three.

As viewed from Slateford Road, the original office premises were in the small stone building on the left. A red brick building on the right, constructed around 1910, masked the working brewery at the back, but this was demolished in 1994 following serious fire damage. This comparatively small site contained the brewhouse, maltbarns, kilns, the cooperage and various cellars and stables. Two wells, sunk by the specialists, R. Henderson & Co., were in constant use up until around 1914, by which time they had become polluted by shale deposits several hundreds of feet below the surface. Lorimer and Clark changed to using town water and relied on the well supply for washing casks only. In 1891 a siding was constructed from the Caledonian Railway to bring in grain and to take away the beer in bulk. Pale and mild ales, beers and stouts were brewed under two main trademarks 'Merman' and 'Old Caledonia'.

In 1919 Vaux Ltd. of Sunderland acquired a majority shareholding in Lorimer and Clark, which reinforced the brewery's strong connections with the north-east of England. The Slateford Road premises were extended in the early 1960s to give a capacity of 2,000 barrels per week, and tankers were introduced to carry beer in bulk to Sunderland for kegging, casking and bottling. Sadly, the cooperage and most of the cask washing was discontinued at Slateford Road. By 1963 the Caledonian was restricted to two main products, most of which went to the north of England: Scotch Ale was sold as Lorimer's Best Scotch, and Gold Strong Ale was produced solely for bottling. The company's trade name for brewing was changed to Vaux Edinburgh Ltd. There was never a substantial bottling plant at Slateford Road and even the maltings were closed in the 1970s. By the early 1980s two of the original brewing coppers were renewed by new ones of the same design, and one, dating from 1869, is still in use. The coppers were changed from coal-fired to gas-fired in 1984.

The greatest threat to the Caledonian Brewery was, however, in 1986, when Vaux announced the intended closure after more than a century of continuous brewing at Slateford Road. What Vaux had not taken into account in its calculations was the remarkable appeal of the Caledonian Brewery itself, and the dedication of its brewery staff. With the assistance of local politicians and the financial community, a management buy-out was completed in 1987. A new company was formed, Caledonian Brewing Co. Ltd., under its first managing director, Russell Sharp. One of its first tasks was the re-introduction of its products to the local market, including India Pale Ale and the traditional 70/- and 80/- Ale. On 21st June 1994 a serious fire at the Caledonian Brewery caused substantial damage and interruption of production. Fortunately it was not sufficiently serious to jeopardise the future of the brewery.

MCVITIE & PRICE LTD.

The McVitie family had been bakers in Edinburgh for almost half a century before a new factory was built in Stewart Terrace in the early 1880s. A few years later, in 1887, a young man by the name of Alexander Grant came to Edinburgh from Forres, where he had recently completed his apprenticeship as a baker. In the hope of finding a job, he went into one of McVitie's shops, in Queensferry Street, where Robert McVitie was behind the counter. On being told that there were no jobs available, Grant apparently replied 'It's a pity, for I'm a fell fine baker', and, on taking his leave, reduced his chances of a job even further by picking up a scone from the shelf and announcing 'Well, onyway, ye canna mak scones in Edinburgh'. Apparently Robert McVitie was so impressed and amused that he offered Alexander Grant a job. He worked well, but unfortunately his youthful exuberance again took the upper hand, and he left McVitie's to return north, where he set up his own bakery business in Inverness. When the business failed through lack of funds, he returned to Edinburgh, undaunted, and asked Mr McVitie for his job back. Robert McVitie's first reaction was to say 'No', but one of his managers persuaded him to take Grant back, with the plea that he was too good to lose. From that day on, a remarkable business association flourished between Robert McVitie from Edinburgh and Alexander Grant from Forres. In the 1890s Grant became the manager of McVitie & Price in Gorgie, where he produced the first 'Digestive' biscuit. Phenomenal growth occurred after 1902 when a new factory was opened at Harlesden, in London, with four times the capacity of the St Andrew's Works at Gorgie. After Robert McVitie's premature death in 1910, Alexander Grant became General Manager of the new limited liability company. Much of the information, and remarkable insight into the character and business acumen of Alexander Grant, would have been lost for ever had it not been for his meticulous habit of keeping a business diary from 1917 until his death in 1937. In 1973 the diaries were 'rediscovered' by the author James S. Adam, when he was gathering material for *A Fell Fine Baker*, the jubilee book about United Biscuits. Later he reproduced an excellent selection, with a historical introduction in *The Business Diaries of Sir Alexander Grant*. The diaries cover all aspects of Grant's busy life, including finance, sales, ingredients and working practices. He was a man of endless energy, who, no matter how hard he may have driven his managers, drove himself even harder. He was firm but fair, and frequently magnanimous to staff in financial difficulties, even in some cases where others would have said that further assistance was not justified. No better example can be found of his inherent modesty than the diary entry for 3rd June 1924: 'I received a Baronetcy'. Sir Alexander was also a public benefactor, who contributed to many worthwhile causes, including the sum of £200,000, in 1923, towards the founding of the National Library of Scotland, where Sir Alexander's diaries are now held.

In the districts of Gorgie and Dalry, and beyond, many people still recall their employment in a firm which maintained many of the ideals first established by Sir Alexander Grant. Although they did not keep formal diaries, their recollections are worth recording.

J started work at McVitie's in 1918 at the age of 14. His father had worked there before him as head stableman in charge of the delivery horses. J's first job was to grease the trays before they were put in the ovens. He remembers Sir Alexander Grant.

W's father was manager of the chocolate department from 1926 to 1951, during which time he worked closely with Mr Morgan Young to perfect Jaffa Cakes. Sir Alexander Grant's son-in-law was the General Manager, Hector Laing, whose son is Lord Laing of Dunphail.

C started with McVitie's in 1927. She was in charge of cooking the fish. She boiled it up, put it into separate dishes and distributed it round the factory. No, McVitie's didn't make fish biscuits, but they did make biscuits which were very attractive to mice. The fish was for the factory cats which kept the mice under control when the factory was closed.

J worked in the chocolate room in the 1930s when Mr Webber was the boss. The work involved dipping chocolate Digestive biscuits and making Easter egg novelties. Discipline was strictly maintained by Miss Dickson who always 'encouraged' the girls to wear a hat—even on journeys to and from the factory. Every morning the staff nurse came round and patted each girl on the head—not as an encouragement for the day ahead—but to ensure that their hair was tucked into their cap, and that they were not still wearing their curlers!

A When A started in the office in 1933 from Daniel Stewart's College, he earned 12/6d (62 ½p) per week and was expected to wear a 'hard' hat (a bowler) and a collar and tie. Later he became what was then known as a commercial traveller. McVitie's always paid their salesmen well—if they were good.

M began as a junior pay clerk in 1936. One of her first duties was to take a salary cheque up to Mr Morton Young, the manager of a subsidiary, Simon Henderson, in Slateford Road. When the girls in the factory got married, they received a wedding cake baked on the premises.

C joined McVitie's as a packer in 1939 at the age of 14. She earned ten shillings (50p) per week but had to pay 4d (2p) for 'the insurance stamp', leaving her with 9/8d (48p) to take home to her mother. Her mother was very pleased with the extra money as father was on a low wage and there were seven children to keep.

E was employed as a message girl, in 1947, at £1:5s (£1.25p) per week, helping the packers. She also swept the floor, kept the place tidy, and weighed the empty tins. The weight was written on the tins so that the checker could be sure that the full tin contained the correct weight of biscuits. E had reached the position of forewoman when the firm closed in 1969: it was a terrible shock to all the staff as closure had not been expected, or even rumoured.

J was a packer in the early 1950s at a wage of £2:10s (£2.50p). Wages were paid in cash at 11.30 a.m. on a Saturday morning shortly before closure at 12 noon. Staff from the cashier's department came round with a tray, on which wage packets were made up in small shiny tin boxes with lids. Each employee's name was called out and the contents of the tin were handed over without comment or ceremony. The amount was confidential and not talked about: people were on piece work.

G's husband worked at Robertson Avenue as a maintenance engineer from 1950 to 1961. McVitie's were excellent employers who were good to their staff and their dependants. They always had a dinner-dance for ex-employees at Leith Town Hall.

B was a packer in the early 1950s, on piece work. A message girl was allocated to every seven or eight packers to fetch the boxes and the lining paper. There was an art to putting biscuits in a box to the proper weight. If a box was underweight the checker sent it back. The McVitie name on the biscuit had to point in the same direction all the time. A small slip of paper was used to wrap the last three biscuits on the top, to form a tab, to help the grocer to unpack them without breakage. A note of the packer's number was put on each completed box so that a tally could be made at the end of the day. Ginger nuts were the worst job: they were very hard and many of the girls had to tape the ends of their fingers to prevent cuts. All the pickers, packers and message girls wore aprons and caps, laundered weekly at Inglis Green Laundry at Slateford.

M worked in the office on stock records from 1959 to 1966. Two girls were employed full time taking orders from the shops and the commercial travellers. The more remote routes in the north of Scotland were mapped out in advance. McVitie's were 'By Royal Appointment', and every time the Queen was at Holyrood or Balmoral there was an order for ginger nuts.

The factory at Robertson Avenue was closed in 1969 as part of a programme to rationalise production and marketing throughout United Biscuits. Production was transferred to other factories in Glasgow, Liverpool and London. At the time of closure the last chairman and managing director of McVitie & Price was Mr Morgan Young, who had been with the firm for forty-four years. After closure the building was occupied by Ferranti for several years, but, at present, it is vacant awaiting redevelopment.

MACFARLAN SMITH LTD

Macfarlan Smith Ltd., manufacturers of fine chemicals and natural extracts, occupies the extensive Blandfield Works, situated within the railway triangle at the north end of Wheatfield Road. Its current position, as a leading manufacturer of specialised products for the medical profession, is the culmination of a long association with the pharmaceutical industry in Edinburgh. The company's roots go back to the late eighteenth century, and include world-famous names, J. F. Macfarlan, Duncan, Flockhart & Co., and T. & H. Smith.

It is frequently difficult to establish the exact date on which a particular firm commences business, but even allowing for that limitation, J. F. Macfarlan is usually quoted as the oldest of the trio. The evidence, is, however, tenuous in certain respects as highlighted in research done by K. C. Reid, recently Head of Research and Development at Macfarlan Smith. In 1815 John Macfarlan was in business as a 'druggist' at No. 139 High Street, Edinburgh. Around 1824 he took over a pharmacy at No. 17 North Bridge, previously operated by John Moncrieff, with whom he had done his apprenticeship. John Moncrieff's business is shown in the Edinburgh street directories from 1788 and is probably the same firm as is shown in 1777 as John Moncrief, Apothecary, Bridge Street. Later John Fletcher Macfarlan took on an apprentice, David Rennie Brown, who gained the Diploma of the Royal College of Surgeons of Edinburgh. Macfarlan concentrated on the commercial side of the business and Brown dealt with technical and production aspects. This division of labour appears to have worked well, allowing the firm, in 1850, to move to much more extensive premises at Abbeyhill, where they remained for many years.

The second part of the equation is Duncan, Flockhart & Co., of chloroform fame. John Duncan, the founder, was born on 26th August 1780 in Kinross, the only son of a country surgeon. In 1794 he was apprenticed to a druggist in the Lawnmarket, Edinburgh for a period of five years, after which he went to London. On returning from the great metropolis in 1806, he opened his first business in Perth—in direct competition with the city's Lord Provost, who was also a druggist. Duncan's big breakthrough came in 1812, however, when he found a quantity of silver coins, whilst making alterations to a new shop which he had acquired in the High Street of Perth. When melted down, the coins formed a useful investment for the future. John Duncan opened his first Edinburgh shop at No.52 North Bridge around 1820. One of the first apprentices at North Bridge was the young and energetic William Flockhart, who became a partner in 1832. The firm, known as Duncan, Flockhart & Co., supplied the chloroform for Dr Simpson's historic experiment on 4th November 1847. In 1846 a new branch was opened at No. 139 Princes Street, the first apprentice being James Buchanan, who became a partner in 1863, and moved to the North Bridge shop in 1865. He remained at North Bridge until his retirement in 1904 at the age of seventy-three. James Buchanan died in 1909 leaving a wife and several children living in Oswald House which had been built for them in the Grange district in 1876. The last surviving daughter, Margaret Buchanan, died in 1988 and was buried beside her parents in Grange Cemetery.

Duncan, Flockhart & Co.'s factory and laboratories were at Holyrood Road where the main products were chloroform and ether. They also had a drug-growing farm at Warriston, started around the time of the First World War. By 1946 Duncan, Flockhart & Co. were employing about two hundred staff, but in 1952 they were acquired by the third firm in the trio, T. & H. Smith Ltd. In December 1946 H. J. Baker, a senior partner in Duncan, Flockhart & Co., wrote the introduction to *The History of Duncan, Flockhart & Co.*, commemorating the centenaries of ether and chloroform.

T. & H. Smith was, for many years, a family firm established in 1836 by the brothers Thomas and Henry, both of whom were qualified doctors. Various members of the family had been in the pharmacy business since at least 1827, latterly at No.21 Duke Street. When the Duke Street premises became too small, the manufacturing side of the business was moved in 1847 to Blandfield Chemical Works in Lower Broughton Road. It was here that the firm established itself on the Edinburgh pharmaceutical scene, although there were several family feuds on the road to success. After lengthy internal squabbles the business was made a limited company, T. H. Smith Ltd., in 1904. By 1906 the premises at Canonmills had outgrown their usefulness and lengthy preparations began to move the various processes out to Gorgie, where Bernard's Brewery had vacated their original premises. In 1952 *A History of T. & H. Smith Ltd.*, by W. F. Martin, was produced for private circulation only.

The modern history of Macfarlan Smith Ltd. probably begins with the amalgamation of T. & H. Smith Ltd. and Duncan, Flockhart & Co. in 1952. This created a formidable pharmaceutical company whose only real competitor in Edinburgh was J. F. Macfarlan. This potentially

Belladona growing at the Blandfield Chemical Works of T. & H. Smith who moved to Gorgie in 1906. J.F. Macfarlan and T. & H. Smith amalgamated in 1960 to form Macfarlan Smith Ltd., who are still at Gorgie. (Courtesy of Macfarlan Smith Ltd. From *A History of T. & H. Smith Ltd.*)

troublesome situation was avoided by the two companies coming together in 1960 to form Macfarlan Smith Ltd. A holding company was created, Edinburgh Pharmaceutical Industries, which in turn was bought over by Glaxo in 1963. Glaxo implemented several organisational changes between 1965 and 1975: pharmaceutical preparations and the manufacture of tablets were moved from Wheatfield Road to Glaxo's plant at Barnard Castle; and the marketing companies, Allied, Duncan Flockhart and Edinburgh Pharmaceutical Industries were moved to London. The name Macfarlan Smith was retained for the manufacture and sale of pharmaceutical chemicals, and in 1990 a management buyout bought Macfarlan Smith from Glaxo. A holding company was formed, Meconic, which was formerly the cable address and trade mark of Macfarlans. More than two hundred years after John Fletcher Macfarlan completed his apprenticeship with John Moncrieff, the apothecary, the name Macfarlan is still a dominant part of the organisation at Wheatfield Road. In the annual accounts for 1994 product sales were £25 million, a figure which John Macfarlan could hardly have comprehended.

WADDIE & CO. LTD

Waddie & Co. Ltd., whose head office is at No.97 Slateford Road, has been at the forefront of high-quality stationery and printing for well over a century. The firm was established in 1860 at No.11 Waterloo Place by brothers John and Charles Waddie to serve Edinburgh's legal, administrative and commercial establishment. The Waddies were not, of course, without competition as, at that time, there were several well-known names in the world of printing in Edinburgh. John Waddie had previously been with Caldwell Brothers, stationers, at Nos. 13 & 15 Waterloo Place where he simultaneously held three appointments as manager, buyer and chief salesman. He had also gathered a lot of experience during his time with Adam and Charles Black and Oliver & Boyd. Rapid expansion of the Waddie business brought a move, in 1867, to larger premises at No.37 Queen Street, where the brothers were joined by their sister Lilias Waddie, or Ward. A few years later, in 1873, John Waddie resigned from the business to take over a coal business in Leith, on the premature death of a younger brother, Alexander. From then on John ran the business of John Waddie & Co., Coal Exporters, and a new partnership was drawn up between Charles Waddie and his sister Lilias Ward to continue the printing business. One of their first tasks was to purchase ground at St Stephen Street in Stockbridge for a new head office, built in 1875 and expanded in 1893 and 1895. A company booklet issued in 1880 gives an interesting insight into Waddie's philosophy at that time:

> Waddie & Co. have much pleasure in submitting a revised list of their manufactures, and can assure their customers that they were never in a better position to supply their wants, or in their experience have they ever found the markets so favourable to buyers. They also beg to remind their friends that their list price is for first-class material and workmanship, W. & Co., as heretofore avoiding all slop work or job lots of damaged goods.

The booklet lists many of the main customers: Preston Gas Company; Town Clerk's Office, Newton on Ayr; North of Scotland Bank, Keith; and manufacturers in tobacco, snuff, fire bricks, and clay retorts. There was a variety of copperplate letterheads, coats-of-arms and fancy scrolls, many of them enhanced by pictures of factories, ships and other illustrations. The book-binding department was also very well established in 1880, basic lines including account books, postage books and letter books.

The Binding and Finishing Department of Waddie & Co. Ltd., Printers, in Slateford Road in 1960, bears little resemblance to the computerised processes now at Slateford and Livingston. (Courtesy of Waddie & Co. Ltd. From One Hundred Years of Print.)

On 1st July 1890 the firm became a limited company with a capital of £30,000. Waddies continued to expand, eventually doubling the floor area at St Stephen Street from the original purchase in 1875. Despite this, a further move was needed in 1950 to No.97 Slateford Road, where 100,000 square feet of space was acquired in a building previously used by Simon Henderson, the baker. Waddies celebrated their centenary at Slateford Road in 1960 under the direction of their chairman, Marcus W. Ward, who had first joined the firm in 1919. To mark the occasion a centenary history of Waddie & Co. Ltd., Edinburgh and London was written entitled *One Hundred Years of Print.* In the book the company's progress is attributed to working practices in 1960. Heralded at the time as revolutionary, most of them now appear very dated given the speed of technological change over the last thirty years. Each of the main aspects of the business is listed: accounts, design and photography, engraving, die stamping, lithography and transferring, composing, letterpress, binding and finishing, storage and des-

William Robertson Annan, c. 1880, founder of Annan's Printing Works which was at Watson Crescent, Gorgie and West Savile Terrace. (Courtesy of Mrs Helen Annan.)

patch. Since 1960 there have been revolutionary changes in the nature of the business, dictated to some extent by advances in the customers' own technology. By far the biggest change has been the introduction of photosetting in the 1970s which removed, almost completely, the need for compositors and the traditional case room. Computerisation now links all parts of the process, doing away with the need for manual alterations to galley proofs and page proofs. At Slateford Road, Heidelberg multi-colour presses were installed, capable of printing up to six colours in one pass through the system. A purpose-built factory in Livingston was opened in 1987 providing 30,000 square feet of additional space to house the latest rotary web presses. The current workforce of over three hundred employees is divided between approximately two-thirds in Edinburgh and one-third in Livingston, and the turnover has increased fortyfold in the last few decades. In recent years export business has been reduced in favour of an increased UK market dealing with brand labels, posters, advertisements, booklets, annual reports and accounts and a wide range of direct mailing material.

*Annie McPherson, née Sutherland, came to Edinburgh from Golspie, Sutherland, in 1905. She is seen here outside the shop at No. 102 Gorgie Road in 1935. The business is still in the hands of the third and fourth generations of the family. (Cour-*tesy of Donald McPherson.)

MCPHERSON THE FISHMONGER

McPherson, the fishmonger, has been in Gorgie Road for almost ninety years. The business was started c.1905 by Annie McPherson, née Sutherland, who came to Edinburgh from a fishing family in Golspie, Sutherland. The first shop, at No.98, had a small staircase at the back which communicated with the family home on the first floor of the tenement at No.96. The nature of the business was such that an early morning start was essential, every day of the week, except Sunday and Monday. The old tradition of the fish market not opening on a Monday was sacrosanct. In Mrs McPherson's time the market opened at 5.00 a.m., which meant rising very early to prepare the horse and cart for the journey from Gorgie to Newhaven.

Mrs McPherson died in 1939, after which the business passed to her son Donald Sutherland McPherson who had worked in the shop since 1920. The third generation, Donald Alexander McPherson, entered the business in 1951 and now runs it with the assistance of his son, Steven, who began in 1983. Four generations of the McPhersons have, therefore, owned the shop since the early part of the century, firstly at No.98 and later at No.102 Gorgie Road. After such a long time in one family, it is hardly surprising that many anecdotes have been passed down about the business and the character of the people who ran it. Mrs McPherson had come from a hard-working family and had spent the best part of her life looking after her own large family, and building up a business at a time when there were many poor families in Gorgie. The story is often told of how a very young girl appeared in the shop one day with only 2d (less than 1p) and asked if she could have some fish 'for the cat'. A dozen herring were counted into a newspaper and the young girl left the shop looking very pleased with herself. Mrs McPherson knew her customers well—the girl had several brothers and sisters and possibly an unemployed father—but no cat. In the 1930s Donald Sutherland McPherson also ran a small fish delivery business supplying fishmongers on the west side of Edinburgh. He also sold mussels in small waxed cardboard containers to the pubs in and around Gorgie. Methods of refrigeration have improved greatly from the days when the desired condition was obtained from a concrete box with layers of ice, and the front window was kept cool in warm weather by spraying cold water on it from an overhead perforated pipe.

At the present day, fish stocks are still bought first thing in the morning at the Newhaven auctions. Whilst there is a wide variety available,

Edinburgh customers tend to be rather conservative, confining themselves mostly to haddock, herring, kippers, lemon sole, ling, salmon
and occasionally crab. The more unusual fish, which could be available,
include brill, coley, dory, hake, halibut, skate and turbot. In 1989 the
McPhersons extended their business by opening the adjacent shop in
Gorgie Road for fruit and vegetables.

8

Sport

The schools, churches and places of employment have played, and continue to play, an important part in the sporting life of Gorgie and Dalry. Most schools participate in one or more of the main sports—football, rugby, hockey, basketball, tennis, badminton and athletics. Annual sports days are held, and there are frequent visits to the established venues, such as Saughton Sports Complex and Dalry Swim Centre. Youth organisations in the churches still have a strong sporting tradition, although the heyday of the local church football team (such as St Martin's F.C. at the Episcopal Church) appears to have passed. On the industrial front, the greatest impact has undoubtedly been in the bowling world. The oldest bowling club in the district, Ardmillan, was formed privately in 1884, but within a short space of time, local employers were instrumental in setting up other clubs. These included the Caledonian Bowling Club in Russell Road, by the Caledonian Railway, in 1899; Gorgie Mills Bowling Club in Alexander Drive, by J. & G. Cox, in 1904; and the North British Distillery Bowling Club, in Westfield Road, in 1909. The brewing industry were also involved, establishing two clubs in Slateford Road. The green at the Caledonian Brewery is no longer in use, but the one farther west, near the Old Maltings, is home to the very active Fountain Brewery Bowling Club, established immediately after the First World War. Bainfield Bowling and Social Club, with very extensive facilities at Hutchison Crossway, began life as a small private football club in 1919, but changed its allegiance to bowls in 1924.

Dalry Swim Centre (originally Dalry Baths), in Caledonian Crescent, has provided swimming and other facilities for almost a century, and Tynecastle Boys' Club began in the late 1920s when the idea of boys' clubs was sweeping the country. The club is now open to girls and boys and has dropped the word 'Boys' from its title. Saughton Sports Complex, administered by Edinburgh District Council, at Saughton Park, offers a wide range of facilities to schools, clubs and individuals interested in football, tennis, rugby, hockey and athletics. The premier sports facility is, of course, Tynecastle Park, home of the Heart of Mid-lothian Football Club, which also has a Young Supporters' Club. Finally, Gorgie's boxing tradition includes Danny McAlinden, Alan Bonas and Danny McKay.

HEART OF MIDLOTHIAN FOOTBALL CLUB

Many people think of the 'Jam Tarts' as having been at Tynecastle from time immemorial, but, in fact, that is not the case. The Hearts were founded in 1874 by a group of young footballers, whose other Saturday passion was attending the Heart of Mid-lothian dance hall. The hall was in Washing Green Court (later known as Holyrood Square) off the South Back of the Canongate, near the present-day high-rise flats in Dumbiedykes Road. The dance hall took its name from the Heart of Midlothian (the old Tolbooth of Edinburgh) beside St Giles Cathedral, and the football club is said to have taken its name (with the hyphen in the word Mid-lothian) from the dance hall. In establishing their own football club, the lads were greatly influenced by watching an exhibition match at Bonnington between Queen's Park Football Club and Clydesdale Football Club in December 1873. The match was played by Association Football rules which the new Heart of Mid-lothian Football Club adopted in 1874. When the club was first established it had no ground of its own, but used the Meadows along with several other clubs, including its arch-rival, Hibernian. By 1875 the club, captained by Tom Purdie, had forty-five members and held its committee meetings at Mother Anderson's Tavern in West Crosscauseway. In the same year it joined the Scottish Football Association and played in the Scottish Cup for the first time, sporting its original strip of long white trousers and white shirts with a maroon heart.

In more than a century of football, Hearts' fortunes have varied enormously. Within two years of being formed they found themselves desperately short of players, as a result of which the club was disbanded. Many ex-Hearts players joined St Andrew's Football Club, but in January 1877 a remarkable recovery saw Hearts re-emerging and absorbing St Andrew's and its players. Towards the end of the 1870s Hearts and Hibs were emerging as the city's two main football teams, forever locked in a battle for supremacy: on 20th April 1878 Hearts eventually showed that supremacy over Hibs at Powburn by winning 3—2 in the fourth replay of the Edinburgh Football Association Cup Final. Whilst Hearts remained at the Meadows, the club's headquarters were in a shop occupied by Tom Mackenzie, the cricket bat manufacturer, in Chapel Street. In the days before the *Pink News* and the *Green Dispatch*, Tom displayed various football results in his shop window over the weekend. After securing their own ground, first at Powburn (where they beat Hibs!) and then Powderhall, Hearts made the big move to Gorgie in February 1881. The first ground, built on the site of present-day Wardlaw Street and Place, was opened on 9th April 1881, where, for a mere 6d (2½ p), the home side could be seen putting eight goals past the Hanover keeper.

Hearts did not remain at 'old' Tynecastle Park for long, the last match being on 27th February 1886. New Tynecastle, on the north side of Gorgie Road, was opened on 10th April 1886 when Hearts beat Bolton Wanderers 4—1, cheered by a crowd of 5,500 fans. In 1890 Hearts were one of the ten founder members of the Scottish League, but in the first League game they were decisively beaten by Rangers, 5—2, at Old Ibrox Park on 16th August 1890. Greater success attended their efforts in the Scottish Football Association Cup, which they won for the first time in 1891. This triumph heralded the start of what has generally been recognised as Hearts' first 'golden era'. They won the Scottish Football Association Cup again in 1896, 1901 and 1906, establishing an enviable five-year cycle which unfortunately went out of orbit and did not return again until 1956. The golden era also brought the accolade of being League Champions during the season 1894-5 and 1896-7. It was a time dominated by such players as Albert Buick, Willie Porteous, Mark Bell, Charlie Thomson, and, most of all, Bobby Walker, who won the first of his record eleven international caps against England on 7th April 1900. Walker played for Hearts from 1896 to 1913, during which time he played in more than 650 games and scored more than 250 goals. He retired in 1913, became a director in 1920, and died in 1930.

Even golden eras eventually fade. No major trophies were won in the years prior to the First World War, which, of course, brought its own problems. In November 1914 the entire first team, and four hundred men from the ranks of the shareholders and season-ticket holders, enlisted to form C company of the 16th Royal Scots. During the war, Hearts lost seven players, killed in action: J. Allan, D. Currie, J. Boyd, E. Ellis, H. Wattie, James H. Speedie and Tom Gracie. Among those injured was Paddy Crossan who played for Hearts from 1911 to 1925. He later opened Paddy's Bar in Rose Street, which still bears his name. The Hearts' War Memorial at Haymarket was unveiled by Robert Munro, Secretary of State for Scotland, on 9th April 1922. Two years

Hearts 'Terrible Trio' from the 'Fabulous Fifties'.
Clockwise from the top left Alfie Conn, Willie Bauld, Jimmy Wardhaugh, (Courtesy of *The Scotsman Publications Ltd.)*

later the mood was jubilant at the fiftieth-anniversary dinner at the Freemason's Hall, where the club chairman, William Brown, presided over three hundred guests, one of whom was Tom Purdie, Hearts' first captain. On the pitch, the year 1926 saw a near record attendance of 51,000 at Tynecastle with 15,000 fans still in the street when the gates closed. Unfortunately, all the strikes were by Celtic, who beat Hearts 4—0 in the third round of the Scottish Cup. The two most memorable players from around this era were Bernard 'Barney' Battles and, later, Tommy Walker. Battles, who came from Fisherrow, joined Hearts in 1928 and retired in 1936, having scored forty-four goals in the 1930-31 season.

Tommy Walker was probably Hearts' most famous footballer, who would have been the club's most capped player had it not been for the interruption of the war years. When he was appointed assistant manager in January 1949 it marked the start of Hearts' second golden era. Much of the groundwork had already been done by manager Davie McLean, who died in February 1951 before seeing the fruits of his labours. When Tommy Walker was appointed to succeed Davie McLean, Hearts were on the brink of the Fabulous Fifties, dominated by the Terrible Trio—Alfie Conn, Willie Bauld and Jimmy Wardhaugh. The team won the Scottish League Cup in 1954, the club's first major trophy since 1906. This was followed in 1956 by winning the Scottish Football Association Cup, exactly fifty years after having won it in 1906. Only one goal was conceded throughout the competition, to Celtic in the final. Hearts attained their peak of achievement in 1957-58 when they won the League Championship for the third time. A string of successes followed: 1958 League Cup Winners; 1959 League Cup Winners; 1959-60 League Champions; and 1962 League Cup Winners.

After such a high-scoring decade it was almost inevitable that decline would follow—and so it did. Even the 1962 League Cup win was tinged with controversy, when Hearts beat Kilmarnock 1—0 at Hampden. With only a minute left to play, Kilmarnock 'scored' what would have been the equaliser, only to find it was disallowed by the referee, after consultation with the linesman. A Kilmarnock player had handled the ball. The euphoria of the 1950s never returned during the '60s and '70s, which were characterised by constant changes in the team, low attendances and even relegation during season 1976-77. The low morale of the players and the fans was compounded by the team's worst ever defeat by Hibernian, 7—0 during the 1972-73 season. The tide did not begin to turn until 1981 with the appointment of Wallace Mercer as Chairman and Alex MacDonald as manager in 1982. A much

A selection of Hearts' team celebrates in the Charlotte Rooms, South Charlotte Street, after winning the Scottish Football Association Cup in 1956. Left to right: Willie Duff; Tom Mackenzie; Willie Bauld; Jimmy Wardhaugh; Freddie Glidden; Alex Young; Ian Crawford. (Courtesy of The Scotsman Publications Ltd.)

improved level of consistency saw the club finish runners-up three times in the Premier League, qualify for Europe on a regular basis, and provide many players for Scotland's international side. It is Hearts' earnest hope that this formula will shortly produce their third golden era to coincide with the new chairmanship in 1994 and the transformation of the Tynecastle ground to meet the stringent requirements of the Taylor Report. When completed the New Tynecastle Stadium will be an all-seated stadium with a capacity of 19,000 spectators.

ARDMILLAN BOWLING CLUB

Ardmillan Bowling Club is situated in Ardmillan Place, within the triangle formed by Ardmillan Terrace, Henderson Terrace and Angle Park Terrace. When the club was formed in 1884, most of the present-day houses had been built, leaving a small area of ground vacant on the west side of Ardmillan Place. For many years, this piece of ground was used informally as a public park. Its potential was realised around 1882 by two ardent bowlers in the district, James Hay and Davie Craigie, who were members of West End Bowling Club in Hailes Street, at Tollcross. Messrs Hay and Craigie soon built up sufficient support in the Gorgie and Dalry area to start a new club. The ground was purchased from Edinburgh Corporation for £760, and a small clubhouse was built. The pioneering spirit of the two West End members was recognised when their former club presented Ardmillan Bowling Club with their first medal. The Challenge Medal (still played for under its new name the Rink Medal) carries the inscription: 'Presented by the Members of the Edinburgh West End Bowling Club as a mark of their sincere respect for Ardmillan's First President and Vice President, Mr James Hay and Mr David Craigie, 19th July 1884'.

Ardmillan Bowling Club was opened on 17th May 1884 by Senior Baillie Roberts of Edinburgh. Two silver-mounted bowls were used for the occasion, which were returned to the club in 1957 by Baillie Roberts' grandson Ian M. Roberts. The bowls, now too old and vulnerable for everyday use, are kept as a memento in a glass case at the clubhouse. Ardmillan has been particularly fortunate in retaining or repossessing its early mementoes. In 1994, a stranger to the club arrived at the ground one day with an ornate horn, which had been missing from the club for the previous hundred years. It carried the inscription: 'Ardmillan Bowling Club presented by William Roberton Esq., S.S.C., won by Mr William Gray 1894'. Mr Robertson was a solicitor at No.14 Young Street, and lived at No.10 Shandon Street.

In 1974, the original clubhouse was in a poor state of repair and was completely inadequate for the size of the club. It was replaced by a new clubhouse on the same site, providing modern facilities for the membership, which is limited to eighty. At the centenary in 1984 a special programme of events was arranged between 17th May and 26th June. The first event was the Members' Game, opened by the President, R.J. Telfer, using the same two bowls as had been used to open the green exactly one hundred years before.

Ardmillan Bowling Club has always been particular about recording the honours of the club. The honours board in the clubhouse is kept up to date, showing the names of the club presidents and club champions in each year since 1884. Some of the leading players are listed in the club's centenary brochure, *Ardmillan Bowling Club 1884-1984*. G.M. Wilson was club champion in 1886 and 1891, and W. Hogg in 1888, 1894, 1895, 1897 and 1905. Winning the club championship in three consecutive years has been achieved twice in the history of the club: John Arnott (who died as a prisoner of war during the First World War)

Ardmillan Bowling Club was formed in 1884. The first clubhouse, seen here, with various improvements, was in use from 1886 to 1973, after which it was replaced by a modern structure on the same site. (Courtesy of Ardmillan Bowling Club.)

won the championship in 1910, 1911, 1912 and 1914; the second person to do so was A. Taylor in 1927, 1928 and 1929. In more recent times, the club championship has been won no fewer than ten times by J.H. Scott, in 1964, 1968, 1972, 1973, 1975, 1976, 1978, 1979, 1984 and 1985.

According to *The Streets of Edinburgh*, published in 1984, the district of Ardmillan is named after Lord Crauford (1805-1876), who became a Court of Session judge in 1854. He took the title of Lord Ardmillan after his parental estate of Ardmillan in Ayrshire.

CALEDONIAN (EDIN) BOWLING CLUB

The Caledonian (Edin) Bowling Club was formed in 1899 in Russell Road, under its first name Caledonian Railway (Edinburgh) Bowling Club. The early minute books confirm its allegiance to the Caledonian Railway Company which permitted committee meetings to be held in the Ambulance Hall of Princes Street Station. The Company also gave general advice as owners of the ground on which the green was situated. In the first few years of its existence, the club arranged matches against various clubs, few of which still exist: North British Railway,

Gorgie Shepherds, Slateford, Kirknewton, New Grange, Corstorphine, Tynecastle and the West End Police.

In 1906, when membership had increased to almost one hundred, a new pavilion was erected for just over £35, a toolhouse for £2 and a press or cupboard from Dowell's Saleroom for £1. Further funds became available from a series of concerts, usually held in St Cuthbert's Hall. Miss Dalziel, soprano, and Miss Nellie Luck, contralto, were cajoled into giving of their best, provided the fee did not exceed one guinea each. It was further provided that if the artistes felt able to waive their fee, then a cab would be provided, free of charge, to take them to and from the concert hall.

Although the club was clearly begun for railway employees only, the committee was frequently under pressure to admit members who had other employment. In 1920, the committee, consisting of representatives of the Parcel Office, Goods Department, Princes Street Station, Dalry, Gorgie and Merchiston Stations, and Loco Department, refused membership to one J. Cockburn because he was not 'a Railway servant'. This topic was brought up again and again over the years before a decision was eventually taken to allow full non-railway members.

The other matter which occupied a great deal of time at committee meetings was the ambition to build a new clubhouse. This was first discussed in 1923 and again at almost yearly intervals during the 1930s. Although a building fund was set up, there was a disappointing response from the membership. At the outbreak of the Second World War the idea was abandoned, post-war activities being confined to extensions of the existing clubhouse rather than a completely new building. However, the idea was re-introduced in the 1970s when the building fund had reached £10,000. After a series of meetings a purpose-built clubhouse, with a lounge and supporting facilities, was constructed in 1977 in conjunction with Drybrough Breweries.

At the present day, the Caledonian has a membership of 123 which includes a ladies' section established in 1966, and a youth section established in 1980.

GORGIE MILLS BOWLING CLUB

Gorgie Mills Bowling Club is in Alexander Drive, fifty yards from the junction with Gorgie Road. The club pre-dates all of the neighbouring buildings. Westfield Court, known locally as the 'Banana Flats' on account of its curved frontage, was designed in the early 1950s. The

Gorgie Mills Bowling Club at the old clubhouse in 1937, winners of the Water of Leith League, Riddle Trophy. (Courtesy of Gorgie Mills Bowling Club.)

former Poole's Roxy Cinema (now County Bingo) was erected in 1937 on the garden ground of Gorgie House, and the red sandstone flats, with the projecting canopy over the shops, were designed by Alex A. Foote, in 1925, and later developed by the Glass family. Before the construction of these flats, Gorgie Crescent was reached from the north side of Gorgie Road. The small group of very old two-storey houses in the Crescent were given a new entrance from Westfield Road, and were not demolished until many years later.

Already the origin of the name Gorgie Mills is becoming less well known. The club was started on 20th June 1904, following a challenge match between the glue and gelatine departments of J.& G. Cox Ltd., of Gorgie Mills. At that time, Cox's Glue Works was a thriving concern, which had made its presence known in the area for many years on account of the pungent odour emitted during its manufacturing processes. Prior to 1904, works' clubs tended to use public bowling greens, but Cox generously provided the green at a cost of £1,000. The cock, the trade mark of the parent company, was adopted as the club's emblem. The green was constructed quickly and was ready for the opening ceremony by Miss Cox on 20th May 1905. The membership was fifty-two factory members and nineteen associated members. The first president was Major R. Bruce of J. & G. Cox, and the first secretary, Robert Linn. Two trophies were donated at a very early stage in the club's history: the Factory Cup was presented in 1904 by patrons W.C. Smith, K.C., and John Scott Tait, C.A; and the Championship Cup was presented in 1905 by Harold B. Cox and Douglas H. Cox. The presentation of prizes and a Smoking Concert were held in the Old School, Gorgie on various dates up to about 1910.

The close link between the firm and the club was maintained even after ownership of J. & G. Cox was transferred to Bryant & May, the match manufacturers, who set up a trust for the continued use of the green. Unfortunately, in 1969, Bryant & May announced the closure of Cox's Gorgie Mills factory, with the resultant loss of about seventy jobs. Following negotiations, the club was successful in buying the green and clubhouse from Bryant & May for the sum of £5,000. That continuity enabled the club to look to the future with confidence: an extra strip of ground was purchased and a new clubhouse was erected in 1976.

Today the club has 120 full members and 48 associate members, but only a handful remain from Cox's workforce. Gorgie Mills has had five internationalists within its membership, the first being J. Galloway in 1932. Currently there are three internationalists, Alex (Tattie) Marshall, William Dyet and Alan C. Brown. Alex Marshall also won three gold medals in the World Championships at Worthing in 1992: he won gold medals in the fours, pairs, and overall winners' medal (Leonard Trophy) in the Championships.

THE NORTH BRITISH DISTILLERY BOWLING CLUB

On 2nd April 1909, several employees of The North British Distillery Co. Ltd. met in the Wheatfield Street Hall to consider the formation of a works bowling club. The meeting, chaired by Peter McLaren and assisted by A.T. Burns of Andrew Usher & Company's Bowling Club, appointed Charles Napier as the first president, with a committee of eight members. The first subscription of 1/-(5p) per annum attracted a very good response of seventy members, almost all of whom lived in the streets near the distillery in Wheatfield Road. Subsequent committee meetings were held in Tynecastle Church Hall and at the 'Distillery Gate'. The green, at the north end of Wheatfield Road, was provided by the company, enabling the club members to concentrate on raising funds for equipment and other items. Unfortunately, the initial enthu-

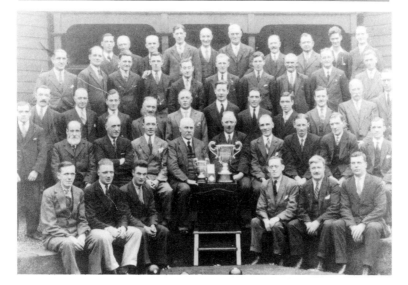

*The North British Distillery Bowling Club, winners of the Usher and League Championship Cups and Open Championship in 1929. (*Courtesy of The North British Distillery Bowling Club.*)*

siasm of the employees was not maintained, causing membership (at 2/- per annum) to fall to only twenty-nine in 1911. When membership dropped even further, to eighteen members during the First World War, the club was temporarily closed in October 1916 and did not re-open until April 1921.

During the 1920s, the club went from strength to strength. New office-bearers were appointed and, by 1930, membership had risen to sixty, each of whom paid a subscription of 10/-, ten times the amount when the club was first started. The annual presentation of prizes was held in the New Markets Restaurant in Chesser Avenue, and donations towards general expenditure were received from The North British Distillery, the Excise Officers, the Green Tree Public House and the Dryburgh Coopers. Matches were arranged, at frequent intervals, against Waverley Rubber Works Bowling Club, Tynecastle Bowling Club, Gorgie Shepherds' Bowling Club and The Grange Works Bowling Club. In 1933, an arrangement was made to allow courtesy membership to the employees of Lorimer and Clark, Caledonian Brewery, Slateford Road, and later a similar arrangement was made with the employees of T. & H. Smith Ltd. (now Macfarlan Smith Ltd.), adjacent to The North British Distillery.

The club celebrated its Golden Jubilee in 1959. A new clubhouse, donated by the company, was officially opened by the Managing Director, Sir Alexander Mathewson, on 20th June 1959. Each of the seventy-six members present received a dram of whisky and two bottles of beer during the afternoon activities, which were followed, in the evening, by a dance in the depot hall. During its long history, the club has played for several cups and trophies. The earliest was the Usher Cup, dating from 1906, which was last played for, and won by The North British, in 1961. The Club Championship Cup was presented in 1949 by George Veitch, a former Managing Director of The North British Distillery.

In 1994 there were fifty-two members, including associate members from Macfarlan Smith. There is also a long-standing arrangement to allow members of the public, of pensionable age, to use the green on most afternoons during the week. They also enjoy the comfort and warmth of the pavilion in the winter months for playing dominoes.

BAINFIELD BOWLING AND SOCIAL CLUB

In 1919, Gilbert F. Nicolson (Gibby) formed the Edinburgh Bainfield Football Club, which took its name from its 'home ground' opposite what was formerly the house of Bainfield in Dundee Street. Bainfield Football Club won the Walker and Cowan Cups in the Juvenile League during the season 1920-21. Despite this promising start, and the comparative youth of some of the winning team, a decision was taken, in 1924, to switch the main allegiance of the club from football to bowls. Apparently, many of those still interested in running the club were getting to the stage where bowls, rather than football, was more in keeping with their physical fitness. The first clubhouse for Bainfield Bowling and Recreation Club was at Harrison Park, at the public bowling green run by Edinburgh Corporation. As membership grew, meetings were held either at Fountainbridge Library or the Keir Hardie Hall, at the corner of Bryson Road and Tay Street.

After many years of deliberation, the club (renamed Bainfield Bowling and Social Club in 1947) secured its own ground in 1951 by the purchase of land from Edinburgh Corporation for the sum of £400. The site was to the east of Hutchison Crossway, and to the north of the railway line which served Cox's Glue Works and Gorgie Slaughterhouses. The unpromising piece of ground was cleared by the voluntary efforts of the members, and the first clubhouse was erected—an old hut measuring 16 feet by 8, expertly divided up to provide a locker

The Edinburgh Bainfield Football Club were winners of the Walker and Cowan Cups in Season 1920–21. In 1924 the club switched its allegiance from football to bowls and moved to Hutchison Crossway in 1951. (Courtesy of Bainfield Bowling and Social Club.)

room, games room, kitchen and function hall. The first green, opened by Councillor Adam Millar on 12th June 1954, was laid at the south-west corner of the ground. The occasion was marked by burying a lead-covered box, containing coins and newspapers, in the south-west corner of the green. From the pedestrian bridge over the railway, the completed green could be seen at a rather oblique angle, which, it is said, was the inspiration for the design of the club badge, the diamond shape representing the green. To cater for increased membership in the early 1950s, the first clubhouse was replaced by two large huts, placed end to end.

At the 1958 Annual General Meeting, the question of improved facilities was raised yet again, as a result of which Willie Lees was elected president, with the remit to erect a brick-built clubhouse. Fund-raising began, and Edinburgh Corporation offered a loan on a 'pound-for-pound' basis against all sums raised by the club itself. After many hours of voluntary labour, led by skilled tradesmen, the new clubhouse on four levels was opened by Lord Provost Duncan Weatherstone, on 25th

July 1964. The complex included a two-rink and a single-rink indoor stadium, locker rooms, toilets, bars, a function hall, and members' lounge, overlooking the original outdoor green.

The most recent development occurred in 1971 when the first outdoor green was lifted and re-laid to the east of the clubhouse. The 1954 time capsule was never found, but a grand six-rink stadium was built on the site, providing all-year-round facilities for club members and visitors from other parts of Edinburgh. To mark the club's sixtieth anniversary, John Wilson, the president, wrote the history of the club, *Bainfield Bowling and Social Club 1924-1984*. In recent years, a video has also been made of the history of the club, based on two 88 mm films, originally shot by club members Peter Whitelaw and John Edwards.

DALRY SWIM CENTRE

The architect, Robert Morham, first submitted his plans, in 1893, for the erection of 'public baths and washhouses', which were completed, in 1895, on the south side of Caledonian Crescent. The petition to the Dean of Guild Court refers to the removal of a small tenement at the east end of the site, and other temporary buildings, to make way for the new baths. The plan provided for a boilerhouse, coal depot, laundry and bath superintendent's house at the west side of the building. The main pool measured 75 feet by 35, and varied in depth from 3 feet to 6 feet 3 inches. There was also a small shallow pool, in which prospective bathers were expected to dally, in the interests of hygiene, before entering the main pool. At pool level, there were changing rooms on the north side, for ladies, and a similar arrangement, on the south side, for men. In accordance with the custom of the times, the pool was fitted with items of equipment, which, in later years, were removed because they were considered to be a danger to the bathers. Perhaps the most adventurous was a series of rings, along the length of the pool, suspended high above the water from hooks in the ceiling. They were used as a trapeze by young boys, and others, who jumped onto the first ring, built up momentum to reach the second ring, and so on until either they fell off into the water, or met someone coming the other way. There was also a chute, a high-dive and a springboard at the east end of the pool.

Hot, private baths, located around the balcony, were very popular with local people, whose houses were built, originally, without baths. Patrons could choose between first class, at 1/3d (6p), and second class,

The staff of Dalry Baths in Caledonian Crescent in 1905, with superintendent Baillie (father of Charlie Baillie) in the centre and his wife on the left. The Baths were opened in 1885 and were extensively modernised in 1993. (Courtesy of Tommy Jamieson.)

at 9d (4p), both of which lasted for half an hour. First-class patrons had the luxury of unlimited hot water, whereas those opting for second class had to make do with the bath being filled once only. A small piece of carbolic soap was provided free, but more refined soap, and towels, could be hired for a small sum. When it was busy, the attendants chalked the expiry times on the outside of the doors, to remind them when to call 'time'. Frequently, there were long queues of people waiting for a bath, particularly on Friday nights at the end of a long week, working with beer, whisky, rubber, sawdust or glue. For many men, and women, it was the only way to prepare for an evening at the Palais de Danse. Some of the older men, who had gone to the pub after their work, frequently fell asleep in their baths, and had to be wakened by the attendant. As local houses were refurbished, the need for the private baths declined, and they were discontinued around 1980.

In 1991 Dalry Baths were closed for repair work and modernisation. It was discovered that extensive maintenance was required, estimated at many thousands of pounds. The old private baths and laundry were removed and new changing rooms, a general purpose room, and a cafeteria were built. Also provided was access for the disabled, a crèche for children, and innumerable inflatable toys for use in the water. The baths were re-opened by Lord Provost Norman Irons on 12th February 1993 as Dalry Swim Centre.

For many years, Dalry Baths have been the home of the Grove Swimming Club. Its exact date of founding is unknown, but it was probably in 1901, under its full name, Grove Swimming Club and Humane Society. The first patron was the Marquis of Linlithgow, and the first president was the Rev. R. Sangster Anderson. Committee meetings were held in the Mission Hall at No. 117 Grove Street, but membership was confined to males only, even although a Miss Boyd was a member of the management committee. A proposal, in 1909, to form a Ladies' Section was postponed for further consideration. The club was very strong in the 1920s and '30s. At the time of its 25th anniversary, in 1926, the question of the Ladies' Section was raised again. Prior to that, the Section appears to have been formed, but allowed to lapse. In 1928, when membership was nearing two hundred, the treasurer announced that: 'We are working to build up our finances to such a point that we would be able to work on the interest which would accrue, and we would strike out and take our place as the premier club of the east'. At the time the balance in hand was £64. To augment that sum, extra funds were raised from various social events, one of which was held in the Westfield Halls in 1932. For 2/- (10p) per head, the committee was promised 'the use of the hall, a presentable tea, fruit and cigarettes'. On a vote being taken, the anti-smoking lobby won the day, and the event went ahead at the reduced charge of 1/6d(7p)— without the cigarettes. In the same year, the Ladies' Section was again re-established, an amount of £31 being advanced for the purchase of eight dozen swimming costumes. It is not recorded what effect that substantial outlay had on the treasurer's interest! At the outbreak of war in 1939, the club was closed and did not re-open until 1946.

During the 1960s, the Grove went through a process of redefining its rules and regulations, with a view to imposing stricter discipline, and improving the performance of the swimmers. A proposal, by the Men's Section, to combine with the Ladies' Section, was considered at length by the ladies, but declined. The question of a joint club was brought up again in 1968 and eventually agreed on 8th August, the committee being 'a little doubtful as to the parents' views on mixed bathing'. As the Grove nears its centenary, membership is now about forty. There is a full programme of events, and competitions are still held for various trophies, including the Boyd Trophy and the Kent Richardson Trophy.

British sportsmen and women at the 1924 Paris Olympic Games. First from the left in the back row is Charlie Baillie, the swimmer, from Grove Swimming Club. First from the right, in the middle row, is Eric Liddell, the runner, of Chariots of Fire *fame. (*Courtesy of Grove Swimming Club.*)*

Throughout the years, the Grove has had many good swimmers, but none better than Charlie Baillie, whose father was the first Baths Superintendent. Charlie, born in 1902, was Scottish champion in the 50 and 100 yards championships every year from 1920 to 1926. He also won several English championships when he later moved to Oldham. The highlight of his career was, however, the 1924 Paris Olympics, the Games in which Eric Liddell, of *Chariots of Fire* fame, also competed. Unfortunately, Charlie was beaten in the heats, but the experience of the Olympic Games remained with him for the remainder of his long life.

In addition to the Grove Swimming Club, other newer clubs use the facilities at Dalry Swim Centre. These include the Edinburgh Octopush Club and the Edinburgh Synchronised Swimming Club. The Edinburgh Octopush Club moved to Dalry Swim Centre in November 1993 after a short time at Leith Academy and South Queensferry High School, where it began, like many other octopush clubs, as a pool exercise for the sub-aqua club. The club now has about forty members (seniors and juniors) made up of swimmers, divers, rugby players, water-polo players and karate experts.

Octopush, or underwater hockey, was invented in 1954 by Alan Blake, a diver with the Southsea sub-aqua club. It began as an enjoyable way for divers to keep fit during the less active winter months, and has developed into a worldwide sport. Originally it was played with eight persons in a team, which is the basis of the name, octopush. It is a non-contact sport, played under water by two teams, not exceeding ten players each, only six of whom are in the water at the same time, while the other four remain as substitutes. Players are equipped with a mask, a snorkel, rubber fins, a pusher, a glove for the playing hand—and a strong pair of lungs. The idea is for each team to keep control of the lead puck, or squid, by passing to one another across the bottom of the pool, until a gull (or goal) is scored. Each team defends a three-metre-wide metal gulley at its own end of the pool: when the puck or squid passes over the metal lip and into the trough behind, a gull is scored. During the match, which lasts thirty minutes each way, players must surface regularly to take in air. The teams also wear different coloured swim suits, gloves and pushers to help with identification under the water. There are two underwater referees and a chief referee who remains at the side of the pool. In 1968 the first National Octopush Championships were held in Great Britain and in 1976 the British Octopush Association was formed to control the sport, which now has nearly 3,000 participants in 120 teams nationwide. The first World

The Grove Swimming Club held their Christmas party at Dalry Baths in 1965.
They have been resident at Dalry Baths since 1901. (Courtesy of The Scotsman
Publications Ltd.)

Championships were held in 1980 in Vancouver, Canada.

The Edinburgh Synchronised Swimming Club was formed at the Royal Commonwealth Pool in 1971, and was affiliated to the East District of the Scottish Amateur Swimming Association in 1972. The club, now with a membership of around forty, settled at Dalry Baths in 1990, after being at several other locations in the city. At least three of its founder members are still prominent in the sport: Mrs Helen Murray has been national convenor for Synchronised Swimming, and was president of the Scottish Amateur Swimming Association in 1994; Mrs May Laidlaw is currently the East District convenor for Synchronised Swimming and has judged several events; and Miss Helen Elkington is also a judge (at national and international level) as well as being a coach and swimming lecturer at Bedford College. The club has two honorary presidents, Lady Heatly and Jack Snowdon, both of whom have been involved in the Edinburgh swimming scene for many years. One of the original swimmers, Cath Fleming, is still coaching at the club. Over the years, club members have participated at national and international level, Caroline Chambers being selected for the G.B. Junior Squad.

Jane Liston and Sarah Burgon were also selected to represent Scotland at the 1994 Commonwealth Games in Victoria, Canada. They took fourth place in the Duet section, a commendable achievement considering that the medallists were all full-time swimmers. The club also had the honour to provide the swimmers depicted on the Single European Market stamp produced by the Royal Mail in 1992. The stamp shows the club swimmers at Glenogle Baths in Edinburgh, forming the shape of a star fish.

TYNECASTLE CLUB (TYNECASTLE BOYS' CLUB)

Boys' clubs began to appear in greater numbers, throughout Scotland, after the First World War. They met in church halls, school halls or wherever accommodation could be found. The earliest recorded boys' club in Scotland was in 1913, in the Pleasance in Edinburgh. In 1927 the Edinburgh Union of Boys' Clubs was formed, to which individual clubs were affiliated for a small annual subscription. The main function of the Union (which changed its name in 1974 to the Lothian Federation of Boys' Clubs) was to train officers and leaders, and to arrange inter-club activities.

Tynecastle Boys' Club had its origins in Tynecastle School in the late 1920s, when Norman Murchison, one of the science masters, held a small informal club in the school building, where local boys could go in the evening to build models from Meccano sets. Other activities were incorporated, as a result of which Tynecastle Boys' Club was formed in 1928. Initially, membership (at 2/- or 10p payable by instalments) was limited to former pupils of Tynecastle School. The headteacher was the honorary president, and by 1930 the club had fifty members involved in gymnastics, badminton, football, swimming and drama. The club leader was assisted by three adult helpers and a boys' committee of four or five members. Meetings were held in a small hut in the playground, although the boys had access to the gymnasium for their main activities. There was very little equipment beyond that which was provided by the school. At the end of the Second World War, the club was run by Jim Aitken who had joined, as a young boy, in 1929. After the war (1945) membership was widened by including boys who were not former pupils of Tynecastle School. Further expansion took place in the early 1960s after Tynecastle Boys' Club amalgamated with Tynecastle Athletic. By that time, the membership was such that new premises were essential. The club moved to Gorgie Road, opposite Westfield

Road, where they occupied the building previously known as 'the tin school' to the west of Gorgie School. The club remained there until 1980 when it moved to self-contained premises in the playground of Balgreen School in Balgreen Road.

The modern history of the club is centred at Balgreen, where an astroturf surface has recently been laid for the combined use of the club and the pupils of Balgreen School. In 1990 the word 'Boys' was removed from the club name to allow girls to join, and there are now more than one hundred members engaged in football, pool and table tennis. Many of the inter-club fixtures involve travel throughout the United Kingdom and abroad. Over the years, the club has produced, and hopes to go on producing, many national and international sports competitors. To date these include: Graeme Souness, who played football for Tynecastle Boys' Club in the 1960s; Peter Cormack who played for Hibernian and several English clubs; and Paul Hegarty of Hamilton Accies and later Dundee United.

GORGIE'S BOXING TRADITION

Gorgie's early boxing tradition has been documented over the years by Brian Donald, author, critic and boxing referee, who lived in Wardlaw Street as a boy, and attended Tynecastle School. Although many young lads from Gorgie tried their hand at the noble art, far fewer made any progress in this highly competitive sport. Among those who did were Danny McAlinden, Alan 'Jock' Bonas and Danny McKay.

The story of Danny McAlinden is told by Brian Donald in his book *The Fight Game in Scotland*, in the chapter entitled 'The Boy From Gorgie Who Biffed Ali's Brother'. The event occurred on 8th March 1971 at Madison Square Garden, New York, where the main event of the evening was Muhammad Ali versus Joe Frazier for the undisputed heavyweight championship of the world, with commentator, Burt Lancaster. On the same bill was Ali's younger brother, Rahman Ali, who was taking on the 'blond bomber' from Wardlaw Place, Edinburgh— Danny McAlinden. Brian Donald recalls that McAlinden won the fight in much the same way as he had fought as a young boy in Gorgie—by wading in with fists flying until his opponent was eventually worn down. Danny McAlinden lost his British heavyweight title to Bunny Sterling in 1972 but won the Irish heavyweight title in 1979.

Alan 'Jock' Bonas was born in Yorkshire in 1919 and made his debut, in 1943, at the age of fourteen, when he was paid the sum of five shillings (25p) for appearing. He acquired the nickname 'Jock' whilst serving in the army with a Scottish regiment, after which he settled in Edinburgh. As a professional boxer in the late 1940s he was rated number seven among the world's featherweights by *Ring*, the American boxing magazine. Jock emigrated to Australia in 1951 where he caused a sensation by outpointing Australia's Empire Championship contender, 'Bluey' Wilkins. In 1954 he returned to Edinburgh where he bought a newsagent's shop at No. 200 Gorgie Road. He continued his interest in boxing by running an amateur club at Dalry House in the late 1950s.

Another great boxer with a Gorgie background was Danny McKay who was born in Bonnyrigg in 1921. When Danny was young, the family moved to No. 8 Stewart Terrace in Gorgie and then to a slightly larger flat, at No. 7. The new flat had a bed-closet which greatly eased the sleeping arrangements for the family of two adults and nine children. Mr McKay sent one of his older sons, John, to boxing lessons at Charlie Cotter's in Leith Walk, and when it came Danny's turn, at age eight or nine, he attended Sid Stanley's gymnasium at Damhead Farm in Gorgie. The 'gym' consisted of the top floor of Sam Robertson's hay loft, which was reasonably well equipped with punch bags and lifting-weights. By age sixteen, Danny had aspired to fight in his first boxing booth (opposite the Palais de Danse in Fountainbridge), run by the Stewart family, who specialised in travelling entertainment. The booth was a fairly temporary structure, made of timber and canvas, capable of holding over 300 standing spectators, with the ring at one end. Sometimes the evening's entertainment would be a professional boxer taking on an amateur 'would-be' boxer, over a few short rounds. Seldom, if ever, did the amateur's ability match his initial confidence, and, frequently, a bout was stopped in time to prevent injury, if not embarrassment. Professional fights were also properly billed and organised, drawing a large crowd, especially on Saturday nights. When the crowd were particularly appreciative, they threw coins into the ring to be shared later between the contestants.

Danny McKay became a professional boxer in 1937 at age sixteen, and boxed at flyweight, bantamweight and welterweight until he retired in 1952. During that time he fought in many of the big stadia throughout the United Kingdom and abroad; he also boxed for the Royal Air Force during the war years; and he won fifty-five of his first sixty professional bouts. In 1946, at the height of Danny's career, the Edinburgh boxing journalist, Bill Cairns, declared that 'in a boxing experience going back to the days of Tancy Lee, Alex Ireland and George

Danny McKay, the boxer, in 1948, when he was fighting at welterweight.

McKenzie, I have not seen an Edinburgh boxer with such a dynamic glove as big, right-hand puncher, Danny McKay'.

Gorgie's boxing tradition has continued to the present day with featherweight Alistair Kidd, who boxes for Meadowbank Amateur Boxing Club. The Club has been very successful, through its trainer, Graham White, in producing three Scottish amateur heavyweight champions in recent years, and several other Scottish amateur champions.

SAUGHTON SPORTS COMPLEX

There have been sports facilities at Saughton Park since Edinburgh Corporation purchased Saughtonhall estate in 1900. Substantial upgrading occurred in 1974, however, on the opening of Saughton Sports Complex on the west side of the playing fields. A commemorative plaque, inside the sports pavilion, confirms that it was officially opened on 16th November 1974 by Councillor Russell A. Fox. The Complex is now administered by the Department of Recreation of Edinburgh District Council. At the time of the Commonwealth Games, in Edinburgh, in 1986, the facilities at Saughton were again upgraded, and used as a warm-up location for the Games athletes. These facilities have since been enjoyed by a large section of the public, but, unfortunately, the intended velodrome was never built. The pavilion provides several changing rooms, showers, equipment stores and a small office for the administrative staff. Outside, there is a six-lane synthetic track for athletic events, an astroturf surface for 11-a-side football, and another astroturf surface for two 5-a-side football pitches, which can be converted to three tennis courts. All facilities are open to the public but, because of their popularity, a simple advance booking system has been introduced. Many schools and other groups use the Complex, which can accommodate most athletic events, rugby, football, tennis and hockey. The Heart of Midlothian Football Club also assists in coaching youngsters on Saturday mornings and during school holidays, when up to 150 children attend each session. In addition to the many individuals and smaller groups, two clubs use Saughton Sports Complex as their home base: Corstorphine Amateur Athletic Club and Edinburgh Athletic Club.

The Corstorphine Amateur Athletic Club (C.A.A.C.) was formed in 1986 from North Merchiston Amateur Athletic Club, by a group of people, mostly resident in the Corstorphine area of Edinburgh. It has since been discovered that the name Corstorphine Athletic Club was in use many years ago by a similar organisation, no longer in existence, but there is no direct connection between the two. A nucleus of thirty or forty people founded the 1986 club, which has since increased to almost two hundred, males and females, from the age of nine, upwards. The club is currently sponsored by T.S.B. Bank Scotland P.L.C., and is administered by a committee of parents and senior athletes of the club. All track and field events are included in the summer programme, and in the winter there is cross-country running, road running and indoor training. Males and females are divided into seven separate groups, by age, the youngest being nine to eleven, and the oldest, 'the veterans', being forty-plus. There is participation in several leagues: Forth Valley Athletic League; Scottish and North West Athletic League; Scottish Indoor League; Scottish Cross Country Union; Scottish Women's Cross Country Union; and others. The club has represented Scotland, the District and the Edinburgh Schools at various events in the sporting calendar. It also makes annual awards to the best Junior and Senior athletes, and operates the Thistle Award scheme promoted by the Scot-

The girls of Corstorphine Amateur Athletic Club at the club's annual award ceremony in 1994. (Photograph by David Kingston, Studio 16 Photography.)

The boys of Corstorphine Amateur Athletic Club at the club's annual award ceremony in 1994. (Photograph by David Kingston, Studio 16 Photography.)

tish Athletics Federation. Corstorphine Amateur Athletic Club is a comparatively young club, which, in its first decade, has established the basic foundations of a progressive athletic club, steadily improving its position in the various leagues to which it belongs.

The Edinburgh Athletic Club was formed in 1961 by the amalgamation of three very famous Edinburgh clubs: the Edinburgh Harriers, founded in 1885, and based at Ford's Road; the Edinburgh Northern Harriers, founded in 1889, with clubrooms at Greenside Place; and the Edinburgh Eastern Harriers, founded in 1922, and based at Meadowbank and Hawkhill. This formidable group was given further impetus, in 1962, when Braidburn Athletic Club also joined.

In the early years of the combined club, the younger age groups did particularly well in cross-country running, the senior boys winning the Scottish championship in 1963-64, and the youths winning in 1964-65. The ladies were equally successful in track events, including Esther Watt, the Scottish internationalist, Marion Donachie, the Scottish champion at 440 yards, and Barbara Tait, the Scottish champion at 1 mile. After the 1970 Commonwealth Games in Edinburgh, club membership grew significantly, at the start of what turned out to be a very successful decade. The men were Scottish cross-country champions for four consecutive years from 1973, and on the track were Scottish League champions each year from 1976 to 1980. It was a time of individual achievement as well as team success: Brian Burgess was Scottish high-jump champion from 1976 to 1981, and won a bronze medal at the Commonwealth Games in Edmonton in 1978; David Wilson was Scottish high-jump champion from 1970 to 1972, and a champion hurdler, representing Great Britain in the Munich Olympic Games in 1972; and Drew McMaster was a member of the team which won the gold medal in the 4 x 100 metres relay, at Edmonton. In 1974, Edinburgh Athletic Club won the world record in the 24-hour ten man x 1 mile relay, the best performance coming from Joe Patton who contributed 31 miles, averaging 4.44 minutes for each mile.

Throughout most of the 1980s, the ladies maintained their position in Division 1 of the Scottish League. Mary Anderson was a strong all-rounder: Scottish shot putt champion; Scottish 400 metres champion; and Scottish Heptathlon champion. Other good athletes included Pat Devine (400 metres), Penny Rother (Scottish cross-country internationalist), Alison Grey (shot putt) and Karen McLeod (10,000 metres). Pride of place among the ladies, and indeed the club, must, however,

go to Yvonne Murray who has competed in every major championship, the Olympic Games, European Games, Commonwealth Games
and World Championships. At the 1990 Commonwealth Games in
Auckland, Edinburgh Athletic Club had three representatives: Yvonne
Murray won a silver medal in the 3,000 metres; Ian Hamer (competing
for Wales) won a bronze medal in the 5,000 metres; and Karen McLeod
completed the 10,000 metres, despite sustaining a cracked rib in a col-
lision with another athlete very early in the race.

At the present day, Edinburgh Athletic Club, which trains at Saughton
and Meadowbank, has over 300 members, males and females, from age
nine to over eighty. The men's team are one of only two Scottish clubs
who compete in the British League, the premier league in British athletics. It is also the only club in Scotland to have two teams in the
Panasonic Scottish Men's Athletic League, (one team in Division 1 and
a B team in Division 3). The boys compete in the Scottish Young Athletes League and the Forth Valley League. The ladies compete in the
Bank of Scotland Women's Athletic League and the Scottish Cup, while
the girls take part in the Forth Valley League and the newly formed
McDonald's Young Athletes League for Girls. Edinburgh Athletic Club
also organises several events each year, including the Octavian Relays
(the largest relay event in Scotland), a 10-kilometer Road Race, and
the Queen's Drive Races. Several members of the club are experienced
judges at both track and field events.

9

Entertainment, Leisure and Education

Between 1912 and 1937 the districts of Gorgie and Dalry saw four cinemas opened: the Haymarket, the Tivoli, the Lyceum and the Roxy. Three of them were closed in the early 1960s because of falling attendances, and the survivor, the Tivoli, lasted for only another decade. Both the Tivoli and the Roxy became bingo halls. Although the demise of the picture houses was unfortunate, their loss has more than been made up for, in other ways. There has been a huge increase in the number of Centres providing activities for a wide range of people—at Dalry House, St Bride's, McLeod Street and Gorgie Memorial Hall. In addition to that, two very different newcomers to the district have attracted a lot of interest, at Gorgie City Farm in Gorgie Road and at the Adult Learning Project in Dalry Road. At the west side of Gorgie, Saughton Gardens has maintained its popularity over the years, as has Balgreen Library, and Fountainbridge Library in Dundee Street.

HAYMARKET CINEMA

In the districts of Gorgie and Dalry, the Haymarket was the oldest and the smallest cinema, but one of the longest to survive. In April 1912 a petition was put to the Dean of Guild Court by James Rae King, C.A., and George Clunie Macgregor as trustees of the Haymarket Picture House Company. They were asking the Dean of Guild Court to agree a scheme 'to take down existing stable and sheds; alter two existing one-storey shop buildings and erect a picture house with brick walls, steel roof and entrance buildings all at 90 and 92A Dalry Road'. Plans, prepared by Alan L. Goodwin, the architect, of No. 12 Queen Street, Edinburgh were approved by the Court on 11th April 1912 and building work commenced almost immediately. The ground on which the cinema was built belonged to Messrs John Watherston & Sons, Builders, whose main works were in the adjacent lane. It was an unusual site to develop, approximately T-shaped with a narrow frontage, and the main auditorium at the rear, parallel to Dalry Road. There was a small entrance hall off Dalry Road, with the pay box on the left, leading to an oval-shaped crush hall, lit by a large cupola. Beyond the crush hall, passageways ran on each side of the manager's office to the main auditorium which seated 675 patrons.

The Haymarket opened on 13th December 1912 and soon acquired its nickname, 'the Haymie'. The early films featured many of the well-known stars of the day: cowboys Tom Mix, Buck Jones and W.S. Hart who 'enjoyed great popularity in a series of Westerns as a mature, solemn faced defender of truth, justice and the honour of good women'; comedians Harold Lloyd, Buster Keaton and Andy Clyde; and Pearl White 'who invariably ended up tied to the rail track or locked in a burning building to be rescued next week'. Between the main film and the supporting one, the Haymie ran variety acts by semi-professional artistes. Monday night was a testing time for all. About half-a-dozen separate acts were included and the best one (judged by audience appreciation but without the refinement of a clapometer) was retained for the remainder of the week. There was no permanent stage at the Haymie, which meant that a heavy platform had to be moved into position at the front of the auditorium at the appropriate moment. Several strong men pulled and pushed to the accompaniment of 'heave, heave' by an impatient audience. Among those who appeared on stage were McNulty, the Dulcimer King, and Bob Williamson who performed his 'light patter routine' to an appreciative audience, some of whom made chocolate biscuits with him during the day at McVitie's along the road. Chorus nights were also a great favourite. The resident band played popular tunes, the words of which came up on the screen, with a small ball bobbing up and down on the words to keep the audience in time—if not in tune! The band violinist, Adam Haddon, was a star in his own right, appearing at the Palladium Theatre in East Fountainbridge in full Highland regalia as Ken Lomond or Mons Haddon.

After the Second World War the Haymie was renamed the Scotia, re-opening with *Bonnie Prince Charlie* starring David Niven in the title role. For maximum effect the outside of the cinema was tartan-clad and a piper played in Dalry Road. The last show was on 29th February 1964 with John Wayne and Maureen O'Hara in *The Wings of Eagles*, supported by Stewart Granger and Rhonda Fleming in *Gun Glory*. When the cinema closed, the Dalry Road frontage was retained as a retail shop.

TIVOLI CINEMA

Prior to 1913 Begbie's Farm and Dairy lay on the north side of Dalry Road, a few hundred yards west of the junction with Murieston Road. Its development potential, in a densely populated area, had not escaped the notice of a group of local entrepreneurs. John Robertson, the builder, R. Raymond and Bobby Walker (of Hearts fame) combined forces to build the first Tivoli Picture House. It opened on 26th August 1913 with the intention of providing a combined programme of films and variety acts, which included Will Fyffe, Harry Gordon, the Houston Sisters and Tommy Lorne. In the days of the silent pictures, the official accompanist on the piano was frequently required to compete with a boisterous and over-reactive audience, especially when there was a breakdown in projection. Alistair James, writing in 1954, recalled that 'the resumption is greeted with a tumultuous roar from the delighted patrons of the Tiv who have been, on the whole, fairly patient and have been for want of a diversion, stamping their feet, lifting bairns to better seats, peeling oranges, whistling or singing the latest hit, discussing the Hearts or trying to read their *Evening News* by the rather dim lights'. Sound equipment was installed at the Tivoli in 1929 and in the early 1930s the cinema underwent a complete transformation. In May 1933 the Robertson family obtained permission to partly demolish and rebuild the old cinema, in accordance with plans drawn up by the architects, John McKissack & Son of No.63 West Regent Street, Glasgow. The new auditorium was planned for 1,146 seats, 882 in the stalls and 264 in the balcony. It opened on 1st January 1934 with *King of the Jungle*, a film of animal life with Buster Crabbe as the leading star. Celebrations included a private demonstration of the new sound system 'R.C.A. Photophone, which relayed orchestral music, dialogue and natural sounds'. A short film was also shown of the demolition of the old Tivoli and the erection of the New Tivoli on the same site. The Robertson family, who had been associated with both cinemas since 1933, sold the New Tivoli in 1961 to Milne Theatres of Dundee. The last show was on 28th July 1973 with Charlton Heston in *Planet of the Apes*, supported by *Escape from Planet of the Apes*. From then on the only escape was a night at the bingo, first operated by Kingsway Minor Bingo.

LYCEUM CINEMA

The Lyceum Cinema was built on the west corner of Robertson Avenue and Slateford Road, its high-profile frontage having a commanding corner entrance and wings along Slateford Road and down Robertson Avenue. The architect was Charles Mitchell of No.2 Randolph Crescent, Edinburgh, who incorporated into the design an orchestra pit, a mezzanine floor to house the projection room, and a balcony floor for an extra 350 patrons. The idea of building a cinema on that corner was first considered by a company called The Lyceum Cinema (Edinburgh) Ltd., of No.7 Merchiston Place, who petitioned the Dean of Guild Court in July 1924. The grand opening, on 8th November 1926, was by the Lord Provost, Alex Stevenson, and the first programme included *The Greater Glory* and *Too Much Wife*. It continued as a popular film venue for a quarter of a century but like many other cinemas suffered badly from reduced attendances in the early 1960s. A report in *The Scotsman* for 1st April 1961 quoted a spokesman for A.B.C. saying that the cinema would close on 8th April 1961 as low attendances had made it uneconomic to continue. Ironically, the last programme was *No Kidding* and *The Man who was Nobody*. After the Lyceum closed it had an unfortunate experience as a bingo hall. It was gutted by fire on 18th May 1963 only hours after 300 bingo enthusiasts had vacated the premises. The following year Leggate & Co., the garage and car salesroom proprietors, obtained permission to have the remains of the old cinema demolished and a new car saleroom built. After Leggate's garage closed in 1990 the site was redeveloped by Teague Homes as Lyceum Apartments. The imposing block, with a strong hint of a modern-day Scottish tenement, was designed by J. & F. Johnston Ltd., of Leith and constructed in 1992. It consists of fifty-two flats on four floors, incorporating a corner clock tower, glazed curtain walling to light the stairways, glazed canopies over the entrances, and iron railings enclosing the small front gardens.

POOLE'S ROXY CINEMA

When the Roxy Cinema opened in Gorgie in 1937 the Poole family had already been involved in the cinema business for several decades. In the late nineteenth century Charles W. Poole had a very successful business, travelling the country with his panoramic shows, from his home base in Gloucester. Edinburgh was one of the main venues on the circuit, where the Synod Hall in Castle Street (now the site of Saltire Court) attracted large attendances. The Diorama show consisted of the re-creation of historic scenes on large painted canvases, which were moved across the stage as the three-dimensional story unfolded. These silent 'moving stills' were accompanied at various stages by learned commentary, bright lights, special effects, and a small orchestra playing patriotic tunes. The show was particularly successful in Edinburgh where it continued long after films were introduced.

The Poole family opened the Roxy Cinema on 20th December 1937 with James Stewart in *Seventh Heaven* and Dick Foran in *Sunday Roundup*. It was an ambitious scheme in that the Roxy was built as a district cinema, far out of the city centre, and in an area already well provided for by the Haymarket, the New Tivoli and the Lyceum. The Roxy, designed by Chadwick Watson and Company of Yorkshire to seat 1,600, was in keeping with the trend towards more sophisticated venues. Its interior was not heavily ornamental, but relied for effect on a unique lighting system which was capable of subtle colour changes at the press of a button. It was particularly effective during the interval, the traditional time for ice-cream and chocolate. The Roxy was planned by Charles W. Poole's son John R. Poole, but on completion the management of it was entrusted to the next generation J.K.S. Poole, known to most Gorgie audiences as Jim. Jim Poole still recalls the comparatively low attendances in the early years when the cinemagoers of Gorgie regarded the Roxy with a certain degree of suspicion. Any lingering doubts were soon swept away, however, when Jim Poole began the Mickey Mouse Club for children. Donning his Mickey Mouse emblem round his neck, Jim would welcome the audience with 'Hi ya, members' and smile broadly at the immediate response, 'Hi ya, Chief'. Once the children were captured, the adults soon followed.

In the early 1950s cinemas in general came under a lot of pressure, both from the film distributors and the public, whose life-time habits were changing. The arrival of television and greater home comforts meant that people stopped going to the pictures automatically but waited to see a particular film of their choice. In 1953 the Roxy installed a wide screen 35 feet by 18 for the introduction of Cinema-Scope by Twentieth Century Fox. The intended stereo equipment was resisted by the Poole management on account of the high costs involved: in fact the Roxy's own sound system coped very well with Cinema-Scope after minor adjustments. Falling attendances throughout the 1950s and early 1960s were eventually responsible for the cinema's closure on 7th December 1963, a mere twenty-six years after it had opened. Prior to closure, Jim Poole had experimented for a few months with cine-bingo which combined a film and a bingo session in one evening, but the idea was not successful. It was found that a bingo audience and a film audience

Poole's Roxy Cinema on the corner of Gorgie Road and Alexander Drive in the late 1940s. The Roxy opened in 1937 and closed on 7th December 1963. (Courtesy of The Scotsman Publications Ltd.)

were not necessarily the same people. After turning the Roxy over to bingo only, in 1964, Jim Poole sold out his interest to Scotia Investments about two years later. The building is now used by County Bingo.

BUFFALO BILL

More than a decade before the first cinema came to Gorgie and Dalry, the district played host to one of the silver screen's biggest attractions—Buffalo Bill. At 5.00 a.m. on Sunday 7th August 1904, three specially chartered trains pulled into Princes Street Station and offloaded 500 horses, 800 staff, a canvas village, tons of provisions, and Colonel William Frederick Cody, alias Buffalo Bill, and his Wild West Show. The entourage quickly spilled out into Shandwick Place for the short journey out to Gorgie, where they pitched their tepees and loaded their rifles, long before most of the citizens of Edinburgh were even awake. The spot chosen was a piece of waste ground near Gorgie Station where the City Fathers, anticipating the ambush, had already erected an amphitheatre, providing cover for 18,000 spectators. During the week-long event, 140,000 people made their way to Gorgie, by train or cable car, for the performance of a lifetime—twice daily, 'rain or shine', with night performances 'brilliantly illuminated by special electric light plants'. Successive audiences were enthralled by re-enactments of Custer's Last Stand, a stagecoach hold-up by Indians, and an attack on a settler's cabin. Between shows, the public could partake of a pipe of peace with Chief Iron Tail and Chief Lone Bear around the many camp fires, whilst the squaws busied themselves about their domestic duties. The event was hugely successful, everyone anxious to catch a glimpse of the legendary Buffalo Bill—an imposing, mature figure six feet in height, with greying hair curling from beneath a white stetson, and wearing a buckskin, festooned with his tools of trade—a hatchet, a long knife, ammo pouches, and a well-notched rifle.

On 13th August the show closed as abruptly as it had opened, and moved to pastures new at Falkirk, Dunfermline and Kirkcaldy. The Wild West Show toured the world for nearly thirty years, by which time Buffalo Bill was at an age where the stirrup presented more of a challenge than the Indians. He died in Denver on 10th January 1917, a few weeks short of his 71st birthday. In 1946 the Edinburgh press highlighted an interesting sequel to the grand Wild West Show of 1904. At the conclusion of the Second World War, the police authorities offered an amnesty for the return of illegally held guns and ammunition. Among the many weapons handed in was one with a potted history of its life and times, a Winchester repeating rifle, owned and used by Buffalo Bill during his visit to Edinburgh in 1904.

Cody was a man of action long before the days of his travelling Wild West Show. Born in Iowa in 1847, he earned his nickname, Buffalo Bill, by hunting the buffalo to provide meat for the labourers building the Kansas Pacific Railway between 1876 and 1878. It is said that he killed over 4,000 buffaloes in eighteen months. He was also a scout for the United States Army and fought in the Civil War.

GORGIE CITY FARM

Gorgie City Farm occupies a two and a half acre site on the south side of Gorgie Road, immediately west of Springwell House. For many years the site was occupied by Edinburgh Corporation Cleansing Department who had railway sidings constructed in such a way that the horse-drawn road carts could tip the refuse straight into the waiting railway wagons. The original cobbled roadways still form the main thoroughfares through the farm. The site subsequently became derelict be-

Gorgie City Farm gives children and adults of all ages the opportunity to see a wide range of animals which they would not otherwise see at close range. The farm was opened in 1982 and attracts over 100,000 visitors, free of charge, every year. (Courtesy of Gorgie City Farm.)

fore being rejuvenated by the establishment of the farm as a Community Project in 1982 from an idea mooted, a few years earlier, by the local people of Gorgie and Dalry. It is now a recognised charity, and in the course of the year it attracts over 100,000 visitors, free of charge, many of them children seeing live farm animals for the first time.

The natural gradient from Gorgie Road enhances the site and provides numerous vantage points. Altogether there are over two hundred animals, including a cow which calves each year, two Shetland ponies, numerous goats, pigs and sheep, ducks, hens, pheasants, turkeys, bantams, rabbits, guinea pigs and tortoises. Depending upon their size and needs, some animals are content in wired enclosures with timber hutches, whereas others, like the pigs, require more robust accommodation. Towards the back of the farm there is ample open grazing for sheep, goats, ponies and, of course, the cow and calf. Whatever their requirements are, they are provided, and there is constant supervision by permanent staff. Regular visits are also made by the staff of the Royal Dick Veterinary College at Bush Estate, to ensure that the animals are fit and healthy. Fortunately, vandalism is rare, but some chickens have been lost to prowling foxes, even in the middle of the day! In addition to the animals, there is a large vegetable garden, a greenhouse, and a wildlife garden adjacent to Gorgie Road. In 1994 a substantial sum of money, granted by Lothian and Edinburgh Enterprise Limited, was used to tidy up the ground nearest to Gorgie Road and to establish the beginnings of a wildlife garden, with a pond, a meadow area, a small coppice and some dense woodland. The vegetable garden produces a wide variety of herbs, potatoes, brassicas and root crops, all grown organically and benefiting from the farmyard manure produced by the animals. Many of the vegetables are sold to a vegetarian restaurant in town, which completes the cycle by donating all its kitchen waste back to Gorgie City Farm, where it is avidly consumed by the pigs.

To the right of the main pedestrian entrance is Jemima's Pantry. Until 1991 it shared the available accommodation with the visitors' centre but when that was moved, the restaurant was extended and upgraded. Its position, adjacent to Gorgie Road, makes it accessible to passing trade as well as to visitors to the farm. Beside Jemima's Pantry is the workshop and craft room where classes are held in woodwork, spinning, weaving, pottery and basket making: and beyond is a picnic and play area laid with forest bark. The largest covered area is in the centre of the farm next to the stable and sheep house. A new interpretive centre with a discovery room and a classroom, costing nearly £70,000, has recently been completed, and was opened on 3rd September 1994 by the television personality, Jackie Bird. The ground floor contains numerous information boards and is to be equipped with an exact model of Boghall Farm, on the Bush Estate, which also has an educational centre and farm trails open to visitors. The upper floor is laid out as a lecture room and project room for visiting school pupils and others. In the course of the year many thousands of school children and college students visit Gorgie City Farm, either as an educational day out or as part of a curriculum project. Conducted tours are arranged for a small charge, depending on the numbers involved. The part-time Education Officer also deals with special projects weeks, which concentrate on specific topics, such as butter and cheese making. There are also three special open days annually, usually in April, June and September, offering demonstrations and activities related to agriculture. Although admission to the farm and centre is free, there is an optional membership of £5 per annum for each family unit which, it is hoped, will build up a nucleus of people interested in the running of the farm.

The administration of Gorgie City Farm is independent and is in the hands of a management committee of about sixteen members. A minimum of six members are elected from the general community, four

Jackie Bird, the television personality, unveils the commemorative plaque at the open-
ing, on 3rd September 1994, of the new interpretive centre, discovery room and
*classroom at Gorgie City Farm. (*Courtesy of Gorgie City Farm.*)*

come from educational bodies and others are invited to attend as experts in particular areas, such as finance and farming, or as representatives of local government. The management committee deals with broad
policy and there are various sub-committees to deal with particular
areas of responsibility. There is a small permanent staff and several volunteers. About 75% of annual running costs are met jointly by Lothian
Regional Council and Edinburgh District Council, but capital projects,
such as the interpretive centre, must be funded from donations and
sponsorship. The farm produces an annual report, maintains a five-year
development plan and has a written mission statement of its objectives.

SAUGHTON ROSE GARDENS

Saughton Rose Gardens extend to approximately 3.5 acres, bounded
on the north by Saughton Public Park, on the south by the Water of
Leith and Gorgie Road, on the east by Balgreen Road and on the west
by Ford's Road. Both the Gardens and the adjacent Public Park formed
part of the estate of Saughtonhall, purchased in 1900 by Edinburgh
Corporation from the previous owner Sir William James Gardiner Baird.

Approximately half of the original 98 acres was used for housing, the remainder being developed for public use. Shortly after acquisition, the land was used for the 1908 Scottish National Exhibition, for which an imposing entrance and bridge were constructed at the junction of Gorgie Road and Balgreen Road. At the present day the bridge is no longer used for vehicular access to the Gardens in view of its proximity to the traffic lights. The new car park entrance from Balgreen Road is much more convenient but has tended to re-orientate the lay-out of the Gardens.

The car park gives direct access to the new Winter Garden. This alloy, single-span glasshouse was erected in 1984 to replace an old nineteenth-century glasshouse, contemporaneous with Saughton Hall Mansion. On 7th September 1984 the new Winter Garden was opened by Lord Provost John McKay, who acknowledged assistance from several do-nors: the Stanley Smith Horticultural Trust; the Royal Caledonian Horticultural Society; the Mushroom Trust; Tom Farmer of Kwik-Fit; the Young Women's Christian Association; Tom Sinclair; and James Crow and Sons. There are also two memorial seats: one for Tom Sinclair and the other for Willie Hall, who was a park patrol officer at Saughton.

Immediately to the west of the Winter Garden there are several orna-mental gardens, traversed by a broad walkway, running north and south, with gate pillars at each end. The walkway divides the available ground unevenly so that the section nearest to the Winter Garden is much smaller. This smaller section, however, contains a Rose Garden, the Italian Garden and the Garden for the Blind. Unfortunately many of the statues and urns in the Italian Garden were vandalised some years ago, but the Garden for the Blind has a wide variety of plants selected for their scent and texture. On the west side of the walkway, the larger piece of ground has another Rose Garden, an area of mixed flowers, dahlias, rose trials and a herbaceous border. In the course of the year about 75,000 annuals are also planted out and replaced in the autumn by spring displays.

In the centre of the westermost Rose Garden there is a ten-foot-high sundial dated 1899. It has a stepped base on which there is a biblical text, a splayed column, and it is capped by a short obelisk. Unfortu-nately, the gnomons, or short projecting angles which cast the shadow, have been vandalised over the years. The number and variety of the inscriptions on the sundial give it a positive identity. There are four proverbs round the base: God is Light; To Die is to Live; Tak Tent O Time Ere Time Be Tint; and the stonemason's conundrum—Goa Bou Tyo Urb Us In Ess. To solve the riddle it is best to forget it and just Go

*This elegant sundial, photographed in 1975, with innumerable proverbs and inscriptions, stands in the centre of Saughton Rose Gardens, on ground once occupied by the policies of Saughton Hall Mansion. (*Crown Copyright: RCAHMS.*)*

About Your Business! Above the proverbs are four additional inscriptions, not obviously designed to encourage frivolity: As a shadow so doth life pass; Alas how fleeting while thou lookest I fly; I mark but the hours of sunshine; How quickly the pleasant days have passed away. There is evidence to suggest that the sundial has not been at Saughtonhall since 1899. In Volume XXVII of the *Book of the Old Edinburgh Club*, published in 1949, A. Niven Robertson reviews the Saughtonhall sundial in his informative article entitled 'Old Sundials in and near Edinburgh'. His description and accompanying photograph do not relate to the sundial now at Saughtonhall.

At one time there was also an ornamental iron bandstand built on open ground between the Rose Gardens and the lodge house at the Ford's Road entrance. The bandstand was removed some time ago because of vandalism, but the main structure is in storage and capable of being re-erected. The only remaining parts of the Mansion of Saughton Hall are the stables and outhouses now used by the Parks Department. The house fell into disrepair and was badly affected by dry rot. In 1952, on the instructions of the owners, Edinburgh Corporation, Saughton Hall Mansion was deliberately destroyed by fire and razed to the ground under the supervision of the Royal Engineers and the Fire Brigade.

DALRY HOUSE DAY CENTRE

The early history of Dalry House in Orwell Place has been dealt with in Chapter 1. The house, dating from 1661, was gifted to the Edinburgh and Leith Old People's Welfare Council, in 1963, by the previous owners, the Scottish Episcopal Church. Almost immediately, an appeal was started to raise £50,000 for renovations, which had increased to £100,000 by the time the building was opened by Her Majesty the Queen on 17th October 1967. A plaque, commemorating the opening, was unveiled by Queen Elizabeth, and a casket, containing objects from the 1960s, was sealed into an old wall. In addition to newspapers for 3rd March 1966, fifty everyday items were buried, including a plastic raincoat, a penicillin vial, a packet of contraceptive pills, a petrol lighter, a ballpoint pen and an electric light bulb.

Since it opened in 1967, Dalry House has been run as a day centre for the elderly, by Edinburgh and Leith Old People's Welfare Council, whose principal aim is 'to promote and assist in the welfare of elderly people in Edinburgh and its environs'. It is administered by an executive committee, elected on a three-yearly basis, and receives funding

An enthusiastic group at the re-opening of Dalry House by Her Majesty the Queen on 17th October 1967. Dalry House is run as a day centre for the elderly by Edinburgh and Leith Old People's Welfare Council. (Courtesy of The Scotsman Publications Ltd.)

from Lothian Regional Council Social Work Department. Other sources of income include membership fees, and donations from a wide range of businesses, trusts and individuals. The Council is a charitable organisation established in 1941, which has two other day centres in Edinburgh: Lamb's House in Burgess Street, begun in 1961; and Stockbridge House in Cheyne Street, begun in 1975. In addition to the three day centres, the Council has two residential homes, Strathearn House and West Coates House, and over forty social and lunch clubs throughout Edinburgh.

Dalry House is run as a day centre and lunch club, offering a varied programme of activities for men and women over the age of fifty. Normal weekly activities include swimming (at Dalry Swim Centre), Yoga, dancing, bingo, painting, handicrafts, pottery, aromatherapy, cooking and a variety of musical entertainment. Most of the 300 members, who all pay a small annual fee, are able to travel to and from Dalry House independently. An additional day care facility is available, at a daily charge, which provides transport, lunch and a caring service at Dalry House. The ground floor of the building contains the dining room, the annexe where the day care people meet, a small shop, offices and toilets. The first floor has a large function hall for dancing and keep fit, and also contains the historic King Charles Room. Its ornate plaster ceiling depicts several crests and shields, the initials C. and R. and the date 1661. The fireplace lintel bears the dates 1668 and 1778. The top floor of the building houses the hairdressers, the chiropodist, baths and showers, a snooker room, a television room and an office for Age Concern Edinburgh.

A number of special events were arranged at Dalry House in 1992 at its Silver Jubilee. An open day was held on 4th September with various stalls, games for children, face painting and a bouncy castle in the playground of Orwell School, next door. Well over £1,000 was raised which was augmented by other activities throughout the year.

ST BRIDE'S CENTRE: SPRINGWELL HOUSE CENTRE

St Bride's Community Education Centre was set up in the former St Bride's Church building in Orwell Terrace in May 1977. Its main objects are the advancement of education and the provision of facilities for recreation, which are in the interests of social welfare, and are intended to improve the conditions of life of the people in the area. In these objects, the two Centres have been eminently successful. There is a controlling Association and a Centre Advisory Group, whose main function is to keep the programme under constant review. Funding is by Lothian Regional Council Education Department, in addition to the income from class fees. The varied programme takes place at St Bride's Centre in Orwell Terrace, and at Springwell House Centre in Ardmillan Terrace.

As over 25% of the local population are at, or over, retirement age, it is appropriate that the Centres provide activities for older age groups. There are film shows, a lunch club, tea dances, carpet bowling and St Bride's Travel Club, which organises coach trips in the summer months. There are also 'over 55' groups for singing and drama. In March of each year, the 'Gie it Laldy Festival' produces a week-long programme of entertainment and educational topics. In the past there have been concerts, photographic exhibitions, cookery demonstrations, talks on old Edinburgh, a music and film quiz, aromatherapy and bingo. One of the most interesting events, in 1994, was a debate under the title, 'The National Health Service is past its sell-by date', between a team of senior citizens and a team of senior pupils from Tynecastle High School.

The adult education programme includes art, keep fit, Yoga, tap dancing, Scottish country dancing, ballroom dancing, musical keyboard,

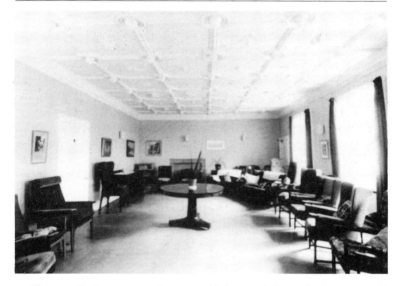

*The King Charles Room at Dalry House with the beautifully restored plaster ceiling, bearing the initials C. R. for Charles II and the date 1661. (*Courtesy of Edinburgh and Leith Old People's Welfare Council.*)*

public speaking, the history of cinema and 'alternative' history. There are also classes for English as a second language, and drama for the unemployed. Classes specifically for women include self-defence, keep fit, art and a mother and toddlers' group.

Young people, between the ages of 8 and 16, are also catered for, all subjects having some degree of creative involvement. These include art, sculpture, sewing, Asian cooking, summer photography and video film-making. Music also features highly, with separate classes for keyboards, guitar, and a junior choir. A newcomer to the field, intended for 15 to 20-year-olds, is Alternative Nightschool, which has a constantly changing syllabus. Past subjects have included Assertiveness for Young Women, Philosophy for Beginners and Reggae Workshop. Drama is represented by the junior drama group, and the Lothian Youth Theatre, which has recently earned itself a reputation well beyond its home base. One of its latest productions, *Deacon Brodie*, by George Williamson, played to a full house of appreciative theatregoers at the end of 1994.

Theatre and cinema have been established at St Bride's and Springwell House for several years. Recent theatre productions have included a wide range of talent and interest: an evening of song, dance and music in the Bright Eyes Variety Show; Savourna Stevenson and Ally Bain, leading exponents of harp and fiddle, with a special tribute to Robert Louis Stevenson; *H. M. S. Pinafore* by Edinburgh University Savoy Opera Group; *A Little Older*, a sensitive play exploring the relationship between Sandy and Isla, through school, adolescence and adulthood, by the Clyde Unity Theatre; and 'physical slapstick, verbal comedy and bare-faced cheek' in *The Wheel* by the Rejects Revenge Theatre Company. Some years ago, the Springwell Theatre Group staged a very successful, and apt, play *The Magdalene*, also by George Williamson, which told the story of Gorgie's own Magdalene Asylum, a home for fallen women, set in nineteenth-century Edinburgh. The St Bride's Film Festival is an annual event which began in 1992. Recent films have included: *Chariots of Fire; Ring of Bright Water;* and *Land of the Pharaohs.*

Both St Bride's and Springwell House actively encourage people with special needs and learning difficulties to get involved with as wide a range of activities as possible. The Centres also provide a focal point for other local organisations, notably the Adult Learning Project and the Dalry-Gorgie Drama Group. St Bride's is also involved in various aspects of multicultural work, which includes Asian sewing, dancing, conferences, and a festival 'Many Rivers', held annually in October, and featuring various shows, talks and educational events.

MCLEOD STREET LEISURE CENTRE

McLeod Street Leisure Centre was set up in 1981 in the former public washhouse building, in McLeod Street, immediately opposite Tynecastle School. It was the culmination of many months of effort by volunteers and professional advisers. The Centre is managed by the Tynecastle Community Association, which is composed of volunteers from the community, and representatives from local government. The building has been converted into a large sports or function hall on the ground floor, and a small hall on the first floor. The building is owned by Edinburgh District Council, who share funding with Lothian Regional Council.

Many of the sporting activities arise from the Centre's affiliation to the Lothian Federation of Boys and Girls Clubs. These include basketball, table tennis, short tennis, uni-hoc (indoor hockey), badminton and volleyball. There is also cross-country running held at Meadowfield, near Duddingston; a golf tournament played at the Braid Hills; rugby sevens at Walkerburn; indoor five-aside football at Meadowbank; a swimming gala at Wester Hailes; and an athletics championship at Saughton, to mark the close of the season. Other events include angling, chess,

*One of the many community activities at St Bride's is an extensive children's pro-gramme which includes a) a film-making class and b) a keyboards class. (*Courtesy of St Bride's Community Education Centre.*)*

six-aside cricket and an inter-club general knowledge quiz held at various venues.

The main function hall, and the smaller hall, are available for children's parties, exhibitions and other events. There is also a regular youth club, for 8 to 16-year-olds, who compete under the title, Gorgie Vale Thistle Club.

GORGIE MEMORIAL HALL COMMUNITY CENTRE

Gorgie 'Mem', as it is affectionately known, occupies the former church building, off Gorgie Road, to the west of Wheatfield Street. The ground on which it was built was originally part of the lands of Murrayfield and Damhead, belonging to Sir Archibald Murray, who granted a separate feu, in 1855, to Archibald Islay Campbell of Succoth. In 1877 the trustees of Sir George Campbell granted a charter to Gorgie Free Church Mission, who erected the present building, known for many years as the 'Little Church in the Field'. Further details of its ecclesiastical history are given in Chapter 4. When the Free Church moved to their new building in 1896, the old church was used by other denominations, before being selected as the site of the Gorgie War Memorial, at the end of the First World War. The building was bought by Edinburgh Corporation in 1938.

Its modern history begins in the 1980s after the hall had gone through a stage of being under-used. It was hoped that a programme of renovation would attract Urban Aid, but, unfortunately, that was not successful. However, the necessary alterations were started in 1983 using people employed on community service. Within a relatively short time the hall was transformed from its previous image of 'a dowdy wee hall with a stage and a piano', to a modern Community Centre. The stage was removed, a coffee bar was installed, the floor was relaid and the decoration was enhanced. The Centre is administered by the Gorgie War Memorial Hall Community Centre Association, which has a management committee composed of members of the community, and is attended by representatives of local government. Funding is by Lothian Regional Council, although the committee actively seeks support from grant applications, and from local businesses for specific projects when required.

Gorgie 'Mem' runs a full programme of daily and weekly events for the community. On a daily basis there is a mother and toddler group, a child-minding group, a lunch club for elderly people, and an after-school day-care facility for children between the ages of 5 and 11. Weekly

Happy smiling faces among 5–6 year-olds from McLeod Street Leisure Centre, in 1988, for the British Amateur Gymnastics Association First Course Certificate. (Courtesy of Davie Cunningham.)

activities include: karate for girls and boys (from age 5 to 11); kickboxing for men and women; step aerobics; Scottish Slimmers; planning meetings for the Gorgie-Dalry Festival; and a Saturday market with individual stalls. It is also a popular venue for birthday parties, wedding parties (including Asian weddings), Asian sari sales, and children's Christmas parties.

ADULT LEARNING PROJECT

The Adult Learning Project (ALP) has been at No. 184 Dalry Road since September 1980. It was founded in 1977 by a small group of local women, supported by a neighbourhood community worker and a community education worker. In its first year, there were more than 200 applicants, most of whom had expressed an interest in classes in O-level English, and Yoga. Lothian Region's Community Education Department made an application, on behalf of the group, for Urban Aid funding, which was granted for an initial period of three years from 1979 to 1982, and then extended for a further period of two years. Urban Aid funding was met 75% by central government (the Scottish Education Department), and 25% by local government (Lothian Regional Council). At the present day, ALP is funded mainly by Lothian Regional Council's Community Education Service, assisted by other grants, and income from its own fund-raising activities. From an early stage, ALP was, and still is, an experiment in applying the principles of the Brazilian adult educationalist, Paulo Freire. This entailed making a conscious decision to move away from vocational and leisure-and-recreation classes, towards classes aimed at exploring themes and concerns identified by the members themselves. Judging by the number of participants, and the variety of subjects tackled, ALP considers, with some justification, that the experiment has been successful, albeit with some modifications. The ALP Association is the organising group, made up of students and staff, which decides broad policy, the curriculum, and charges. By joining a project group, each student automatically becomes a member of the Association. ALP differs from most educational establishments in that students have a greater say in what they will learn, and in the choice of activities undertaken by ALP. To assist in the running of the organisation, the Association is always keen for people to get involved in any of the three main task groups, namely the Business Group, the Communications Group and the Social Group. Staffing consists of two education workers, one administrator and about a dozen part-time tutors.

The first major investigative project carried out by ALP, over a six-month period in 1980, was Living in Gorgie Dalry, which in turn led to three learning programmes: The Family Today; You and the School; and On Being Scottish. Later investigations included Health and Wellbeing, Parents and Authority, Popular T.V., and Living with Change in Gorgie Dalry, all of which produced other learning programmes. A Writers' Workshop was established in 1981 and a Photo Workshop in 1982.

ALP's programme for 1994-95 has been arranged under the general title 'Making Sense of Scotland', which deals with the economic, political and social aspects of life in Scotland. In the History section, a new group, Rootes, is undertaking an oral history project, recording the living memory of Scotland's most recent past, by interviewing ordinary people who have lived through significant events of the century. There are also classes on Politics, Scotland's Cultures, and Gaelic. Photography Groups in ALP have already held a number of local and national exhibitions under the titles, Tenement Life, Scotland and its People, and Images of a Generation. The Writers' Workshop continues its programme of poems, stories, songs, plays and novels. Participants are encouraged to share their work in a supportive atmosphere. Women's Studies are also included, with separate sections for Writing, Music and

*The Photography Group of the Adult Learning Project discusses the selection of photographs for another exhibition, 1991. (*Courtesy of the Adult Learning Project.*)*

the study of Scottish Women, Past and Present. The Scots Music Group is particularly strong, covering a variety of instruments and abilities, but all contributing to a programme of concerts, ceilidhs and pub sessions. ALP also runs residential Study Breaks, Weekend Schools and Summer Schools.

Over the years, ALP has been involved in various publications: *From Margaret to Mary*, by Rose Brown, is a tour of the Royal Mile, featuring the contribution of women to national and local history. Over forty women are mentioned including Lady Glamis, of witchcraft fame; Susan Ferrier, the novelist; and Flora Stevenson, the pioneering educational-ist, whose name is remembered in Flora Stevenson's School at Comely Bank. *Unco Fou in Auld Reekie* is a short, but interesting, study of the history of alcoholic over-indulgence in eighteenth-century and early nineteenth-century Edinburgh. The most recent publication is *The ALP History Journal*, first issued in 1994. It plans a series of articles on the social and economic history of Scotland. The most comprehensive book is, however, *Living Adult Education*, with the sub-title *Freire in Scotland*, by Gerri and Colin Kirkwood. It provides a very detailed description of the work of the Adult Learning Project in Dalry, with particular emphasis on how it has adopted (and adapted) the philosophy of Freire.

FOUNTAINBRIDGE PUBLIC LIBRARY

When Thomas Nelson, a son of the founder of the famous printing works in Edinburgh, died in 1892 his philanthropic work was already well documented. Among many other ventures, he provided £50,000 to build the Nelson Halls in Edinburgh. By a useful coincidence the city's library services were looking to expand into new areas, and the opportunity was, therefore, taken to combine the two aims. Libraries and Nelson Halls were established at Dundee Street in 1897, Stockbridge in 1900 and McDonald Road in 1904. In 1914 a Nelson Hall, without a library, was built at St Leonards. The Nelson Halls, administered by the library service, were open to the public from 9.00 a.m. to 9.00 p.m., excluding Sundays, as reading rooms and a place to play games, such as draughts, chess and dominoes. Although the Halls were principally reading rooms, they were also used for a variety of meetings, particularly music evenings first established at Dundee Street on 21st February 1901.

The first library and Nelson Hall, on the corner of Dundee Street and Murdoch Terrace, was a comparatively modest building of two main storeys, but it was well patronised. By the mid-1930s, when the library was bursting at the seams, a decision was taken to demolish the building and erect a new library and Nelson Hall, more in keeping with local requirements. In August 1937 tenders were called for, to demolish the old building and to build a new one following the drawings of the architect J.A.W. Grant. Readers were advised to return books by Saturday 9th October 1937, otherwise they would need to take them to Central Library on George IV Bridge. Progress was remarkably good in the early stages. No sooner were the books safely removed to other libraries, than Charles Brand, the demolition contractor from Dundee, was selling off the more valuable fittings: cheap for immediate removal; apply to the foreman on the job; panelling, leaded glass, lino, tiles, sinks and even w.c.'s. On 24th November 1937 a photograph appeared in *The Evening Dispatch* showing the shell of the old building being demolished.

During 1938 work proceeded satisfactorily on the new Art Deco-style library. The sculptor, Charles d'Orville Pilkington Jackson, was commissioned to design an ornamental overdoor for the main corner entrance. Following initial instructions, he produced drawings showing an elegant fountain and a bridge, which he exhibited to members of the library committee. To his dismay he learned that the proposed name Fountainbridge Library had been changed to Dundee Street Library. However, as the drawings were at an advanced stage, and had won the general approval of the committee, it was decided to revert to the more picturesque name of Fountainbridge. What the committee does not appear to have done was to research the origins of the name Fountainbridge. Its earliest derivation is, in fact, Foullbridge, taken from a bridge near the top of Grove Street which crossed the Dalry Burn, a tributory of the Water of Leith. The burn was little more than an open sewer, but gradually the more acceptable name Fountainbridge was adopted from the well of spring water near the old Foull bridge. Confirmation of the name Foullbridge can be found in a Scottish Record Society publication *Monumental Inscriptions in St Cuthbert's Churchyard* which lists Baillie Robert Mitchel, portioner of Foullbridge, who died on 20th May 1730 in his 63rd year. Fortunately, aesthetics triumphed over historical accuracy and Pilkington Jackson's completed work depicts a fountain below a bridge, rather than a sewer pipe!

By May 1939 the library was at an advanced stage of construction, but as no announcement had been made about an opening date, Councillor Mrs Graham decided to make an official complaint at a public meeting in the Keir Hardie Hall in Tay Street on 18th August. By the end of the year, despite the outbreak of the Second World War, the opening date was set for March 1940. At 3.00 p.m. on 11th March the new library and Nelson Hall was opened by Lord Provost Henry Steele. From the stock of 30,000 books, the Provost was presented with the first book issued by the library—a specially bound copy of *Haunting Edinburgh* by Flora Grierson. In a sobering speech, Treasurer Darling alluded to wartime restrictions by reminding the assembled company that 'many of us would have found these months of black-out intolerable had it not been for the consolation and comfort of books'. The Nelson Hall, incorporated in the building, provided a reading room and a games room with thirty tables. The children's room and a reference library for thirty readers were located on the top floor. A commemorative plaque, brought from the old building, carries the inscription:

> The first of the Nelson Hall Concerts was given here on 21st February 1901 by Robert Finnie McEwen of Bardrochat who as a trustee of the Nelson Halls Bequest initiated the concerts and inspired them.

The musical evenings were particularly popular for many years and are still held on an annual basis at McDonald Road Library.

At the present day, to provide equal opportunities for all individuals, Fountainbridge Library is contained on the ground floor of the building, with good access and facilities for the disabled, ethnic language collections, integrated children's and reference sections, and a large newspaper and magazine selection. Increasingly, access to information is gained by computer networks. There are computers, accessible to the public, for catalogue searching, community information, word processing and printing facilities, and children's games, in addition to the library's own online book issue and cataloguing system. Part of the library accommodation has recently been refurbished as a meeting room, named the Bainfield Room, after the mansion of Bainfield, which stood to the south of the library building. The Bainfield Room is available for community meetings, as well as being used for library events such as multicultural evenings, children's entertainments, 'meet the author' sessions, and large travelling displays. The first floor of the building is occupied by the Scottish Book Centre.

THE SCOTTISH BOOK CENTRE

The Scottish Book Centre opened on 24th January 1992 on the first floor of the Fountainbridge Library building. The idea of the Centre was first mooted in 1988 to meet the growing needs of the publishing industry in Scotland. The Centre is home to the Scottish Publishers' Association, the Edinburgh Book Festival, Book Trust Scotland, the Scottish Book Marketing Group and Readiscovery 95. It also incorporates the T.C. Farries Room, equipped for meetings and conferences of up to forty people, which was gifted to the Centre by T.C. Farries & Co. Ltd., a major, Dumfries-based book supplier to libraries. In the main corridor of the building there is a list of the Centre's sponsors, which includes the Scottish Arts Council, T.C. Farries, the Foundation for Sports and the Arts, Scottish Enterprise, and a host of other firms, publishers and individuals.

The Scottish Publishers' Association was established in 1973 by a group of twelve publishers under its first name, the Scottish General Publishers' Association. In 1991 the Association vacated its cramped and awkward premises in Thistle Street Lane and moved to a much more convenient space at the Scottish Book Centre, where it now has around seventy members. Its main aims are 'to help publishing concerns in Scotland to conduct their book publishing businesses in a professional manner, to market their output to the widest possible readership within Scotland, the U.K. and overseas, and to encourage the development of a literary culture in Scotland'. Many of its services, such as marketing, publicity and advertising, are offered on a co-operative basis, which suits many of Scotland's smaller publishing houses. The Association promotes Scottish publishing at the Frankfurt Book Fair and publishes, annually, the *Directory of Publishing in Scotland*. It was also responsible, along with the Scottish Branch of the Booksellers' Association, for setting up the Scottish Book Marketing Group, which issues a fortnightly Scottish Bestseller List and co-ordinates the annual summer brochure (a free holiday guide to Scottish books). The Group also organises the Scottish Book Fortnight, which has free author events and displays in bookshops and libraries throughout Scotland.

The Edinburgh Book Festival also has its base at the Centre. The Festival was established in 1983, the initial intention being to have a 'one-off' event to represent books and literature at the same time as the other August festivals. The main aims of the Book Festival are to extend the interests of new and existing readers, and also to give them, and authors, the opportunity to meet one another. Its venue in Charlotte Square Gardens, on a biennial basis, has proved even more popular than the organisers first envisaged. The sixth Edinburgh Book Festival in 1993 attracted 65,000 people. In addition to the major book display, there is a Children's Book Fair and two theatres, set in a double-court-yard layout of marquees. Since 1983 there has been a gradual build-up in the number of discussions and readings by famous authors. These have included Jung Chang, Roddy Doyle, Doris Lessing, Ben Okri, Salman Rushdie and Joanna Trollope. Younger readers have also met Roald Dahl, Rolf Harris, Shirley Hughes and Joan Lingard at the Children's Book Fair.

The need to encourage young people to read books is recognised, and met, by Book Trust Scotland, which transferred from Glasgow to Edinburgh when the Scottish Book Centre was opened. The Trust has its origins in the Scottish section of the National Book League. The aim of the Trust is the general promotion of books, with particular emphasis on younger readers. It operates on the premise that if young people acquire the habit of reading at an early age, that habit will remain with them throughout their adult life. Among the Trust's recent publications are several colourful and arresting posters, intended for display in schools and libraries: *Radical Reading* was a campaign to encourage teenagers to pick up a book; and the *Books for Babies* campaign relied on health visitors and carers to pass on the message. Another continuing series is *Now Read On* which highlights a selection of the best contemporary and classic writing from Scottish libraries. The Trust has also produced a series of exhibitions over the years, two of the most popular being *Twentieth Century Scottish Writers* chosen by Edwin Morgan, and *Glasgow Books and Writers* based on a bibliography prepared by Moira Burgess.

Readiscovery was an idea, backed by the Scottish Arts Council, for promoting books and reading all over Scotland during 1995. Its main focus was the Book Bus which toured primary schools in Scotland, particularly those in more remote areas. The idea was to stimulate interest in reading, especially in children who do not live near a bookshop or a library. On each tour an author was on board giving talks and readings at the various schools. Readiscovery was launched at Discovery Point in Dundee on 6th January 1995, and was part of National Book Day on 12th August 1995 and National Poetry Day on 12th October 1995. Also included was a project 'Posters in Public and Private Places', which advertised books and literature, with a different poster each month, in swimming pools, theatres, halls, leisure centres, hospitals, prisons and ferries.

BALGREEN LIBRARY

Balgreen Library, adjoining Balgreen School, was established in a way quite different to Fountainbridge Library. In 1926 the Education Committee and the Library Committee of Edinburgh Corporation agreed to formalise a working arrangement which had existed between them for at least the previous two years. The idea was to form branches of the public libraries in schools under the control of the Education Committee. Following a report from the City Librarian, the Education Committee agreed to incorporate a library room in two schools about to be built, namely, Bellevue Technical and Commercial School and Leith Academy Secondary School. The basis of the agreement was that the Education Authority would provide and equip the room, and the Library Committee would provide the books and the staff. A further proviso, which was really the basis of the whole experiment, was that the library had to be open for the issue of books at hours convenient for day pupils, and students attending Continuation Classes, and for the preparation of home lessons and the consultation of reference books. When libraries at Bellevue opened in 1929 and Leith Academy in 1930 they were very successful, but they had one main disadvantage: they could only be reached through the school building, which meant that they were closed when the school was closed. Unfortunately, the construction of Bellevue and Leith Academy was too far advanced by the

The rather austere-looking Balgreen Library, photographed shortly after it was opened on 8th February 1935, has changed out of all recognition, to a much more user-friendly environment at the present day. (Edinburgh Education Week, 1936.)

time the two Committees had worked out the details. What was needed was a library which was both accessible from the school and directly from the street.

Such a library was provided at Balgreen, and also at Craigmillar and Granton. Edinburgh Corporation already owned the old mansion of Balgreen House, situated in the triangle formed by Balgreen Road, the Water of Leith and the railway. Early in 1933 the Corporation obtained permission from the Dean of Guild Court to demolish the old rambling house and its stables, and to erect Balgreen School and Library on the site. The plans, by the architect J.A. Carfrae, show the intended school on the site of the house, the playground on the site of the stables, and the library on the shrubbery. The completed library was a plain, single-storey, rectangular building, measuring approximately 58 by 33 feet, with a slatted belfry in the centre of the pitched, slated roof. To conform to the requirements of the Committees, there was a main entrance from Balgreen Road, and an internal door giving access from the school corridor. The books, all 7,000 of them, were arranged on shelves around the walls with wooden roller shutters which could be drawn down and locked. There were no island bookshelves, the centre floor space being occupied by functional tables and chairs for reading. The library was opened on 8th February 1935, about five months after the school, and attained nearly 73,000 book issues by 1937. School pupils used the library by day and adults used it in the evening. Its popularity was maintained through the years of the Second World War with the help of events like *Story Hour*, when local children between the ages of 7 and 9 came to the library on Saturday mornings to hear readings from English literature: apparently the favourites were *Alice in Wonderland* and *Dr Dolittle*.

Over the years Balgreen Library has maintained its service as a branch library, having abandoned the restricted hours for adults many years ago. In 1993 the book stock was 18,301 and the book issues were 109,050.

10

The Twentieth Century

In this final chapter a number of related observations are brought together to give some idea as to how the district has evolved during the twentieth century. Many references to the present century have already been made in the chapters dealing with specific topics, such as churches, schools, sport and entertainment. But there remains additional material which falls naturally into the pre-War and post-War periods. Before the Second World War, Gorgie and Dalry was characterised by the existence of a fairly stable population, most of whom worked in local factories and lived in small tenement flats. Many lacked the basic amenities which were provided, as a matter of course, in tenements built at the same time in more affluent areas, such as Bruntsfield and Comely Bank. The immediate post-War period was one of stagnation, but in the last twenty-five years very considerable progress has been made in improving the area. To maintain and build on that progress is the challenge of the remaining years of this century and into the next, with special emphasis needed on the environment, housing, traffic congestion, provision of more open spaces, and the rejuvenation of small retail outlets.

A GORGIE CHILDHOOD BEFORE THE FIRST WORLD WAR

Recollections of Gorgie and Dalry before the First World War are not easy to come by, but, when found, they are worth the time spent in searching. The Wilson family lived at Murdoch Terrace until 1906, after which they moved to Wheatfield Street. The flitting was in May as many people still moved house at one of the term times, Whitsunday or Martinmas. There was no removal van as we know it today. The family and their friends got the use of a horse and cart, or a handcart, for the day, which was piled high and lashed with ropes, leaving just enough space at the front for mother and father. The children walked and carried something with them: no-one was allowed to arrive empty-handed. All the china and other breakables were wrapped in newspaper and placed in a wicker clothes basket with two handles, but it was not entrusted to the horse and cart.

The family unit consisted of mother, father and three children—two girls and a boy. Mr Wilson was a joiner in Watherston's, the joiners, off Dalry Road where he worked for several years. The working day started at 6.00 a.m. and at 8.00 a.m. there was a break of one hour for breakfast. It was the habit of the men who lived locally to walk home for a breakfast of porridge and something fried. They also went home at lunchtime but, in all, the working week was forty-eight hours, which included Saturday morning. Mrs Wilson did not have any formal employment. She spent all her time and energy looking after her husband and family in the days when there were no electrical gadgets to assist, and no motor cars for school journeys, social events or shopping. To begin with, the children attended the 'tin school' located in outbuildings in the playground of Gorgie Public School, where streaming, by ability, was done at quite an early age. School bags were not usually carried, there was no school uniform, but girls wore pinnies which had to be changed for old clothes for playing when they arrived home.

The elder daughter of the family recalls that Sunday was very different to other days of the week. Her parents were not over-religious but they followed the conventions of the day. The children attended the Mission Sunday School at Wheatfield Terrace where they had to learn a small piece of text for the following Sunday. There was also a short sermon usually aimed at the evils of drink. At home, some families read from the Bible and most children said their prayers at bedtime. At age seven, bedtime was 6.30 p.m. during the week and slightly later at the weekend and during holidays. On Sunday afternoon the whole family got dressed up for a family outing, which usually consisted of a walk to Longstone or Saughton Park. The sisters, with straw hats, long buttoned-up boots and parasols, walked in front with their brother, whilst mother and father walked behind. On returning home, there was a full meal of meat and potatoes, most of which had been prepared the day before. House chores were reduced to a minimum, no sewing or knitting was allowed, and although Sunday newspapers were in the house, reading them was either done furtively later in the day, or delayed until Monday.

The Wilson's accommodation consisted of a room and kitchen and a bed-closet. Like many other houses in the district it was comfortably, but not lavishly, furnished. Lighting was by gas mantles on long brass brackets which swung out from the wall. A large, black range in the main room was used for heating and cooking. The children were allo-

The workforce of joiners at Watherston & Sons of Dalry Road in the early years of the twentieth century. (Courtesy of Mary Wilson.)

cated daily and weekly chores in return for pocket money. Mrs Wilson did not approve of her daughters delivering milk or newspapers, but Mr Wilson allowed the son of the family to deliver morning rolls. Most of the milk deliveries were done by older boys, in their early teens, who were strong enough to carry several pitchers (with looped wire handles) on each arm. At home the girls would remove beetroot and other stains from the knives, using bathbrick and a knife board, before the days of stainless steel cutlery. There were, of course, no refrigerators, nor was there any central heating. Milk and butter were bought in small quantities and replenished frequently from the numerous dairies in the district. In winter, modest heat, to thaw out the pipes in the bathroom, was supplied by using a candle inside a clay plant pot, with another placed over the top, rim to rim.

Several children in the district attended piano lessons from Miss Robertson at Damhead Farm, and later at Harrison Road after Miss Robertson got married. Immediately prior to her marriage Miss Robertson had a farewell picnic for all her former pupils. Two or three horses and carts, packed with budding musicians, left Gorgie for Cramond, via Roseburn and Davidson's Mains. Journeys on holiday were sometimes not much further. The Wilsons usually went by train to Aberdour to a self-catering holiday house rather than a boarding house or hotel.

All in all, the Wilsons lived a secure and contented life at Gorgie with a strong emphasis on education and moral values, but not significantly different to many other families.

AROUND CALEDONIAN CRESCENT IN THE 1920S

Like other parts of Gorgie and Dalry, Caledonian or 'Caley' Crescent was a close-knit community with many large families living in fairly modest accommodation. Frequently, grandparents, uncles and aunts lived in the same stair or street. Many stairs had up to sixteen separate flats, each consisting of a room and kitchen, and a small toilet. There were also larger flats with an extra bedroom, but few, if any, were equipped with baths. Fathers worked on the railway, in the rubber mill, or in one of the many firms of joiners and engineers. The Scott family lived in Caley Crescent before the First World War, but moved to a larger flat in Orwell Terrace, around 1923, where they had the benefit of another room. Tom Scott still recalls life in and around Caley Crescent in a family consisting of mother, father and seven children.

The large, diverse population sustained several small businesses and shops, most of which have now been closed and converted into flats. One of the many dairies was run by Mrs Brown on the corner of Caley Crescent and Road. The shop was divided into two sections, one for the dairy and one for the general store. The milk was kept in large open-topped vessels without any form of refrigeration. Customers brought their own jug or pitcher, which was filled by using a large deep ladle: if cream was required it was skimmed off the surface with a flatter ladle, and charged separately. The milk was delivered to the shop from outlying farms many of them in the Corstorphine area. The farmers charged an extra halfpenny per pint between October and April to cover the cost of winter feeding for the cows. Finlay, the family grocer, was on the east corner of Caledonian Place and Caledonian Crescent. Most commodities were sold loose. Lentils, peas, barley and sugar were all in sacks, near the door, with the sides of the open sacks neatly rolled down to give easy access using the metal scoops. Butter was kept in bulk on a cold slab behind the counter, beside the big rounds of cheese. The butter was served with the use of ribbed, wooden pats, frequently dipped in water to prevent the butter from sticking. The cheese was cut using long wires held tightly between small wooden handles. Treacle was a messy business, poured, as carefully as possible, into the customer's own jar. While this was going on, general back-chat between the

A group of children with a few treasured possessions in Duff Street in 1922. (Courtesy of Dalry Primary School.)

customer and the assistants gave the skilled grocer just enough time to wrap or bag each item.

There were also one or two shops on the south side of Caley Crescent, close to the westmost pend. One shop was occupied by Mr Ross, who hired out bicycles at 3d (1p) for half an hour—frequently extended if the hirer was a local lad and business was slack. For more adventurous travellers, a better bicycle could be hired for 3/6d (17 ½d) for a full day. Near the cycle shop, an elderly lady eked out a modest living by combining a general store with a much more strenuous occupation. For 2d she would take in a large basket of washing and caw it through a large cast-iron mangle which stood in the middle of the shop floor. Also nearby was Mr Boyce, who had a roaring business selling briquettes (small bricks of compressed coal dust) which burned reasonably well in domestic grates, provided the chimney had a good 'draw'. At the start of the day, the briquettes were stacked high on a small cart drawn by an even smaller donkey. Housewives, alerted by Boyce's dulcet tones, would open their windows and shout down the order, which arrived, sometimes up three flights of stairs, carried on a short wooden board. Occasionally, Mr Boyce was given a hand by local boys keen to learn the trade—until their mothers found them later in the day cov-

A hostelry has stood on the site of the present Ryrie's Bar at Haymarket from time immemorial. It was the Haymarket Inn from at least as early as 1862 and was remodelled for Messrs Ryrie & Co., in 1906. (Courtesy of Ryrie's Bar.)

Staff and customers at Nisbet's Bar, Dalry Road, in the 1920s. In the back row, second from the left, is F. H. Kumerer, the pork butcher, at No. 26 Dalry Road, and fourth from the left is Tom Scott Snr., engine driver with the North British Railway Co. The gentleman with the hat, third from the right, is Sam Drennan, the boot repairer. (Courtesy of Tom Scott.)

ered in coal dust. White & Boland, the long-established boot repairers, also in Caley Crescent, repaired army boots, as well as ensuring that the local population kept on an even heel.

In addition to the established shops, there were many traders who hawked their wares round the doors, usually from small horse-drawn carts. One man, who always arrived in Caley Crescent on a Sunday, sold soor dook (buttermilk) by the jugful, to those housewives who were keen to spend their weekends making scones. Some traders, of course, had handcarts only, such as Skinner's bakery. Their delivery man hauled an old handcart, laden with pies, from the bakehouse in Dalry Road to the branch shops in Orwell Terrace and Gorgie Road. His determined expression, and his preference to pull the cart by inserting a cross-beam between the shafts, earned him the nickname 'Skinner's horse'.

RECOLLECTIONS OF DALRY ROAD SHOPS

The section of Dalry Road from Haymarket to Dalry School was always intended to be the main shopping area to serve the people living in the tenements above the shops, and in the numerous side streets. The middle section of Dalry Road had fewer shops, but they were more numerous in the westmost section opposite Dalry Cemetery. Nearest to Haymarket, the main retailers were moving in as early as 1874, including James Archibald, the stationer; David Imrie, the newsagent; Christine Wilson, the fruiterer; and George Melvin, the grocer. The presence of shops like George Dunnet, the tailor, suggests that a fairly large population was expected to settle at Dalry. As the population increased, shop proprietors jostled for position, frequently moving either to larger premises or to a position with better passing trade.

The shops, operating near the west end of Dalry Road from the 1930s, are nostalgically recalled by many senior citizens, some of whom are still resident in the district. Basic provisions were obtained at St Cuthbert's Co-operative which had a butcher, a fishmonger and a grocer in a row of shops on the south side of Dalry Road, between Orwell Terrace and West End Place. In addition to St Cuthbert's, there was the Argentine Meat Co; the Maypole Dairy Co. (nearer to Haymarket); the Buttercup Dairy Co; and several small grocers, one of whom sold soup stock at 2d per jug. At Easter, the Buttercup Dairy had a great attraction for the local children—a batch of different-coloured 'dyed' chickens chirped about in the front window only a few days after hatching out. Among the many bakeries were Leadbetter, whose pies were apparently second to none, and the Innovation Bakery on the corner of Orwell Terrace, whose hot doughnuts, at 3d per bag, were essential eating on the way to 'the Tiv' in Gorgie Road. Some shops were more conspicuous than others: Hardie's, the drysalters, frequently had huge wooden crates and straw lying on the pavement outside the shop on the days that a consignment of crockery was being delivered; Mr Pearson, the boot repairer, near Orwell Terrace, always had a huge boot in his window; and Councillor Buckner's tobacconist's business at No.82a had a small gas jet burning at the doorway to allow passers-by to light their cigarettes and pipes. David Hall also started his first butcher's business at No.151 Dalry Road, which now operates at Broxburn under the name David A. Hall Ltd.

Carpet Susie was one of Dalry's great characters: she ran a shop dealing in new and second-hand carpets on the west corner of Caledonian Road and Dalry Road. Her shop was so full of carpets that inspection, and any necessary cutting, was usually carried out on the pavement. Equally crammed with merchandise was her other shop on the east corner of Caledonian Place and Dalry Road, which was given over to

John McBain, the fruiterer, ready for his rounds, photographed at Murieston Lane outside the timber yard of Scott Morton, the cabinetmaker. (Courtesy of Bill McKenzie.)

the sale of pianos of all shapes and sizes. Dalry residents were also well catered for in the clothing department. The men went to Thompson, the gents' outfitters, or to Mr McKenzie, the Gaelic-speaking tailor, between Orwell Place and Orwell Terrace. The women frequented Vanity Fair on the corner of Dalry Place, or for very special occasions, Dumas, who sold wedding dresses and ladies' outfits.

Some shops have no obvious modern equivalent, although the service which they provided appears to be well catered for in other ways. On the south side of Dalry Road, west of Haymarket, was the *Evening Dispatch* office and farther west, in direct competition, the *Edinburgh Evening News* office. Each of these branch offices dealt with intimations from the public of births, deaths and marriages, and also classified advertisements. They also received bulk deliveries of newspapers for collection by the local news vendors and newsagents. Crowds of men and boys, anxious to learn the latest sports results, would gather on Saturday evenings, poised between the two offices, waiting to see if the *Green Dispatch* or the *Pink News* was produced first by the rival presses.

LIFE IN 'THE CASTLE'

The history of Stenhouse Mansion and a description of its architecture is given in Chapter 2. It will be recalled that in 1929 the *Tenth Report of the Royal Commission on the Ancient and Historical Monuments of Scotland* stated that the Mansion was 'reduced slightly in area and greatly in degree as it provides labourers' dwellings'. The author of the 1929 Report could never have imagined that one of the children, who had been living there at the time of his Report, would still be residing in the Stenhouse area sixty-five years later. Bill Rigby, the last surviving member of a family of two adults and eight children, can recall aspects of living in Stenhouse Mansion as though it were only yesterday. In those days the Mansion was always known locally as 'the Castle'.

The building was divided into apartments for four separate family units, the Rigbys having three rooms on the ground floor. The kitchen was the centre of activity with a large open range containing ovens on both sides. Mr and Mrs Rigby slept in the kitchen, which gave access to a small room where the two youngest members of the family slept. The only other habitable room was a large bedroom (to sleep three boys and three girls) divided down the centre by a heavy curtain to provide a modicum of privacy. Each room had an open coal fire, not always lit, but otherwise there were no amenities. The Castle had no electricity and no gas: lighting was by paraffin lamp in the kitchen and candles in the bedrooms. There was no water, either hot or cold, and no drainage. There was no toilet, either for the Rigbys or anyone else in the building. The toilets were a range of brick-built cubicles, some distance from the main building. Each cubicle was fitted with a rudimentary lavatory seat and a pail. Toilet requisites came in the form of a bag of lime and a sheaf of cut-up newspapers. From time to time the pail had to be emptied into the midden, which was later removed by Edinburgh Corporation Cleansing Department. All water, for drinking and washing, was carried in enamel pails from a tap at Stenhouse Cottages, a hundred yards from the Castle. With eight children there were plenty of 'volunteers' to carry water, but then eight children needed a lot of water, especially on wash days. In winter there was the added problem of the water freezing over, which meant that it had to be thawed out by lighting a small fire under the pipes. The family washing was done in a communal boiler which sat in the open and was fired with sticks and coal.

Mr Rigby was a flour miller to trade at Inglis Mill, Juniper Green. He rose at four o'clock in the morning when his wife cooked a good

Stenhouse Mansion, off Gorgie Road, c. 1930, about the time that it was inhabited by a number of tenants, including the Rigby family. (A. W. Brotchie Collection.)

breakfast and made up his piece. He then walked to Inglis Mill to start work at six o'clock and returned about seven o'clock in the evening—covered from head to toe with white flour. Mrs Rigby did most of the cooking, washing and ironing for ten people and still found time to make her own butter and cheese. She helped to eke out a modest standard of living by milking the cows twice a day at Kerr's Dairy nearby.

The family budget was tight, occasionally loosened by 'Provi' cheques and the Store dividend. Most of the week's food was bought at St Cuthbert's Co-operative Association in Gorgie Road. Clothes and shoes were often hand-me-downs or donated from the Edinburgh Police Boot Fund, which supplied new boots for deserving families. On the inside flap of each boot were three small puncture holes, not sufficiently conspicuous to be embarrassing, but obvious enough to be refused by every pawnbroker in the city. Birthdays were not special days: no cards and no presents, but Christmas was better. Each child of the family received an apple, an orange and a new shilling. At New Year the house rang with noise and laughter, while the whisky flowed freely. There were other lighter moments throughout the year. Every Saturday night Mr and Mrs Rigby took a tram to the East End of Princes Street and walked up the Bridges for their weekly visit to the Empire Theatre. Earlier in the day most of the children went to the old Tivoli where the seats, near the front, were only long rough benches. The 'usherette' was a big man who packed more children into the row by prodding them with a long pole. The annual holiday was a one-day outing by tram to Portobello beach. For Bill Rigby, however, one of his lasting memories is of Miss Sarah Inglis, a kindly, elderly, infirm lady who lived alone at the top of the Castle. Every Friday, after school, Bill earned 3d (slightly more than 1p) by walking back to Longstone village for Miss Inglis' messages—a noggin of whisky and an ounce of Kendal Brown snuff.

The Rigbys and other families endured the rigours of the Castle until 1932. By modern standards it is a story almost beyond belief—that the absence of basic amenities could be accepted as the norm. It could even be argued that the Castle, in 1932, actually offered fewer facilities than it did in 1623 when it was built. In that year it had a well of water inside the building, and, being at least partly defensive in design, probably had some kind of toilet facilities inside. In 1932 the Rigby family, less two, who had left home to be married, were offered a Corporation house in the new and growing district of Stenhouse. It was a dream come true—electric light, water and a bathroom—but no hens, no nanny goat and no midden.

PUBLIC WASHHOUSES

Public washhouses were established in Edinburgh in the first few years of the twentieth century. Before the Second World War they were operating in most of the inner city areas: Lochrin; South Gray's Close; Simon Square; McLeod Street; Henderson Row; Abbeymount; Union Street; Murdoch Terrace; Livingstone Place, Portobello; and Bonnington Road. Those at Murdoch Terrace and McLeod Street were, of course, extensively used by women living in and around the districts of Gorgie and Dalry. To appreciate just how important these public utilities were, it is necessary to remember that many tenement houses, built around the turn of the century, did not have hot water, baths or double sinks, and were so small that it was almost impossible to dry a family washing indoors. Fabrics at that time were also much heavier and not nearly so easy to wash and dry as they are nowadays. The 'drip-dry' world had not yet been invented. Many women, young and old (but never men), were seen at almost any time of day, scurrying along Gorgie Road with a child's push-chair or pram, stacked high with a tin bath full of the week's washing. On most occasions the bundle bulged over the top of the bath, and was held in position by a large towel or sheet, tucked

Councillor Betty Mackenzie at McLeod Street Public Washhouse, c. 1980. In 1981 the building was converted to McLeod Street Leisure Centre. (Courtesy of ex-Councillor Betty Mackenzie.)

down the sides. The covering was selected with care to give the best impression, and to ensure that the neighbours and any well-wishers saw only what was good for them!

Public washhouses eventually went into decline for a number of reasons: houses were equipped with hot water and baths; washing machines and spin-driers became commonplace; and launderettes began to spring up all over the town. Many women, in Gorgie and Dalry, and other districts of the city, still recall the good times, and the bad times, during visits to the public washhouses.

It was normal practice to book a place at a particular time and date. The usual duration was one hour, but two hours could be reserved if there was a washing for a big family. The superintendent in charge kept a note of the bookings and got used to some customers coming at the same time every week. Charges were fairly static, usually around one shilling (5p) for a one-hour session. Payment of the fee allowed the use of a double tub with as much hot water as was necessary. Above the tubs was a boiler where whites could be washed separately. The women brought their own soap powder (Persil, Oxydol or Rinso) or cakes of Sunlight washing soap, usually bought from McKenzie's, on the corner of McLeod Street. Wash boards were supplied, guaranteed to ensure that manicuring nails, either before or after, was a pointless exercise. Rubber gloves were not generally used. The tubs were in lines across the breadth of the floor with a wide passageway down the centre. Duckboards were laid on the floor, beside the tubs, and many women brought their Wellington boots with them to wear during the washing process. Large vents were installed in the roof, and the window spaces had metal grilles instead of glass, to allow the steam to escape. After the clothes were washed and rinsed, they were put in a spinner, which removed the excess water, but did not dry them. The clothes were dried on 'horses'—large metal frames on wheels, which were drawn out from the wall. Once the horse was loaded with wet washing and pushed back into its slot, it was fanned by a continuous flow of hot air. The drying process took about half-an-hour, during which time the women had a short respite for social chat, taking care to avoid the sharp eye of anyone keen to aspire to the title 'bully o' the washhoose'.

THE SECOND PART OF THE CENTURY

The districts of Gorgie and Dalry did not suffer physical damage to any extent during the Second World War. There was an isolated incident in

*McKenzie's Manufacturing Tinsmith and General Ironmongers, 1932, was on the east corner of Gorgie Road and McLeod Street, ideally placed for local women on the way to McLeod Street washhouse. (*Courtesy of Bill McKenzie.*)*

Duff Street, but otherwise the district escaped serious damage. The schools were disrupted by evacuation procedures: there was rationing of all basic commodities; and local firms were greatly reduced in capacity by the workers being called up to the Forces. The firms' reduced capacity was usually channelled into War-related contracts. In the decade or two after the War, Edinburgh was not famed for its thrusting capacity for redevelopment, and Gorgie and Dalry were no exceptions. Indeed, the closure of some of the district's big employers had an adverse effect on the locality. Scott Morton, the cabinetmakers, closed in 1966, and Cox's Glue Works and McVitie & Price, biscuit manufacturers, closed in 1969. These were followed by Macandrew, the builder, in 1971 and Mather, the engineers, in 1972. Between 1951 and 1971 the population of Gorgie and Dalry fell from 29,000 to 23,000, and in the 1971 Census 10,000 dwellings, or 54% of the total, were classified as sub-standard. Edinburgh District Council responded to the growing problems with the Gorgie Dalry Local Plan of 1978, one of its main aims being 'to restore confidence in the residential nature of large parts of Gorgie Dalry, by all means possible'. Following widespread concern at how effectively the Report would be implemented, the Gorgie Dalry Local Plan Association was formed. At a Public Enquiry in 1982 the Association succeeded in making substantial alterations to the Plan.

*Cable car No. 107 travelling west in Gorgie Road, c.1912. The high wall on the right is at the Magdalene Asylum, now Springwell House. The building on the left, with the pointed roofline, is the original Tynecastle Toll, converted to a newsagent and tobacconist's shop under the name Wilson. The building was demolished for the construction of the first Tivoli Picture House in 1913. (*Courtesy of Wilfred Grubb.*)*

*Several cable cars in Dalry Road, near Haymarket, packed with Hearts supporters returning from Tynecastle, 1920. (*Courtesy of Bill McKenzie.*)*

Conductress Helen Hutcheon (later Andison) and her driver at Saughton cable car terminus, near Ford's Road, c.1919. (Courtesy of Jim Andison.)

The No.4 electric tram on Slateford Road, in the 1950s, negotiates the overlapped rails outside the Caledonian Brewery. The rails were overlapped at that point to allow space for the brewers' lorries to park. (From the A.W. Brotchie Collection.)

In the latter part of the 1970s, throughout the '80s, and into the '90s, the districts of Gorgie and Dalry have established a wide range of amenity, action and housing groups, which have brought great benefits to the area. Some of them are discussed here.

CANMORE HOUSING ASSOCIATION

The Canmore Housing Association was constituted in April 1975 as a limited liability company, not trading for profit, under its founding name, Gorgie Dalry Housing Association. At that time Housing Action Areas were being declared in the districts of Gorgie and Dalry, which meant that substantial grants were available to the Association (and others) to improve the housing stock. The opportunity was taken to acquire and improve nearly 700 tenement flats, many of them in and around Caledonian Crescent. The comprehensive improvement work, carried out between 1975 and 1991, involved the replacement of old plumbing, the installation of baths and showers, the provision of damp-proof courses, and repairs to roofs and stonework. As well as increasing the number of houses to rent, the Association provided a service to nearly 500 owner-occupiers, who were participating in the overall improvement of the tenements. In 1991 the Association changed its name to Canmore Housing Association, and widened its geographical area of operation to include locations within one hour's travelling distance of its base at Dalry Road. In practice this now includes the whole of Edinburgh, West Lothian and Fife. Canmore has over one hundred and thirty voluntary members, about half of whom are also tenants. Anyone with a non-commercial interest in the Association's business can apply for membership, and stand for election to the management committee.

Canmore's main object is the provision of rented accommodation for people on low incomes, or with special needs. In pursuing this policy, many links have been made with organisations such as Barnardos, the Edinburgh Association for Mental Health, the Edinburgh Council for the Single Homeless, the Church of Scotland, and Freespace Housing. In its Annual Report for 1993, Canmore stated that 62% of its housing units are occupied by single adults, and that nearly 68% of its housing stock has two apartments only. This situation follows closely past and anticipated trends in housing requirements. In Edinburgh there is a very high proportion of owner-occupier housing, which is increasing as the number of local authority houses and private-let houses diminish. The trend has created a significant gap in the housing market which

The headquarters of the Canmore Housing Association (previously Gorgie Dalry Housing Association) was built in Dalry Road in 1992, to designs by the architect, Ronald Cameron. (Courtesy of Canmore Housing Association.)

Canmore is well suited to fill. In doing so the Association is conscious of the large number of single people, elderly people and those with physical and mental disabilities who require help to find affordable accommodation. The number of applicants annually far outnumbers the available houses.

Although Canmore has extended its operations beyond the districts of Gorgie and Dalry, it has certainly not neglected its home territory. It has almost 500 tenement flats built before the First World War, and about 170 new flats in blocks built by the Association itself. In recent years several sites have been developed, including 75 flats, mostly for families, in Duff Street in 1991, on the site of the famous whisky bond which was bombed during the Second World War. In 1994 a similar-sized development was built at the Dalry Road end of the former Morrison Street Goods Yard, and a much smaller one at Orwell Terrace to provide ten flats for the elderly. At the Orwell site a further 28 flats, to let at market rents, were constructed by Canmore's sister organisation, Malcolm Housing Association. Further west, on the site previously occupied by Waverley Tractors, at the junction of Chesser Avenue and Gorgie Road, construction started in 1994 on 69 flats for the elderly, some of which will provide extra care facilities. The most recent site is at the former Gorgie Goods Yard, to the west of Robertson Avenue, where a mixed development of 72 flats was started in 1994. It will include shared-ownership accommodation and eight workspaces intended for use by small businesses. The Association's own headquarters at No.193 Dalry Road, designed by the architect Ronald Cameron, and opened in 1992, also has four flats on the upper floors. The building is diagonally opposite the new St Colm's Church, on the site of the original Dalry Free Church dating from 1881. In 1988 the opportunity was taken to demolish the old church and halls, and construct an integrated building including eight family flats, two wheelchair flats and twenty six flats for the elderly.

One of the most interesting sites to develop was in McLeod Street in the early 1980s. Two blocks, with open balconies, on the east side of the street, were designed in 1896 by the City Architect, Robert Morham, for the Public Works Office of the City Chambers. Each block, built on what was then known as Dalry Meadows, contained one- and two-apartment flats, with bed recesses, ventilated pantries and coal closets. There was one W.C. for every two houses, and six washhouses and four baths to serve 32 dwellings. Gorgie Dalry Housing Association acquired one of the blocks in 1980 but the other was not economic to restore and was demolished. A time capsule, buried on 4th June 1896 by Mrs McDonald, wife of the Right Hon. Andrew McDonald, Lord Provost of Edinburgh, was found during demolition and is in the possession of Canmore. The retained block was restored to create twenty modern flats.

GORGIE DALRY COMMUNITY FESTIVAL

The Gorgie Dalry Community Festival was started in June 1980 by a number of local volunteers and community projects coming together on a regular basis. The main aim was to provide the community with an annual Festival of the arts and entertainment, to be enjoyed by people of all age groups. The first Festival, funded from the proceeds of jumble sales, raffles, car-boot sales and donations, was very successful, leading the way for more adventurous programmes in later years. At the present day the Festival is administered by an elected committee of twenty people, consisting of four officebearers, eight members of the public, and eight representatives of the local community organisations. Funding is by Lothian Regional Council, Edinburgh District Council, and a host of business and private sponsors in and around the district.

*A carnival atmosphere prevails at the Gorgie Dalry Community Festival in Murieston Park. (*Courtesy of the Gorgie Dalry Community Festival.*)*

Between 1980 and 1987 the Festival was confined to a week-long event in June each year, but since 1987 a co-ordinator has been appointed (funded by Lothian Regional Council) with the remit to extend the Festival to an all-year-round programme.

The Festival traditionally opens in June with a parade of floats, bands, majorettes, and children and adults in fancy dress costume. It starts at St Bride's Centre in Orwell Terrace, and proceeds along Dalry Road and Gorgie Road to the car park at the Gorgie Memorial Hall, where it turns and goes back along Gorgie Road to the main venue in Murieston Park. A different theme is adopted for the Festival each year: in 1994 it was Famous Families, which portrayed the Broons, the Waltons, the Ewings and several others; in 1995 it was the Mardi Gras, giving great scope to the Festival's musical interests. At Murieston Park, every inch of space is taken up with stalls, side shows, bouncy castles, road safety displays, pony rides, face painting, the children's corner, the 'bonny baby' competition and the fancy dress competition. Over the years, many celebrities have been present, including Big Daddy, the professional wrestler; Andy Cameron, the comedian; and Glen Michael of Cavalcade fame. Music has been provided by a variety of bands: Daniel Stewart's Melville College Pipe Band; Tynecastle Jazz Band; 50th Edinburgh St Michael's Boys' Brigade Pipe Band; Linlithgow Reed Band; and the Pipes and Drums of the 2nd Battalion Scots Guards. A long and sometimes tiring day at Murieston is concluded with the Litter Race, where everyone is encouraged to leave the Park as they found it!

The Festival is by no means confined to Murieston Park. All the main indoor and outdoor venues are involved, including the Adult Learning Project, Gorgie City Farm, Gorgie Memorial Hall, McLeod Street Leisure Centre, St Bride's Centre, and Springwell House. The Jazz Festival, which has grown quickly over the last few years, has been held at various locations, particularly the Blue Lagoon, the Haymarket Bar, Ryrie's Bar and the Stratford Bar. There is also a snooker competition at the Locarno Snooker Club in Slateford Road.

All the main denominational churches are involved, the Festival Service being held at St Martin's Episcopal Church in Dalry Road. The district schools, and many from other parts of Edinburgh, participate in the five-aside indoor football competition held at McLeod Street Leisure Centre. This is now a two-day event to accommodate almost thirty teams. Gorgie City Farm has a special open-day where there is sheep clipping, pony rides, basket making, spinning and, of course, the opportunity to see over two hundred animals, most of them at very close range.

Although the main part of the Festival is in June, many events now take place at different times of year. At Christmas, the Gorgie Memorial Hall is the venue for the children's party, which has included live reindeer appearances. Each November, schoolchildren enter the Christmas Card Design Competition, the winning entry being adopted as the official Festival Christmas card for that year.

GORGIE DALRY COMMUNITY COUNCIL

Under the Local Government (Scotland) Act of 1973 local authorities were required to submit to the Secretary of State for Scotland a scheme for establishing Community Councils in their area. Although authority was given for fifty-five Councils to be set up in Edinburgh, by 1995 the number operating was twenty-four. The main purpose of each Council is 'to ascertain, co-ordinate and express' the views of the community to the local and public authorities on matters which are within the responsibilities of such authorities.

Gorgie Dalry Community Council held its first meeting on 1st April 1981. Its postal address is No.258 Dalry Road but monthly meetings are usually held in McLeod Street Leisure Centre. Funding is by Edinburgh District Council, which makes a lump-sum payment of £700, plus 2p for each person on the electoral roll within the Community Council's area. The area involved is bounded on the north by the Edin-burgh—Glasgow railway line; on the east by Morrison Street car park; on the south by the West Approach Road, Angle Park Terrace and Slateford Road; and on the west by Robertson Avenue, via Gorgie Road to Balgreen Road. The Council has a maximum of twenty-one members, fourteen of whom are appointed at elections held every three years. The remaining seven members represent organisations in the area, registered for Community Council purposes. Although the organisa-tions do not all appoint a representative, they are kept informed of the action taken.

A wide variety of issues comes before the Gorgie Dalry Community Council, many of them common to other areas, such as traffic pollu-tion and density; cleanliness and condition of pavements and roadways; clean-up campaigns; local cemeteries and open spaces; and the closure of local retail shops. The Council has also contributed ideas and com-ments on the Central Edinburgh Plan; various local and central gov-ernment reports, such as the proposal to build another Forth Road Bridge; and the reorganisation of local government, with particular reference to Community Councils. The Council also has representa-tives on the board of the Better Gorgie Dalry Campaign. It was also instrumental in setting up the Gorgie Dalry Credit Union Ltd., a sav-ings and loan scheme for residents of Gorgie, Dalry, Moat, Hutchison and Shandon. The registered office is at No. 258 Dalry Road and the collection points are Fountainbridge Library, the Citizens Advice Bu-reau and the Better Gorgie Dalry Campaign office.

WOMEN UNLIMITED

Women Unlimited are an energetic voluntary project based at No. 4a Downfield Place, which concentrates particularly on health issues for women. Their aim is 'to provide opportunities for women to develop their skills and confidence, to enable them to have greater control over those issues which affect their health and well-being'. In pursuit of that aim they meet together in a friendly environment to identify their health concerns, and to find ways of meeting these needs. The idea of the group originated from the Scottish Women's Health Fair which was held in Princes Street Gardens in 1983. As a result of the Fair, a Well Women Centre was set up, on a temporary basis, in the Gorgie Dalry

area. It was soon discovered that there was sufficient interest to maintain the idea on a permanent basis. Meetings were held at St Bride's
Community Education Centre, where pilot sessions on women and
food, assertiveness, and body image, found appreciative audiences. A
newsletter was circulated with the assistance of the Adult Learning Project,
and the Centre drew up a list of visiting speakers. As the Centre became
better known it established links with other women's organisations, and
attracted limited funding. In 1988 a small office at St Bride's was secured,
a management committee was set up, and the Centre became more locally orientated, although women from other areas were still made welcome. At the end of 1989 the Well Women Centre changed its name to
Women Unlimited and moved to its present address in Downfield Place.

During the '90s there have been several new projects and courses.
These have included Alive and Kicking (events for older women in the
district); Women and Food; Self Defence; Being a Mum; Dealing with
Doctors; Women's Safe Transport; and the Gorgie Dalry Anti-Racism
Campaign. There is also close liaison, and joint activities, with Nari
Kallyan Shangho, the Scots Asian Women's Group. One of the most
rewarding activities was the Community Health Survey in Gorgie and
Dalry in 1991, which gave local women a voice in determining their
own health needs. Women were encouraged to view problems in a
wider context and to see the benefits of self-help groups. The need for
a more equal relationship between health service users, and providers,
was also highlighted.

At the present day, the two main groups are the Middle Years Group
and the Open Space Group. The Middle Years Group was set up as an
informal support network with a strong focus on health issues relating
to the menopausal years. The Open Space Group has a crèche to enable
mothers to participate in the programme of discussions and workshops.
The subjects include homeopathy; women's changing role in society;
photography; breast screening and jewellery making. Women Unlimited receives funding from Lothian Regional Council for running costs
and from a variety of Trusts for specifically agreed projects and courses.

CITIZENS ADVICE BUREAU

The Gorgie Dalry Citizens Advice Bureau was set up at No. 268 Gorgie Road in October 1983, under its first chairman, Bill Scott. Impar-
tial and confidential advice is given free to 'ensure that individuals do
not suffer through ignorance of their rights and responsibilities, or of

the services available, or through an inability to express their needs effectively'. In its first full year of operations, the Bureau dealt with almost 5,500 queries: income was £19,833 and expenditure £17,904. A decade later, the 1993-94 Report highlighted the increased complexity of queries, caused, in part, by the introduction of new legislation covering a wide range of social issues. In all, 6,324 cases were dealt with, divided into fourteen categories, of which 'money matters' was the largest single group at 39% of the total. Other large groups related to goods and services, employment, housing, and family and personal matters. Within the 'money matters' category, the largest subdivision was 'negotiating debt', which accounted for 25% of the total, followed by queries on the Community Charge at 19%. This workload is dealt with by a team of over thirty volunteer advisers, two volunteers involved in administration, and five home visitors, all under the guidance of a manager whose responsibility it is to ensure that the Bureau reflects the particular needs of the community. During the financial year to 31st March 1994 the income was £30,823 and the expenditure £34,535. A legal clinic was established in 1984, staffed in rotation, without charge, by qualified solicitors from various practices in Edinburgh. There is also a management committee of approximately fourteen members, drawn from the community, local government representatives, and other public bodies. For several years now, the Bureau has outgrown its premises in Gorgie Road, which has had some effect on the comfort and speed (but not quality) of service available to the public. This will be rectified in 1995 when the Bureau moves into new purpose-built accommodation in the same building as Fountainbridge Library, in Dundee Street. Scotland has over sixty Bureaux which deal with half a million enquiries every year. Each Bureau operates independently within the framework of the national association, Citizens Advice Scotland, which has bases in Edinburgh, Glasgow and Inverness. The Bureaux in Scotland cost approximately £2m to run annually, almost half of which is met by the Department of Trade and Industry. Most of the remainder is met by funding from local authorities to Bureaux within their area of administration. The annual cost would be many times greater if it were not for the efforts of 1,600 voluntary staff.

GORGIE-DALRY GAZETTE

The *Gorgie-Dalry Gazette* was founded in 1984 as a community newspaper to serve the districts of Gorgie and Dalry from Haymarket to

Stenhouse. The northern boundary for circulation is the main Edinburgh—Glasgow railway line and the southern boundary is the Union Canal. Within this area the *Gazette* is delivered free, once a month, to approximately 17,000 households, and is also stocked at public libraries and other outlets. In the early years the *Gazette* was administered by a management committee, but in 1990 it became a non-profit-making limited company, with a board of directors made up of local people. It receives approximately 50% of its income from advertising, and the other 50%, in equal proportions, from Lothian Regional Council and Edinburgh District Council. The *Gazette* also helps to produce a twice-yearly newspaper for the Canmore Housing Association, which is circulated to all the tenants.

The *Gazette* is a member of the Edinburgh Community Newspaper Trust, which also includes the *Wester Hailes Sentinel, North Edinburgh News, Craigmillar Festival News*, and the *Central Times*. The Trust was set up in 1989 to administer funding on behalf of its members, and to distribute grants in accordance with the annual business plans submitted by each newspaper. It also organises a two-year training scheme for journalists which involves a three-month secondment to Napier University. Funded jointly by Edinburgh District Council and the European Social Fund, the training scheme is recognised by the funders as a model of its kind.

The *Gazette*, first and foremost, is a vehicle 'of the community, for the community'. It prides itself on keeping in close touch with the organisations of the district, and ensuring that the people of Gorgie and Dalry are kept informed about what is happening in their district. They are encouraged, through the columns of the newspaper, to contribute views and ideas on local issues to ensure that the paper is truly representative of the district.

NARI KALLYAN SHANGHO

Nari Kallyan Shangho, or N.K.S. as it has become known, operates from fairly small premises at No. 200 Dalry Road. It is a Women's Welfare Group, established in 1987, mainly, but not exclusively, for Asian women. The staffing consists of a co-ordinator, an administrative worker, two health workers, a support worker and a playgroup supervisor and assistant. Upwards of one hundred women and children are attracted to N.K.S. from throughout Edinburgh and beyond. It is funded by Lothian Regional Council.

A high proportion of the work undertaken is health-related with a female Asian doctor available for consultation and advice on all aspects of women's health, including family planning, diet and healthy eating. One of the special qualities required of the doctor is the ability to speak Urdu, Bengali, Arabic and Persian, as well as English. N.K.S. also hold language classes to teach spoken and written Urdu, and there are similar, future plans to teach English. Other activities include cooking, sewing, swimming, Yoga, various educational outings to hospitals and health clinics, and a playgroup at Springwell House. Advice on various aspects of housing and welfare rights is also available.

BETTER GORGIE DALRY CAMPAIGN

The Better Gorgie Dalry Campaign was officially launched on 5th April 1988 with the aim of providing a local forum 'to promote, develop and sustain the economic and physical regeneration of the Gorgie Dalry area'. It is administered by a board of management, elected annually from representatives of local government, the Gorgie Dalry Business Association and the Gorgie Dalry Community Council. The committee meets once per month to consider a wide range of proposals put to it.

In recent years two important projects have been adopted—Local Employment Initiative and Property Support—assisted by funding from Lothian Regional Council and Edinburgh District Council. Help is given to local people with job applications, interview techniques and information on training courses. Particular attention is paid to recruiting local people, where possible, for local jobs through 'Jobs Local', a public noticeboard giving details of job vacancies in the district, which attracts three hundred callers each month seeking employment. Property Support was set up with a number of separate aims: to co-ordinate ideas for the improvement in the appearance of properties in the district; to draw up a register of vacant shops and units with a view to having them occupied; and to identify and develop property which could be classified as 'workshop' as opposed to retail.

Various initiatives, over the years, have produced good results. The railway bridges, across Dalry Road and Gorgie Road have been painted in various colours, depicting the design and structural details of the Victorian railway architecture. The bridges, Gorgie City Farm, Dalry Road and Gorgie Road are also adorned with lights at Christmas time. Many shop fronts and stair doors have been repainted and repaired, and the exterior render on Westfield Court has been repainted to enhance its rather plain façade. The orange-coloured Gorgie Dalry logo has now been affixed to all the street signs in the district. The Campaign has also been involved in the implementation of traffic-calming schemes, and the introduction of a police surgery, undertaken at No.258 Dalry Road, on specific dates, by three community officers. In 1991 a study by the Campaign revealed that there were sixty-four advertising hoardings between Haymarket and Robertson Avenue, many of them inappropriate in size, position and the message they conveyed. It was considered that the number of hoardings was generally detrimental to the district and following the study, many of the more unsightly ones were successfully removed. The Campaign also played a leading role in cleaning up Dalry Cemetery, which was 'reopened' at a special ceremony on 14th May 1991 as part of the City's first Festival of the Environment.

One area in which the Campaign spends an increasing amount of time and effort is Planning Applications. The district has several areas of ground suitable for redevelopment, some resulting from the closure of railway sidings and factories. Whilst the opportunity for redevelopment is welcomed, the Campaign is keen to ensure that it is appropriate to the existing and anticipated needs of the community, with particular application to housing, jobs and the need, or otherwise, for more retail shop outlets.

From its offices at No.258 Dalry Road the Campaign also offers several services to the public. These include: photocopying and faxing; following up complaints on street lighting and road and pavement defects; the supply of leaflets and information on such matters as Welfare Benefits, Trading Standards, stair cleaning cards etc., to what's on in Gorgie and Dalry. The Member of Parliament and the local councillors also hold their district surgeries at the Campaign's offices.

THE WEST EDINBURGH DEVELOPMENT GROUP

The West Edinburgh Development Group was established in 1991, firstly in Manor Place, then Murrayburn Road, and latterly at No. 255 Dalry Road. Its principal aim is to provide services for people with learning disabilities, as well as their parents and carers, in the west of Edinburgh. It is a recognised charity, funded jointly by Lothian Region Social Work Department and Lothian Health Board. A small staff, and about twenty voluntary workers, from a wide spectrum of society, deal with several hundred enquiries every year. There is a monthly meeting of the Man-

Does my bus stop here, or just my watch? (Crown Copyright: RCAHMS.)

agement Committee, which consists of eight people, representing the main funders, other voluntary organisations and parents.

The main object of the work is to help people with learning disabilities to take part in local activities and to make more use of the community facilities around them. After suitable selection and training, volunteers can be of great assistance in a wide variety of ways, from helping out at day-centres for a few hours each week, to a full week of shared local activities in the summer. There are several other specific areas of interest: on the educational side, accompanying someone to an adult education class and providing support with learning; joining in a men's or women's group; or becoming a member of a music group and helping others to play or sing.

IS 'ONLOOKER' LOOKING ON?

In the Introduction to this book, reference was made to a series of articles written in 1911 by 'An Onlooker', who expressed the view that between Dalry and Saughton, 'there [was] less to attract attention . . . than in almost any part of Edinburgh'. With the benefit of hindsight, and almost another century of history, it can safely be said that 'An Onlooker's' view no longer accords with the facts, even if it ever did.

Gorgie and Dalry have again reached an important stage in their development. The heyday of the mass employer has passed, but there are still important and efficient industries in the area. Almost all the schools have remained open, and the churches have made substantial progress in facing the problems of maintaining expensive buildings, coupled, in some cases, but not all, with declining membership. Housing has improved immensely, as have facilities for sport, leisure, recreation and care. But there is no room for complacency. The community has come through the first stage of giving the districts a new identity. That impetus must be maintained if all the progress is not to be dissipated. It is for the community, its leaders and its organisations to participate: it is not a time for onlookers.

Suggestions for Further Reading

Adam, James S., *A Fell Fine Baker*, 1974

Adam, James S. (Ed.), *The Business Diaries of Sir Alexander Grant*, 1992

Adult Learning Project, *The ALP History Journal*, 1994 on

Baker, H.J., *The History of Duncan, Flockhart & Co*, 1946

Brown, James, *The Epitaphs and Monumental Inscriptions in Greyfriars Churchyard*, 1867

Brown, Rose, *From Margaret to Mary*, 1994

Cowper, A.S., *Historic Corstorphine and Roundabout*, 1992

Chambers, Dr Robert, *Traditions of Edinburgh*, Reprint, 1980

Donald, Brian, *The Fight Game in Scotland*, 1988

Dunlop, Rev. A. Ian, *The Kirks of Edinburgh*, 1988

Gardiner, Leslie, *The N.B.—The First Hundred Years*, 1985

John Gifford, Colin McWilliam & David Walker, *The Buildings of Scotland—Edinburgh*, 1984

Grant, James, *Old and New Edinburgh*, 1882

Kay, John, *Original Portraits*, 1887

Kirkwood, Gerri & Colin, *Living Adult Education*, 1989

Lyon, David T., *Memorials of Gorgie Mission and Free Church*, 1899

McKean, Charles, *Edinburgh: An Illustrated Architectural Guide*, 1992

Macandrew & Partners, *Colin Macandrew & Partners Ltd.—A Story of Achievement, 1882–1955*, 1955

Martin, W.F., *A History of T. & H. Smith Ltd.*, 1952

Royal Commission on the Ancient and Historical Monuments of Scotland, *The City Of Edinburgh*, 1951

St Cuthbert's Church, *St Cuthbert's Parish Centenary*, 1989

Shaw, Donald, *The Balerno Branch and the Caley in Edinburgh*, 1989

Smith, John, *The Book of the Old Edinburgh Club*, Vol. XX, p26–60, 1935

Stenhouse Saughton Church, *Stenhouse Saughton Parish Church, Semi Jubilee, 1928–1953*, 1953

Thomas, Brendon, *The Last Picture Show: Edinburgh*, 1984

Tollcross Local History Project, *By the Three Great Roads*, 1988
Tollcross Local History Project, *Waters Under the Bridge*, 1990
Waddie's, *One Hundred Years of Print*, 1960
Wilson, Dr Daniel, *Memorials of Edinburgh in the Olden Time*, 1891
Wilson, John, *Bainfield Bowling and Social Club, 1924–1984*, 1984

Index